CALENDAR BOY

In memory of
Duncan Dallas
1941–2014
X. Y. T. V.

CALENDAR
BOY

Austin Mitchell

PEN & SWORD
POLITICS

First published in Great Britain in 2014 by
Pen & Sword Politics
An imprint of
Pen & Sword Books Ltd
47 Church Street
Barnsley
South Yorkshire
S70 2AS

ISBN 978 1 47382 844 5

Design and artwork: Nigel Pell

Printed and bound in England
By CPI Group (UK) Ltd, Croydon, CR0 4YY

Pen & Sword Books Ltd incorporates the Imprints of Pen & Sword Aviation, Pen & Sword
Family History, Pen & Sword Maritime, Pen & Sword Military, Pen & Sword Discovery,
Pen & Sword Politics, Pen & Sword Atlas, Pen & Sword Archaeology, Wharncliffe
Local History, Wharncliffe True Crime, Wharncliffe Transport, Pen & Sword Select,
Pen & Sword Military Classics, Leo Cooper, The Praetorian Press, Claymore Press,
Remember When, Seaforth Publishing and Frontline Publishing.

For a complete list of Pen & Sword titles please contact
PEN & SWORD BOOKS LIMITED
47 Church Street, Barnsley, South Yorkshire, S70 2AS, England
E-mail: enquiries@pen-and-sword.co.uk
Website: www.pen-and-sword.co.uk

CONTENTS

EXCUSES
FOR
EGOMANIA

Hiya. And welcome to my Calendar years.

This is not a history of Yorkshire Television (YTV [1968-2003]). That is being written by Graham Ironside, its long-time News Editor, and very good it will be too. This is a personal memoir, one of those mixtures of fact, anecdote and egomania which political flesh is heir to, particularly as senility approaches. It is the 'alibiography' of a Calendar Boy and his part in the forming of YTV and its key programme, *Calendar*, the regional magazine which became Yorkshire's favourite.

I was one of the talented and enthusiastic team privileged to participate in the early, exciting years we spent devising and creating the best of programmes for the best of companies in the best part of the country; which in case you have not realized, is Yorkshire. It was the time of my life and the greatest privilege I've had to be part of a team of child prodigies who created the most successful regional news magazine programme in the television network and built the best of companies. We put YTV and Yorkshire on the nation's screens; at long last.

Calendar was a marvellous programme; the pride of Yorkshire. Insular southerners might find this a little boastful. They do not understand that when Yorkshire folk are accused of boasting they are speaking nothing but the unvarnished truth. The sad reality is that so far as Londoners are concerned we are but a faraway county of which they know nothing and care less. So their views about 'God's Own County' and the 'God Zoners' who live there are as irrelevant as they are condescending. They should remember that Yorkshire is the centre of the universe, not 'The Great Wen' (a disparaging name for London coined by William Cobbett in the 1820s) they inhabit. *Calendar* was more important, had a bigger impact and audience and inspired more affection within Yorkshire's boundaries than many BBC programmes had on the whole country. Its presenters were bigger figures in their county than such BBC equivalents as Michael Barratt or Jeremy Paxman could ever be in Yorkshire. Or any part of the country. We were the concentrated essence of stardom. They were the diluted extract. We did not reach the huddled masses living outside the 'Broad Acres' (Yorkshire) but we did not want to. Why bother? Condescending southerners tend to sneer at Yorkshire and its endeavours but *Calendar* was not Alan Partridge-type television. It was simply Yorkshire's programme where Yorkshire folk could speak truth unto Yorkshire; with a Yorkshire accent. There may be other aims and destinies but none higher.

That is why it was such a great privilege, such an achievement and so much fun to have been in at the birth and the first stage of *Calendar*'s lusty rise. Creating something new, be it programme, company, product, project or technology, is the most exciting thing anyone can do in life. Perhaps not as rewarding as Silicon Valley's start-ups, like the creation of a Facebook, a Microsoft, a Google or a Twitter, but certainly creating *Calendar* was big and exciting enough for a modest Yorkshire lad. Together we created a triumph. I was lucky enough not only to be part of it but to be one of the public faces of the team that did it.

This was all 40 years ago. Since then I have faded into a blur on Yorkshire's subconscious, or at least that of its older folk. Once universally recognized, albeit sometimes for the wrong reasons, as a lost relative, ex-husband or photograph in the *Police Gazette* rather than Yorkshire's star, today I am a slow moving, hospice ready, with a face that would not even look good on radio. Yet I am still occasionally recognized by other 'oldies' with their Zimmer frames and by others who struggle to remember where they have seen me before – perhaps in the next allotment years ago. Or did I once sell them that dodgy car which broke down so badly?

All things fade, particularly fame and photos, but we British do love nostalgia. It is better to live in the past than in our declining, messy present. So there is no harm and some pleasure in this reminder of what was television's great decade and Yorkshire's own 'Indian Summer' before it all went wrong and television became the 'Kardashian' country of celebrities, egomaniac pygmies and glamour girl reporters it is today. The nubile nymphs who trod the boards in Studio Two at YTV must now be pensioners, grandparents and senior citizens. Many of the men have been reshaped by beer and chips. Yet *Calendar* gave them and me 5 minutes of fame and gave Yorkshire years of interesting programmes. That's a far better deal than the 15 minutes of fame proposed by Andy Warhol or several years of being talked down to by London. So Yorkshire deserves this chance to look back on the great and happy days of the 1960s and 1970s when something new and exciting was born in Yorkshire.

This part of the past, when it is not being ignored because it did not happen in London, has been maligned and portrayed as amateur TV: insular, parochial, rough and unpolished. Something to be laughed at: not with. Such views are indicative only of London's sense of superiority and its abiding ignorance of what's going on in the rest of our over-centralised country. Who cares what London thinks? *Calendar* had better ratings and stronger roots in its audience than any London-produced programme. No need to talk down to our audience. We were Yorkshire and closer to it than any London-based programme could ever be. Now that TV offers fifty choices of grey London priorities: cooking and food programmes, property, war, and pornography, the days of a two and a half channel black and white television broadcasting might look like 'Logie Bairdland'. But they were the time of our lives and the best of mine.

The second part of the record which should be put right is the more sordid story now brought to light by the arrests of so many presenters and stars from that period, all dragged from plush homes to face charges arising from what they claim were the affectionate gestures of a different age. Indeed, I am one of the few presenters who has not been helping the police with their enquiries. So far this sordid sequence of disinterment makes it look as though television, and particularly television outside London, was an orgy of rape, 'inappropriate touching', paedophilia and general promiscuity, all carried out in a crude northern fashion while Frank Bough was more elegantly and quietly taking his cocaine-fuelled trips round London call girls. Today, the 'heroes' of my age are on trial and pilloried by a press which once glorified them. None of that happened in Yorkshire where we managed to make pretty good television programmes even without Ant and Dec, drugs or any hired prostitutes. There was an absolute minimum of inappropriate touching, mainly to move people into or out of a good camera shot. Indeed, the only bit I remember was the occasional blow from John Wilford whose motivation was more disciplinary than sexual. This was a pre-'kissy kissy' age and Yorkshire a non-'kissy' county. The limits of what was permissible and acceptable to the 'touchee' (male or female) were vaguer and broader but I'm sure we did not exceed them, though we might have feared violence back if we had.

Autre fois autre moeurs, as they say in Harrogate. Attitudes were different then, particularly in chauvinist Yorkshire, but in any case while Manchester may have been dodgy – always was – Yorkshire was clean, straight-laced; even puritanical. Our programme was relaxed and family orientated and, like Yorkshire itself, a little chauvinist. We did not know what the feminist cause was until Germaine Greer turned serious, dropped out of *Nice Time* and decided to tell us; for a fee.

It is true that Jimmy Savile was a Yorkshireman and that he made no secret of his passion wagon. We occasionally travelled up to Leeds Infirmary where he worked as a porter and parked his 'sexmobile' outside. He appeared on *Calendar*, but there was never any indication that he was anything more than a raving lunatic with tartan hair who posed as Yorkshire's gift to sex. Indeed, he boasted of his sexual prowess and conquests to such an extent that made it seem to me that he was overcompensating for not getting any. For the rest we were – most of the time – as seemly as a Sunday school. Hardly surprising as most of the team were former Boy Scouts, now newlywed with small children and resolute wives who would have raised a row had they thought their newly acquired husbands were coming to work at a den of iniquity like *Look North* in Manchester. Either that, or I and everyone else, was as blind as a bat.

The first Calendar *set: Austin wondering what to say. Note the overcrowding and the all-male crew.*

As we wander down memory lane together, please remember that the past is another county and television, being in black and white, another medium. We did things differently then. People watched less television (even when I was on), but they probably did so more intently and watched together in one-set households where the TV set sat in the living room like a domestic god. When Yorkshire Television began broadcasting there were only two, or more accurately two and a half, channels since BBC Two (established only in 1964) had only a small audience. So the audience divided between the duopoly where in today's multi-channel situation there is an anatomical division. Hundreds of TV channels compete for eyeballs, cinema and theatre compete for bottoms on seats, scores of cookery channels compete for stomachs and numerous pornography channels compete for other parts of the anatomy. The two main channels are still dominant, though their audiences are smaller.

Channel loyalty was greater. Most switched on one channel and watched it for the entire evening, partly because of the absence of channel change remote controls (which came in only in the 1970s and are almost certainly responsible for

Yorkshire: Lovely to look at when not watching Calendar.

the spread of obesity), but also because each channel was aimed at a different social group and designed to hold their attention by clever scheduling to allow later programmes to inherit the maximum audience. Independent Television (ITV) lived by mass advertising of mass products to a mass and mainly working-class audience and Britain then had a large working-class, many of them in the North. The BBC was more upmarket and metropolitan and middleclass, broadcasting safe opinions to the respectable. Like the newspaper one read, you said something about your class and concerns by the channel you watched.

The regional magazine programmes and their stars played a bigger part in all our lives than they did in studies of TV and its effects, all of which are London based. They were a unique aspect of television art and *Calendar*, like other regional programmes, played a vital part in audience recruitment. 'Give me a child until he's seven and I'll give you the Catholic,' said the Jesuits. The masters of ITV echoed this with 'Give me an audience for *Calendar* and I'll give you the peak time audience.' In viewing, as in marriage and voting allegiance, people were much more loyal in those dim and distant

Runswick Bay: Civilisation's frontier with Tyne-Tees.

Scarborough: Deserted while people watch Calendar.

Shipley Glen.

1960s. So the art of scheduling was to build and then hold this audience by providing a succession of interesting material and programmes for it to watch, or at least keep the set tuned to while the audience indulged in all the other dimensions of human activity which can (and regularly did even then) go on in front of a TV screen. From 6 to 6.30pm the audience were mainly eating as they watched.

Building the audience was crucial. That audience was general, watching and waiting for something interesting to come on. Today in our multi-channel situation where literally hundreds of channels are available and new ones start up (or close) all the time, they are more selective and specialization prevails. Viewers choose between six main channels, with BBC1 and ITV still dominant, but they also follow more specialized interests through news channels, comedy, stand-up, arts and culture, history, geography or a plenitude of pornography. Production skills are more specialized. Back in my good old days, the basic requirement for magazine programmes was to produce interesting items which would hold the attention of the audience until the next interesting item which could be completely different. Music, news, history, sport, art, folk ways, even cooking, were all mixed in one programme all aimed at building a larger audience to hand on to the next programme. The keynote had to be quality and interest: not too specialized or pedantic to put people off but sufficiently interesting to keep people watching.

Bolton Abbey. Duke of Devonshire not visible. Probably watching Calendar.

That meant a more crowded studio than today's regional magazines, which all look as though they are served in a chill pack by a 'mom and pop' duo sitting in a designer waiting room. We covered a wider variety of subjects than the trivia they now offer and we served them up all hot in a crowded studio. All human life was there; or most of it. *Calendar* was not just a skip into which any rubbish could be piled but a carefully calculated mix of news, events, music and entertainment which always handed on a much bigger audience, regularly over 1,000,000 and sometimes 2,000,000 or more, to its successor programme. On occasions *Calendar* paid for itself, with the advertising revenue generated round our very expensive programme. Because regional programmes are almost as expensive to produce as national ones but have a smaller audience, most were treated as a loss leader to draw in the viewers. Ours actually paid its costs. No regional programme today can say that. Indeed under Michael Grade, ITV spent a lot of time trying to persuade government that regional programming was an expensive liability which ITV could no longer afford to bear, and which government hoped initially to slough off to new local TV stations, run on shoestring budgets, some of them certain to go bust, as all their cable predecessors (except Grimsby's Channel 7) already had by 2013. The new local TV is important but no substitute for strong regional companies of which only Scotland's now remains.

In the 1960s, we made different (and better) programmes for a different Yorkshire: still God's own county but closer to 'Him' then than it is today after the depredations of Margaret Thatcher who believed that phoenixes rose from

Hardraw Force before privatisation of water.

ashes, so that the best way of regenerating Britain's basic industries was to create more ashes; particularly in the North. That and New Labour neglect have turned a north–south gap into a gulf. Our beloved north country has more poverty and unemployment, more areas of deprivation and under-privilege than it had then. Fortunately it retains much of its spirit, toughness and simple bloody mindedness.

It has been a privilege to have served the North and another to have had so much help in writing what is essentially a personal memoir of my Calendar years. The team spirit lives on as (mercifully) do most of the team, and they have been very generous with their recollections. They are too numerous to list but a special thank you to Simon Welfare who saved me from a whole series of clangers and contributed his own happy memories, to John Fairley, Paul Dunstan, John Wilford and Duncan Dallas (who died in April 2014). Credit all praise to them, blame for remaining errors to me; which is the reverse of the deal we had on *Calendar*. Thanks also to Joyce Benton who put it all in order, to Kiwi Jackie Hay who did the proofs, to Ian Bloom, 'showbiz' lawyer, and to Steve Burnip of Huddersfield University. Steve is a former YTV producer who had the brilliant idea of doing an oral history of YTV which is now on the internet and he has been generous in making his material available, though I cannot say the same of YTV (RIP) whose records and archives appear to be scattered, depleted and possibly discarded and dumped. Old men forget but my old mates have all helped me to remember. So my thanks to Steve, the friends who have read and advised on the manuscript, and to you, the reader of these geriatric ramblings.

Welcome to my Calendar years.

CHAPTER ONE

YESTERDAY'S YORKSHIRE

In 1968 Yorkshire was a county with seven cities, five universities, three ridings, and no television station. It was awaiting the belated arrival of its own television station announced the year before and busily building in Leeds. The county which looked forward to this was different to today's motorway crossed county with its gleaming city architecture, its big booming universities, its shopping malls and energetic tourist promotion. It was black, soot grimed, flat'atted and dirty. Many of its 5,000,000 people were housed in grim rows of back-to-back and terrace housing, rushed up by Jerry builders in the industrial revolution. The mills, pits and steelworks created in that revolution were working busily. Its people were employed and much better off than before the war and it was proud of its superiority in industry, cricket, football and beauty. A Yorkshireman was Prime Minister, Labour (the party of the North) was in power and the working-class of a working county were enjoying what turned out to be their 'Indian Summer' basking in a county, both more self-sufficient and self-satisfied than any other, having been the first to industrialize, the one whose industry had made Great Britain wealthy and which still contributed most to paying the country's way in the world. Yorkshire was the proudest land symbolized by its boastful joke: to be born British is to be a member of the world's best club. To be born in Yorkshire is to be on the committee. Symptoms of decline were appearing but were largely ignored.

'Basking' is the word. Yorkshire was on the cusp and the biggest county, Britain's Texas, had been the slowest to modernize. Swinging Britain began as a London phenomenon. Media came from there and fashion was set there. The North swung later, and with The Beatles emerging from Liverpool, The Animals from Newcastle, Yorkshire seemed to swing more slowly than most. We were, still are, the most beautiful county with spectacular hills, dales, national parks and a dramatic coastline, but also a 'black' county where the detritus and poor housing of the industrial revolution had not been swept away and where black grime accumulated on our buildings. 'Where there's muck there's brass', we said, but there was also brutality, some of which emerged in the 'Rhino Whip' police brutality scandal in Sheffield with the rest posthumously portrayed in the *Red Riding* books by David Peace. Slum clearance to rid the cities of the acres of back-to-back and terrace housing was getting going. Sand blasting the massive black-stained town halls came later. Motorways ran up to and through Lancashire and the Midlands but were only just reaching Yorkshire. The BBC had no Yorkshire regional production centre because it served the North from Manchester. The first BBC local radio stations arrived only in 1968. Yorkshire was the only large region without its own commercial TV station. Unlike Manchester where Granada ruled the whole north and unlike Birmingham or even Anglia and Tyne Tees. Modernization, the great change process of the 1960s, came late to Yorkshire, still content to live in a better past.

By the 1960s, modernization and motorways were changing Britain. Harold Macmillan tried a massive dash for growth and entry to what was then called the Common Market. Harold Wilson turned to the white heat of technology with devaluation, new universities, incomes policy and a botched trade union reform. Britain succumbed to television becoming the first TV nation as set ownership leaped from two out of three to nine out of ten households and Britons were glued to the box for a total of four hours every night. Even the church people and academics, who had condemned television on its arrival, soon began to watch and even appear, though it was more respectable to appear on BBC than ITV.

Television privatized life and brought the nation home to watch it. Community activities and outdoor events, from children's play to visits to the cinema and playing sport as opposed to watching it, all declined as entertainment transferred to the living room and the family TV set whose screen size grew from 10in to over 20in, a sort of 'phallic' competition where screen size reflected income. All TV's competitors, the cinema, the churches, the theatre and outside social life generally, suffered proportionately. Britain was seduced (and was content to be so) by the least worse television in the world. The climate almost certainly helped. Unlike the largest TV nation, the USA, British weather encouraged people to sit at home watching television rather than going out. We became a stay-at-home nation and a better entertained one than any other. The Germans worked harder to rebuild their battered nation and its powerful exporting industries. The British workers sat back, job done, to be entertained, feeling that after fighting to make the world fit for British cars to break down in they could relax and enjoy the fruits of victory presented by personalities such as Hughie Green, Michael Miles, Gilbert Harding and others.

Modernization, commercialization and the television revolution began in the south, affecting Yorkshire, as they did the rest of the country, but not to the same degree. Being more content than the South, Yorkshire folk felt less need for modernization and their television arrived late. The Holme Moss transmitter had started up only in 1952 and their commercial transmitter was not built until 1968. As an industrialized county with a higher proportion of manual workers, Yorkshire was a natural audience for TV and then ITV but a series of lesser regions without the same pride, such as Anglia, Tyne Tees, and even tiny Border, received their own ITV franchises and stations, some barely financially viable, while proud Yorkshire, a county with the same population as Scotland and double that of Wales, got nothing; until 1967.

That was the year the Independent Television Authority decided to create a new franchise. The result of the delay was that there were no local TV skills, no employment prospects and none of the benefits and stimulus their regional stations had brought to Birmingham and Manchester. There was less local news, fewer locally inspired programmes to bring the county and Yorkshire to the national screen until March 1968 when the BBC set up a Yorkshire version of *Look North* in a small regional studio, symbolically a converted chapel, to transmit its regional programme, *Look North*, as a spoiler operation to build the audience before Yorkshire Television could get on air. Granada and the BBC produced a few Yorkshire programmes, usually with lots of 'trouble at t'mill', such as *The Master of Bankdam* or Phyllis Bentley's *Inheritance*. But most of their local programming was Lancashire inspired and Yorkshire news was minimal, because it was so much easier to get film back from the towns around Manchester than over the Pennines from Yorkshire. Most productions came from Manchester or Liverpool, created by staffs living in and around Manchester and presented by Lancashire personalities, such as Stuart Hall. Manchester had long been the media centre of the north and the only part of the area they knew well.

Yorkshire lagged in a modernizing world. The motorway network spreading spaghetti junctions round the country started with the Preston bypass (opened by 'Super Mac' [Harold Macmillan] in 1959) followed by the M6. Eventually it linked to Birmingham and Lancashire. Yorkshire still depended on the congested A1, the 'Great North Traffic Jam'. It received only one of the new 'white-tile' universities, York, to join its nineteenth century red bricks. Fashion, always stimulated by the media, radiated from London and came North more slowly, an unacceptable delay for the male population which could not wait for hot pants and mini-skirts. We were suited by Burton's, not tailored by Savile Row; flat 'ats died more slowly here.

Yorkshire was more insulated than either Lancashire or the prosperous South. It was conservative which was why it voted solidly Labour. It was not stricken like Lancashire where the cotton industry had largely collapsed. Nor did it get the diversion of car production from the south. That went to Liverpool and Scotland, while the aid and restructuring to save cotton went to Lancashire. Unlike the northeast, Yorkshire was not hit by the decline of shipbuilding but nor was it as prosperous as the southeast where the new industries: plastics, electrical, automotive, had gravitated in the 1930s. The North-South gap which later widened alarmingly, hardly gaped in the 1960s because Yorkshire was solid, like its building societies and town halls. It was content, a state which comes easy to the best.

But it no longer led either; once Yorkshire and the North generally had led the way to the future as the industrial revolution transformed society and built its great cities. The industries which had created that revolution were still producing powerfully but they were in slow decline, under-invested and un-modernized as international competition intensified and the consequences of British complacency, our reluctance to invest and the inefficiencies of family capitalism came through. This was an 'Indian Summer'; a prelude to tougher times to come but not yet felt.

Leeds backstreets: waiting to be pulled down.

Confidence was less secure than in the boastful years of the industrial revolution. Though less powerful and getting outdated, Yorkshire's great cities and industries were still strong, and being more self-sufficient than other parts and more insular, it was more self-satisfied. Yorkshire folk were less concerned about or interested in London and the South and less inclined to visit it. They had never emigrated on the scale of the Scots, the Irish or even Lincolnshire folk. Indeed, they had less reason to go outside the 'Broad Acres' for holidays, tourism, trips or even business. Yorkshire was less interested in the rest of the country, more preoccupied with itself, its issues and its people, being more complete in its good Yorkshire self than any other county. Why bother with the rest? Not quite a nation but still different and less dependent, it did not quite have its own language but the Yorkshire accent distinguished us from both the South and the received pronunciation of the media. You can always tell a Yorkshireman but you cannot tell him much. Indeed he probably would not listen unless it was told him in a Yorkshire accent. That could always be identified by the 'sher' test. The natives called their home county 'Yorksher'. Outsiders called it 'Yorkshire,' a nice place surely, though 'Yorksher' folk do not live there.

For staff coming north to start a new company, Yorkshire was a new world and a different one. Our north country was, is and, hopefully, ever shall be different to the comfortable south and particularly to overcrowded cosmopolitan London, a city which belongs more to the world than to England. In Yorkshire life was harder, tougher, more basic, and people worked harder for less money which was why 'brass' (money) was

Leeds: still waiting.

more cherished. Yorkshire folk were more respectful of 'brass' because they had less, though the less charitable took this for meanness, with Yorkshire folk seen as being as generous as an 'Aberdonian with no arms.'

This tough north/soft south dichotomy reflected the fact that the North was the home to heavy and basic industries, the South to finance, consumer industries and commerce. We were the producers, they the traders. In literary terms the South was Jane Austen, the North the Brontës or, perhaps in more modern terms, the South was *James Bond* and Lady Docker compared to the North's Joe Lampton and *Billy Liar*. The North was ugly and black, visualized as back-to-backs and terrace housing while the cleaner South was portrayed as commuter villages, sleepy rural scenes, thatched cottages or gleaming modernity. The North was industrial cities surrounded by the detritus of the industrial revolution. Our people lived in the debris of the past. The South lived with its riches.

The North was less well off. Ownership of washing machines (still twin tubs), televisions, refrigerators and the other gadgets of affluence, was lower in the North. But the ties of community remained stronger with the solidarity of the pit villages and the remaining working-class neighbourhoods, like Hunslet, whose life Richard Hoggart chronicled in *The Uses of Literacy*, or *Huddersfield*, chronicled by Brian Jackson. The old order of Working Men's Clubs, Co-ops, Miners' Welfare Societies, pigeon lofts, allotments, chapels and brass bands had 'held its ground not least because of the strong suspicion of the new and strange'. Northern girls complained that it took six months

Wish we had a playground until Calendar *comes on.*

No playground. So the kids made their own.

or more for southern fashions, like the mini-skirt or the 'Pill', to reach them. Northern men still wore suits, with wide-bottomed trousers, from Burtons or John Collier.

This was no place for the sophistication which YTV's new friends thought themselves to be bringing North. A few joked that they had to put their watches back ten years. Some could not wait to escape back to London every weekend. All complained of the black ugliness of Leeds and Bradford because subsidized sandblasting had not yet reduced our magnificent public buildings to fifty shades of grey. They found Yorkshire less sophisticated, less pretentious, harder and more basic. Yorkshire folk saw it as more open, more honest and certainly more beautiful. They found the North less respectful of and less concerned with education, a disconcerting discovery for Oxbridge graduates who got less deference.

Incoming staff for YTV were venturing into a new world. As day trippers to paradise they had to observe the unwritten rules incumbent on would-be residents. Do not make fun of Yorkshire. Praise is due and welcome, especially if it is lavish. Criticism is not. Laugh with us not at us (which means you will not laugh much). Do not expect anyone to enthuse about what you do. Praise is given grudgingly, except to cricketers. Avoid hype. The Yorkshireman is always 'fair to middlin' whether he's slowly dying or has just won the Euro Millions lottery. Do not praise London, the South or Manchester. Be objective and express your dislike for all of them. Do not talk too much; touch too much or go in for 'kissy-kissy' routines. They transmit germs and as an outsider you have probably got too many.

The North still retained the pride, the pomp and some of the power built up in the nineteenth century when it had been the engine house and wealth generator of

Woodhouse Mill, Todmorden.

the country. Huddersfield still boasted of having more Rolls-Royce motorcars per capita than any other city, the silk hats still sat uneasily on the heads of the wool merchant millionaires of the Bradford Exchange, the 'Squirarchy' still ruled in the North Riding and upmarket Harrogate flourished as the Cheltenham of the North, too rich and posh to be 'reet' Yorkshire. Best of all, Yorkshire was in its rightful place as the top cricket team. Yet a touch of insecurity was creeping in because the cradle of the industrial revolution had fallen behind in the twentieth century. Wealth, talent, and the new industries had moved to the more prosperous South, and the old basic industries which had built Britain were beginning to lose out in a more competitive world. London was sucking the wealth and talent out of the rest of the country. That sucking sound grew louder in the 1960s, though still not loud enough to disturb the settled routines of Yorkshire life.

By the mid-1960s, the pace of change was building to a level from which there was no turning back to the older, steadier, tightly corseted society Britain had been, and Yorkshire still was. Most changes were due not to government but social trends over which the public had little say. Immigration on a growing scale was making Britain a more pluralistic, multicultural society. More women were at work as full employment opened up opportunities and domestic appliances gave them time. The slums were being cleared, as people moved out to new towns and the suburbs. The spread of car ownership meant longer travel to work rather than living near 't'mill' or 'ower t'shop' as Yorkshire had traditionally done. Affluence meant the rise of the consumer society,

Squatters move in as the terraces are cleared.

criticized by J.B. Priestley as 'admass,' by Labour as greedy and moralists as 'live now pay later'. This filled the shops with luxuries, many of them imported as householders purchased a refrigerator, washing machine, toaster or a television set. The producer society was morphing into a consumer society, some of it so trendy that it made Britain swing with new music, relaxed morality, and the more casual sexuality fostered by the 'Pill' and the miniskirt. Yet when *Time* magazine announced (1 April 1967) that Britain swung it was about 'London the Swinging City' not Hull or Bradford the staid cities of the North. There change came more slowly.

Yorkshire felt the trends but their impact came later and was less on what was still a producer society with family capitalism, particularly in textiles, rather than dominant corporations. We were less dissatisfied with the old ways. 'Trendies' coming north (not really a habit of southern 'trendies') interpreted all this as backward and unfashionable but both characteristics were in fact more a manifestation of the contentment of stability than of self-satisfaction. Yorkshire was a society in transition: a safe generalization because Yorkshire, despite its images of rock-solid certainty and solidity, is always in transition. But the transition was slower and the vestiges of a proud independence symbolized by the great black-stained town halls of Leeds and Bradford which were the testaments of indifference to the soft South. The basic industries were still there, producing strongly, less strike prone than the motor industry but also less profitable, less confident and less competitive, while in the archetypal Calder Valley, the valley of a hundred chapels, mills were closing, co-operatives going bankrupt and chapel attendance was dwindling away.

They're hanging out the washing on the Hunslet line.

The county was coasting not climbing, its dominant characteristic complacent satisfaction rather than drive. A nation of producers was become one of consumers, but in Yorkshire 43 percent of employment was still in manufacturing, 10 percent in primary industries and 7 percent in construction, compared to 41 percent in services (48 percent nationally). Here was the essence of the difference, for Yorkshire was more working-class and the 1960s the apogee of working-class power with full employment, a greater share of national income going to wages and salaries, greater equality than in other parts of the country, a supportive welfare state, strong unions and the Labour Party in power. The working-class was not in its heaven but as near to it as it was ever to get before Margaret Thatcher destroyed the unions and the post-war settlement and tilted the balance back to wealth and its owners.

Yorkshire's solid middle-class were content but the North's working-class culture had created a new school of writing and a new realism to displace the old family sagas of wool barons and cotton kings. Northern working life was now described in books such as *Billy Liar*, Stan Barstow's writing, and even John Braine's *Room at the Top*, the story of the rise of a working-class lad into Yorkshire's middle-class society up to the top in a land when the height of a suburb indicated its wealth. This was paralleled by the growth of a new working-class entertainment developed out of the club and institute affiliated clubs and the Miners' Welfare Societies, particularly Greasbrough Working Men's Club, which was the first club to go 'big' in the 1960s by replacing local talent with national stars paid high fees to bring in the crowds.

How we used to live.

This led to the flowering of clubs, such as Batley Variety, Wakefield Theatre and the Fiesta Clubs in Sheffield and Stockton. Working-class audiences were brought in by coach from all over the country to be entertained by top artists from London and overseas, even by Jayne Mansfield who struggled to stand upright. Indeed, I remember one occasion when the hypnotist, Martin St. James, who had hypnotized six of the audience asked what dancers he should get them to imitate. A Yorkshire joker shouted 'Douglas Bader'.

Yorkshire has always been and remains more insular, less interested in the rest of the country or the world, more self-sufficient. Since the happy days of the 1960s northern industries, and even its building societies, had become less powerful, more dependent on southern capital and the city while the growth of national media, and particularly national television, eroded the North's distinctness and undermined its local media, like the *Yorkshire Post*, the *Sheffield Morning Telegraph* and *The Northern Echo*, all declining in circulation and authority. In the 1930s the *Yorkshire Post*, denouncing appeasement, had been a power in the land. Now it was the voice of a stodgy northern conservatism. Yet there was still a feeling of superiority and a greater interest in things domestic to Yorkshire than things southern and, by definition, unimportant. Complacency lingered on and Yorkshire was best, its people the proudest, its industries still proud. Complacency ruled: not OK.

The industrial revolution which built Yorkshire's industries had left deep scars on some of the ugliest, dirtiest, least attractive parts of Britain, outside Lancashire.

And how we used to play.

The landscape was littered with spoil heaps, some still burning, the hills were pock-marked with mines and grim-looking power stations were served by a merry-go-round of coal trains from local pits which made Yorkshire Britain's powerhouse. The cities were black monuments with the buildings rushed up in the nineteenth century to house the migrants drawn to the cities by the rise of industry. Most of it had still not been cleared and the terraces of basic back-to-back housing, built for an underpaid workforce, was deteriorating but too extensive for the clearance programmes.

Yet the ugliness was easy to escape. What Priestley had written about Bradford thirty years before in his *English Journey* still remained true of that city, and of all other large Yorkshire conurbations, even the city of Hull. 'Bradford' he wrote 'is a city entirely without charm though not altogether ugly...but it has the good fortune to be on the edge of some of the most enchanting country in England... However poor you are in Bradford you need never be walled in, bricked up as a round million folk in London must be. These great bare heights with a purity of sky above and behind them are always there waiting for you...However small your office or warehouse was, somewhere inside your head the high moors were glowing, the curlews were crying...That is why we did not care if our city had no charm, for it was simply a place to go and work in until it was time to set out for Wharfedale or Wensleydale again. We were at heart Wordsworthians to a man.'

New staff coming to YTV were more inclined to view Kirkstall Road as T.S. Eliot's *The Waste Land*. They escaped it in their housing. Instead of living in town and getting the tram out to the moors, to Wharfdale or even the beauty of the Dales, they purchased homes in those parts of the county which were more like the South, such as Ilkley, Harrogate or the up-market North Leeds rather than the industrial west which is where Duncan Dallas and I moved to. There they lived a kind of Yorkshire 'Lite' life, like Donald Baverstock who bought the fifteenth century Low Hall with his wife's, Enid Blyton, money, or Menston near the asylum where the company purchased a house for Ward Thomas. It was convenient for Harry Ramsden's, the biggest fish and chip shop in the world. I doubt if Ward ever ate there.

Yorkshire is a state of mind as well as a geographical entity. Sometimes it is a bloody one. The 'awkward bugger' syndrome is endemic in Yorkshire shown in an obstinacy and a stubbornness which several of the new colleagues complained about when meeting angry Yorkshiremen on narrow roads who refused to reverse or give way but just blocked the road. Yorkshire has produced more mass murderers. Christie (who grew up in the same street as my father – Chester Road, Halifax – where his father scandalized the Mitchell neighbours by keeping rabbits in the bedroom), Donald Nielson and Sutcliffe, the 'Yorkshire Ripper', and the first man to utilize the opportunities brought by the M62. This obstinacy and awkwardness was the cause of the prolonged and bitter fratching and quarrelling which crippled Yorkshire County Cricket Club for much of the period. It's demonstrated by the long stone walls Yorkshire farmers built over worthless hills and down miserable dales just to show who owned it. It also produced all the jokes about meanness, being blunt to the point of obtuseness (I say what I mean and I mean what I say) and all their boastful claims of superiority (why ask someone if they are from Yorkshire? If they are, they will tell you in minutes; if not, why humiliate them?)

In the industrial world people were what they made. It dictated the lifestyle and the housing. Yorkshire was heavy industry: power generation, coal, steel, wool and clothes, all basic industries which made for a basic way of life, with workers living close to the mill or mine and home early for tea and the kind of basic attitudes shaped by work which was hard and tough. No point in coming to Leeds looking for the sophistication of metropolitan man. Yorkshire's defensive shield of assertiveness and contempt for the 'arty farty' and 'posh' accents took pride in its own Yorkshire accent. In Chaucer's day, that had been the national Received Pronunciation (RP) but until Wilfred Pickles and Harold Wilson made it more acceptable it had been caricatured as a symptom of lower-class origins

There was an element of defiance in this. Yorkshire folk knew some of their world was ugly but did not care. They knew their accent was laughed at. So they exaggerated it. This defensive defiance made them uneasy in the South, happy at home, and happier with their friends than strangers who were an object of suspicion and guilty until they proved themselves OK. This was a difficult hurdle for outsiders to jump. Those who never did, did not stay long. Those who jumped it were welcome and well received – eventually.

One new YTV employee took his wife into a Leeds pub to give her a taste of the North. He ordered a pint for each of them but was amazed when he took her pint to his wife to have the barman snatch it back, announcing 'We don't serve pints to ladies.' The implicit assumption was that any woman who drank it was not one. Immigrants were numerous, particularly in Bradford where people from Pakistan and Bangladesh had been brought over in large numbers to provide cheap labour for the mills. Yet they had not then brought an element of variety to Bradford and Huddersfield because they lived mainly in ghettos rather than integrating and became more assertive about Islam. Indian restaurants, music, specialist shops and films did not emerge and flourish until later.

The prevailing ugliness was so great that one member of YTV staff driving his partner north up the A1 road to their new home felt he had to chatter loudly and wave his arms vigorously to prevent her noticing the 'beauties' of Ferrybridge. Those who came and stayed realized that Yorkshire was a better place to live, work and enjoy life well away from the overcrowding, pressures, high costs and sullen snobbery of the South, but it took time to realize this and for most new recruits Yorkshire was a far-away county of which they knew next to nothing. A few read Graham Turner's new book, *The North County*, as if it was a *Lonely Planet* guide to a foreign country. They could not even make the standard joke that they were seeking the source of the M1 or the M62 motorways. Neither was complete.

They were coming to what was almost a country not just a different area, but one where inhabitants saw themselves as independent, plain spoken, bluntly honest and more friendly and better than southerners, if only because they were. They had all the virtues Harold Wilson sought to make his trademark in the early 1950s when he abandoned the posh RP accent of the social climber for the plainer and blunter tones of Yorkshire. Why should Scots be the only people deemed sufficiently honest looking to sell patent medicines on TV? Because Yorkshire folk will not lie for money! 'You can live next door to folk in the south for years and never get to know them' was the claim of Yorkshire folk. With a few significant exceptions, such as Lords Harewood, Wharncliffe and Fitzwilliam, that did not apply in Yorkshire. It certainly did outside of the county.

Yorkshire folk, particularly those who had moved south, liked to present a bluff face to the world as a caricature: the stage Yorkshireman acted to disguise their lack of assurance but the differences were real. Yorkshire folk were more self-sufficient, more phlegmatic and probably more stolid and less excitable and volatile. It was more difficult to win their trust and YTV's new staff came from London, the production centre for sophisticates and the pretentious. Even the recruits from Manchester felt a touch superior to the universal 'flat 'ats' to 'snagging' in the street and to the Greenwoods tailoring which surrounded them. John Fairley had written fashion articles for *The Observer* - at £200 a time. That could have bought him ten suits in Greenwoods or eight from Burtons had he been tempted to wear native dress.

Some new chums were shocked by their new surroundings. An unfinished TV centre built on a vast weed-growing wasteland (no Common Agricultural Policy set-aside grants then), surrounded not by shops, pubs and restaurants like Granada or BBC Manchester, but by wasteland, grime-covered factories like Yorkshire Screw, a second-hand television centre and rows of terrace housing rising from Cardigan Road behind and beyond the 'Lowry-style' railway arches to the west. Good, cheap restaurants (as opposed to the pretentious and posh) such as the Jumbo from Manchester and Leonard Cohen's Get Stuffed (where many of us did) only came later.

New staff had to put aside any sense of superiority for the privilege of being in at the start of a new television station and discovering a part of the country they did not know, making them like explorers venturing into a strange world. It may have been similar to Rochdale where Barry Cockcroft came from or Liverpool where John Fairley grew up but it was very different to London, Scotland or even Birmingham. Even the Yorkshiremen among us were rediscovering their county. Richard Whiteley and I had taken the middle-class route out, me as a grammar school boy to Manchester, then Oxford and New Zealand which I saw as a kind of Antipodean Yorkshire, Richard via the public school route to Cambridge. Yorkshire had to be rediscovered, particularly working class Yorkshire, mining Yorkshire, wool and fishing Yorkshire; the real world of work and 'brass' which even in this most egalitarian of counties was new to its new arrivals.

In the rest of the world (which I stopped calling the real world because that was us) revolution was in the air, the student revolt in Paris, the siege of the American Embassy in London. When Duncan Dallas arrived in Leeds one of the first things he saw was graffiti proclaiming 'Today Paris; Tomorrow Leeds.' Dream on 'Leeds Lefties'. It was not to be. Nor was it part of the expectations of any of the new employees who thought they had gone back in time not forward and were focussed on their own career prospects. If they were missionaries it was for commercialism, an ITV station bringing the commercial message and the better entertainment that Yorkshire, always the last county to benefit, had got at last.

It takes all types to make Yorkshire...

...but only the toughest to be a Yorkshire miner.

Hard work at t'mill. *Hard life outside it.*

Yorkshire was not fertile ground for political radicalism. It was small 'c' conservative. Why change when you're the best? Yorkshire's most powerful union, the National Union of Minerworkers (NUM), was cautious and conservative not militant, Yorkshire's wealthy were cautious, canny and small minded, its local government solid, stolid and unexciting, its Co-operative shops closing because they were slow to develop as supermarkets. Britain had begun to change. Labour created a National Plan to improve the country's lame economic performance. Even in Yorkshire tradition faded. Councils were corrupted by big builders. Wakes and feast weeks, where each town closed down totally for holidays, faded away. Communities were pulled down. Yet all this was slow and Yorkshire changed less than the rest. Its white heat remained coal fired (no nuclear plants in the 'Broad Acres'), its mood complacent and self-satisfied.

Basic industries dictated Yorkshire life. Mining was concentrated in villages of National Coal Board housing; effectively little urban patches in the country where poaching flourished. The fishing industry was concentrated in Hull and Grimsby with their terrace houses surrounding the docks and angling flourished in the canals, not the elaborate art of fly-fishing for trout, that went on north of the 'Wharf'. Wool workers were housed in back-to-backs around the mills with social facilities, pubs, chip shops and Working Men's Clubs, everything life could offer, all nearby. Everywhere the workers took home samples of their produce, be it fish, a length of suit cloth or coal, as a pay supplement. During the war, parts to build a complete tank had been stolen piece-by-piece from the Leeds factory where they were produced.

It's easy to tell when wool's not doing well.

Basic industries made for a basic lifestyle. It was hard but the industries also supported beauty for many proud mills and mines had their own brass bands bearing their names like John Foster's Black Dyke Mills Band or Grimethorpe Colliery. Wool and clothing were not yet hit too hard by the intense competition which had destroyed Lancashire's cotton industry but faced a growing threat. Wool was diversified into specialized production units: spinning, combing, weaving, dying (amalgamated into the Bradford Dyers' Association) rather than integrated. It had remained so since the second half of the nineteenth century when most of the dark 'satanic' mills were built. Bradford buyers still dominated the New Zealand wool market, wool barons dominated the Bradford Exchange and the mills (except for Illingworth Morris) remained mainly family firms employing cheap female or Asian labour and providing a living for the founder family, but when things became difficult or the mill less profitable that family were all too ready to sell up rather than invest, as Richard Whiteley's family firm, Thomas Whiteley & Company of Eccleshill, had done in the mid-1960s. They would put their mill on the property market and get out, or burn it down for the insurance rather than investing and upgrading to keep abreast of the times – 'Red sky at night, a woollen mill alight' and the skies were reddening more often. New processes were

Fishing was good before the Common Fisheries Policy.

coming in, developed by the Woollen Industries Research establishment at Ilkley. Integrated production, with all processes under one roof, was developed by the new Bulmer Lumb factory in Bradford, but the industry kept going by low-wage labour rather than by investment, new machinery or moving upmarket. As for garments, Montague Burton's large factory in Leeds still clothed and suited many Britons. Marks & Spencer still boasted that 90 percent of what they sold was British made and Bradford's Textile Society, to which my father belonged, was still dominated by producers not merchandizers. You could tell when the wool industry was in trouble because the skies of Bradford turned red at night with mill fires started to claim insurance. In 1968, fire brigades were busy.

Coal was more prosperous and was still exported to the rest of the world through the port of Immingham. Mining was a powerful, proud industry, vastly improved by nationalization and the investment it brought and not yet weakened by the closures of the 1970s. It dominated South Yorkshire, fuelling Britain's power stations with a rail merry-go-round from the pits to Ferrybridge and back. Massive investment had mechanized coal. Smaller and older mines were closed, an ongoing process which provided many a sentimental film for *Calendar* as I desperately tried to make closures a moving occasion, only to have the miners confess that they were glad

Yorkshire: centre of world walking stick production.

And national tripe production.

a small, difficult to work pit like Waterloo (described by one as 'the scabby back pit') had closed so they could move to larger, easier to work pits like Kellingley, the newest and the largest mine in the country. The new mines, opened in the 1960s, were worked by advancing face-cutting machinery, all of it manufactured in Britain, making Kellingley and other new mines the most efficient in Europe and very profitable. Yorkshire was the best and proudest part of a National Coal Board empire run from Coal House in Doncaster and in close co-operation with the strong union. Its confidence was manifested by the posters all over the coal field – 'Mining: A Job for Life'. It was not but no-one saw that in the 1960s and only the insane and unsound could have believed that mining would be closed down, as Margaret Thatcher's revenge.

Steel, concentrated in Stocksbridge, Sheffield and Rotherham had been nationalized then denationalized. Though not as well invested or as effectively modernized as coal or overseas competitors it was striding ahead with the huge new integrated steel plant, one of five in Britain, being built in Scunthorpe at the Anchor plant. It was facing more intense competition from Germany and from the Far East, particularly in finished products like cutlery, or coming in on wheels in the form of cars, but progressive companies like Viners were still trading profitably.

Fishing was the realm of Hull and Grimsby from where a large fleet sailed to fish in Icelandic waters. They made huge catches, though Grimsby claimed it caught quality while Hull took 'shit fish' by going for quantity. Both were increasingly disputed by the Icelanders who were building up their own industry and gradually extending the limits, and by the weather which in 1968 sank three Hull vessels, all of which capsized as heavy ice accumulated on the superstructure. This resulted to protests, led by Lilly Bilocca, which produced more effective safety regulation and investment with newer diesel-powered vessels replacing the last coal-fired trawlers. The catches held up; supplies to fish wholesalers and retailers all over Yorkshire were maintained. The fishing crisis was to come later.

These basic industries, their lives dramatized by *The Price of Coal*, and in Grimsby *The Price of Fish* or Bentley's *Inheritance*, determined the Yorkshire pattern: conservative, slow to change and coasting. Yorkshire did not realize in its contentment that its industries were less competitive and dynamic. Other countries invested, reorganized, co-operated and competed to build strong exporting sectors and national champions. Yorkshire was more complacent and self-satisfied and less dynamic, the workers better entertained with the best sport and television but working longer hours for less money and facing worse economic prospects because the need to invest and modernize to compete in an increasingly competitive world was ignored on the complacent assumption that Britain was best.

Like Caesar's Gaul, Yorkshire was divided into three parts: the historic Ridings. The spectacular coastline was dotted with lovely, but failing, seaside resorts running down from Whitby through Scarborough, Bridlington and Filey to Cleethorpes where people from Sheffield went for their holidays. All were struggling because of the trend to cheap package holidays in Spain. Rural North Yorkshire stretched as far as Wharfedale and there were the homes of county society, a down-market Cheshire, their halls and houses accommodating what had once been Yorkshire's

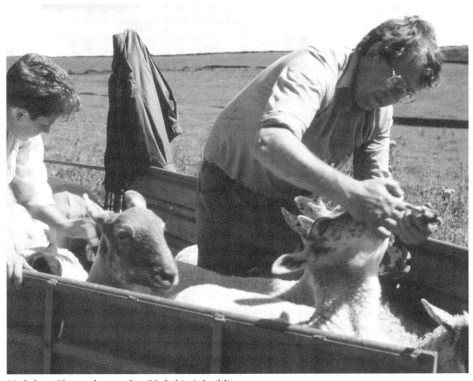

Yorkshire Sheep: cleaner than Yorkshire's buildings.

traditional leadership, though the county's gentry had never been quite as fashionable or influential as their southern counterparts. In the West Riding, they had been displaced by an industrial 'elite' of wool barons and also mill owners, great and small, many of whom became landowners. Some, in the case of Lord Masham or Lord Somerleyton, succeeded.

Yorkshire had less class differentiation than the South with its wider social range from enormous wealth to the poverty of London's East End. The North of England was an area where it was possible to live a life more ordinary, more like other people's lives and more contented. It had fewer extremes and less visible class demarcations, but you could see the divisions everywhere: in the division between the rough and the respectable working-class, described by Hoggart, or between those who ate in the chandeliered dining room at Harry Ramsden's and those who took their 'take-away' in the glass roofed lean-to at the side or between the motorists and the car-less. The real elite was smaller, often public school educated, but ranging from the few who were sent away south to the major public schools, to the majority who paid less (and got less), educated in the county's minor public schools, such as Woodhouse Grove, Giggleswick, Queen Ethelburga's, and Rishworth. Beneath these were the grammar schools ranging from King Edward School in Sheffield and Bradford Grammar School, both direct grant schools taking only a small proportion of the local school leaving population, down to grammar schools like Bingley, Heath, Batley and other local grammars which took up to a third of primary school leavers, a proportion equalled only in Wales. These grammar schools were the production line of the Yorkshire elite, typified by Harold Wilson, the many managers of Yorkshire's businesses and the staff of its schools and financial institutions: the dutiful, devoted grammar school elite. At the bottom the secondary modern schools educated the majority as the skilled and semi-skilled workers for the Yorkshire economy. Most Yorkshire folk had been educated for that and no further, for there was a prevailing lack of aspiration which high pay in sole industry towns had bred and an all too common feeling that 'You can educate folk until they're daft'. Or, more accurately, until they go south.

The brightest Yorkshire children left to go on either to university, often outside the county (only a minority of them to Oxbridge), or to seek better careers in London, a 'brain drain' which became more serious as Britain became more centralized. All career ladders led to London's bigger stage and too much talent went south, a process which raised the IQ of both regions. Much of Yorkshire's top talent, from J.B. Priestley, James Mason, Eric Portman, Henry Moore, John Braine, Ted Hughes and A.S. Byatt, emigrated to the South's softer clime. David Hockney had gone to California and Alan Bennett commuted between London and the Dales. Only a minority stayed in Yorkshire to buy houses and raise families in its settled community, though some of its writers, from Larkin, Stan Barstow and Alan Plater stayed loyal to Ossett or Hull. No TV production centre checked this 'brain drain' by providing opportunities in the North.

Yorkshire TV was not created by Yorkshire Nationalists to argue for Home Rule, desirable as I, personally, began to think that was. The aim was to multiply

Getting ready to read the news.

Yorkshire money and keep it in the county to stimulate Yorkshire business (and pride), make Yorkshire complete, stop the drift of talent south and put the best (and most boastful) county on to the television screens of the nation; at a profit. As for the collection of child geniuses, including me, we came north to advance careers, in the best and most interesting job in the world, making television programmes. The basic purpose was to provide good TV programmes and make Yorkshire's the top TV station. Every county should have one. We did, at last.

When I was at school the few locals in radio all had to go to Manchester. Wilfred Pickles, Phyllis Bentley from Halifax and Bertha Lonsdale, the librarian from my village Baildon who we treated with awe. Now thirty years later, the county awaited its own television station to keep Yorkshire talent at home and provide opportunities for every pop group, singer, entertainer, comedian, reputed television star, journalist and writer in Yorkshire. At last the great county was to televise its talkers, its tragedies, its characters, its heroes and villains as well as its beauties, hills, lakes and history. They were the best. All that was lacking was the opportunity to draw their superiority to the attention of the world.

Glyn Hughes in his book, *Millstone Grit*, argued that 'millstone grit defines also the nature of the people who dwell on it. Rough, truculent and dour they might appear, but this as well as their stone, is only a forbidding exterior; break it open and just as the millstone grit is gold inside so these people sparkle with human courage and kindness.' YTV was to bring these virtues to the screen and demonstrate them to the nation. Or to change images. The basking county was to be woken up.

THE BIRTH
OF YTV

In 1967, the Independent Television Authority announced only twelve years late that Yorkshire was, at last, to get the major boost to modernization which would come from its own TV production centre to put Yorkshire on the nation's screens, a major step towards undermining the excessive centralization which has made us the most over-centralized country in the world, outside of Monaco. London contains a higher proportion of the population than any other capital. It overflows into the 'Home Counties', so called as if other counties were alien. Far too much money is spent on it and in it, it gets disproportionate attention and far too much is centralized there. Other countries spread power around through federalism, like Germany, Australia and the US, or create regionalized structures, like France and Italy. In Britain centralization was getting worse and London was draining the country. The other great cities, whose proud town halls had once been the symbols of their independence, their power and wealth, were all losing out to London.

There were sporadic, but always feeble and failing, attempts to reverse this centralization by regional aid: the Kilbrandon Commission's proposals for regional government in the 1960s, the Hardman Report in the 1970s urging dispersal of the Civil Service, and finally devolution to Wales and Scotland, along with Regional Development Agencies for the rest of the country. None of it did much for Yorkshire or the North. So ITV's federal structure was the only successful attempt to breathe life into the regions and stimulate regional identity. It took TV production out of London to put it into regional companies, and last, but most important of all, to Yorkshire which got its own ITV company and production centre in 1968. At last Yorkshire could make programmes, present itself to the world, take production and people out of London and bring them to Leeds to promote Yorkshire pride and give the North something to be proud of.

Independent television or, as Labour preferred to call it, 'commercial television', was created in the 1950s after a brilliant public relations campaign which I used as a model when I taught political science. Presented as providing choice and a free alternative to the state-funded BBC, the Television Act which created the system and the Independent Television Authority to regulate and control it, was passed by Parliament in 1954 over the obscurantist, backward-looking opposition of the Labour Party. The Labour spokesman, Ness Edwards, warned that 'We regard this Bill as a great danger to the mental and cultural outlook of the people of Britain.' The ageing Herbert Morrison, grandfather of 'Modernizing' Mandelson (who would almost certainly have disowned his grandfather on this and many other counts) claimed that the Conservative Party had ceased to be the Party of 'aristocratic culture' and become 'the Party of capitalist commercialism'.

Morrison urged that sordid commercial TV should be rejected in favour of 'properly balanced alternative programmes with national coverage' which the Conservatives rushed to point out would have to be paid for by the taxpayer rather than by a small increase to the price of a packet of soap powder. Labour eventually came to love ITV more than the BBC but at the beginning was fighting on the side of the establishment, the church hierarchy, the universities and all that was respectable and boring. Fortunately it was outvoted, though the taunt of being anti-ITV still stuck, to the extent that just before the 1959 election *The Daily Sketch* newspaper terrified readers with the warning that if Labour won their beloved ITV would be 'abolished in six months'.

The Independent Television Authority worked under the guidance of its first chair, Sir Kenneth Clark (of *Civilisation* fame) to give commercial TV a touch of culture. The ITA chief executive, Robert Fraser, the first (and the best) of the Australians who shaped British TV, was the real architect of Independent TV. He saw it as 'People's TV' and devised its new structure on regional lines, not so much through any intellectual commitment to regionalism but to have the new service run by as many independent companies as possible rather than one large company like the BBC which would inevitably have been based in London. This suggested the creation of a series of regional companies, each financed by a regional monopoly of commercial TV and the revenues from advertising. Because the new transmitters served only the three largest population centres he started with three initial regions each supporting two companies, a weekday provider like Granada in the North and a weekend provider in ABC. The six initial companies shared what turned out to be a financial bonanza, created by regional monopolies which sustained it for nearly fifty years when digital broadcasting allowed anyone to watch anything from anywhere.

Birmingham, London and Manchester were the starting point for ITV federalism. Its ethos was populist not metropolitan. ITV gave the people what they were assumed to want, not what the BBC and the establishment thought they should have. This populist, low-brow approach with its endless quiz shows offered amusement rather than education or information but the British, particularly those at the broad base of the social pyramid, fell under its hypnotic spell, 'amusing themselves to death'. ITV won a majority share of the audience from the more staid, serious and public service orientated BBC. By 1957, the audience share in households which could get both channels was 35 percent BBC and 65 percent ITV. When I returned home from university in the 1950s, I occasionally suggested that my parents might like to watch some programmes on the BBC. The answer was always '…we don't watch BBC.' A majority of the nation said the same. After once monopolizing viewing the BBC faced declining audiences until, in the late 1950s and early 1960s it was revived by a new generation of producers, like Donald Baverstock and Alasdair Milne, with such hits as *Tonight, Z Cars* and *That Was the Week*.

By the 1960s, federalism was becoming coherent with smaller companies set up to serve smaller areas, like Tyne Tees and the wealthier Anglia region in the East, though transmission areas could not conform exactly with regional identities so the borders were 'flexible' and the identities sometimes confused. Tyne Tees reached well down into the North Riding. Yet this growth made the omission of Yorkshire all the more indefensible. It was the only region without its own TV station, a failure rectified in only in 1967 when the ITA, chaired now by the 'radio doctor', Lord Hill, decided to split the North, take Yorkshire away from Granada and ABC and set up the last great region as the fourth network company and a main producer of programmes for the network.

This upset the Bernstein brothers who had taken great pride in their northern TV 'empire'. They had even considered erecting 'Granadaland' signs on its boundary, having given Granada a northern anti-London bias and set out to show the North to the North in regular outside broadcasts, though these mostly came from the towns round Manchester. Their North was Mancunian and Lancastrian rather than 'Tykonian'. The news, too, was devoted more to areas round Manchester because the need to get film back over the Pennines restricted Yorkshire coverage. The soap-opera *Coronation Street* set the tone by not being set in Hunslet or Huddersfield. Sidney Bernstein threatened an appeal to the United Nations where he may have thought the USSR would exercise its veto to protect lefty Granada but he could have been joking. Lancastrian dominance was broken. His consolation prize was the closure of ABC at Didsbury, giving Granada all of the beloved North West for a full seven-day week. A White Rose Day for us: Red Nose Day for Sidney.

The ITA called for bidders for the Yorkshire contract. Paradoxically the winning bid was fashioned in Blackpool and developed by a Lancastrian, Stuart Wilson. This bid, first to be made, was from Telefusion, a Blackpool-based television rental company with a significant customer base in Yorkshire. The chairman of Telefusion, J.C. Wilkinson had long been interested in owning a television channel, largely because of the money which he (and many others) hoped to make out of what Lord Thomson, the Canadian owner of the Scottish franchise, rightly called a 'licence to print money'.

For Wilkinson it was an ego trip – 'Lancastrian wins Yorkshire contract' sort of pride. He saw Yorkshire as a prime target and was not averse to outsmarting the Bernsteins. He gave that job to one of his young graduate managers, Stuart Wilson, the 27 year-old marketing manager for Telefusion. Wilson was told he could spend as much as required to win the contract. He set forth from Blackpool to the 'Promised Land', pockets bulging with cash, mind obsessed with the 'Broad Acres'.

Donald Baverstock: presiding genius of Yorkshire Television.

The *Daily Mail* newspaper dubbed Wilson 'The Butcher's Boy from Blackpool'. In fact he was an economics graduate from Nottingham and astutely sought the advice of Frank Copplestone, a fellow Nottingham graduate who had become head of programming at the ITA. Copplestone advised him to recruit a managing director from within the system who knew how it worked rather than some 'glamorous' outsider and pointed Wilson in the direction of Gwyn Ward Thomas, former bomber pilot and currently successful managing director of the small ITV company, Grampian, located in Aberdeen. Thomas, whose home was in London with a wife who did not want to move, cautiously agreed to negotiations, met Wilson who encouraged him by saying that his own aim was just to be a shareholder not to run the company. Ward Thomas agreed to take on the job. Leeds was nearer London than Aberdeen, the money far better and the power far greater. He would have preferred to combine it with the job of programme director as well but whereas that was feasible in a small company like

Grampian it would have been amateurish in the big league. Wilson recruited a more prestigious figure, Aubrey Singer, from the BBC as programme director.

Lynch pins in place, Wilson added Sir Richard Graham, a former Lord Lieutenant of Yorkshire and present High Sheriff, in the figurehead role of chairman. He was already on the board of Telefusion and now added dignity and a touch of history to the new company. Graham's family legend has it that when at the commission's interview with the YTV bid team, Lord Hill sourly remarked 'Promises, promises, promises. How do we know you won't break them?' Sir Richard stood on his dignity to reply that 'My family has generations of service and has never broken its promises': collapse of one 'radio doctor'.

TV expertise came with Geoffrey Cox, the creator of ITN, who was recruited as vice chaiman. Wilson also hired a consultancy, Voice & Vision, run by Hugh Thomas, an ITN reporter keen on greater things, to guide his steps and write the appropriate papers on the type of television the new company would provide. These became a major source of strength because the ITA was anxious to move ITV upmarket and away from the endless quiz shows and endless 'miles' of Michael Miles. Documentation produced by Telefusion emphasized the need for higher standards and fewer quiz shows on ITV. Phil Parker was hired to be the engineer. By this time Wilson, who still had money to burn, had spent over £100,000 (as much as £2,500,000 in today's terms) in the run up to the contract on public relations, publicity, opinion surveys. It all went to create the best documented and most publicized bid.

But not the only one, there were other major contenders. The favourite was a bid based on the The Yorkshire Post Group, which changed its ownership name (but not its nature) from Yorkshire Conservative Newspapers to appear more impartial. It combined with the local Star Cinema Group, anxious to emulate the success of Granada cinemas ten years earlier. Another local group was headed by Professor McGregor who had made a failed bid for Tyne Tees five years before. There was also a 'Yorkshire TV Producers' Group', a curiously named bid (since there were not any) led by Wyndham Cinemas with Decca. Then along came Trans-York TV organized by local businessmen and larger than most, plus a London-based bid organized by the then ubiquitous Lord Goodman who had fingers in every available business 'pie'. His bid was intellectually powerful and included *The Daily Telegraph*, London equivalent of the *Yorkshire Post*, Penguin Books and British Lion Films, making a highly-respectable group which offered a prospectus of heavy programmes; rather like the BBC with commercials. It was not very Yorkshire.

The rise of TV had produced a gadarene-like rush of cinema and film businesses anxious to get out of their declining industry and into the more profitable field of television. A final manic touch was added by Ken Dodd's *Diddy TV.* Sadly, the 'Diddymen' (who were Lancastrians in any case) only reached their peak of popularity in the 1970s and Dodd's bid was withdrawn in weeks. Yet it could have appealed more to Yorkshire audiences than to the serious, heavy earnestness of Lord Goodman's team. Dodd's interviewing technique would certainly have been more fun for the ITA.

Faced with this galaxy of greed the ITA opted, as it usually did, for compromise. The Yorkshire Post Group and the Goodman Group came together before the interviews to make a group heavy with talent, such as Donald Baverstock, but drawn mainly from the BBC, while the Telefusion bid now brought in Peter Willes, the well thought of head of drama at Redifusion, also Alan Whicker, as a major shareholder and programme contributor, making it more ITV orientated. Both groups promised to spread their shareholdings around Yorkshire. Both included Yorkshire newspapers, with Telefusion having rather more, although smaller newspapers also had shares. Both proposed shareholdings for Yorkshire universities. Both produced programme plans which emphasized originality, though Telefusion was smart enough to criticize the London bias of existing television and to propose a 'People's Television'. The Yorkshire Post Group, heavy on London talent, could do neither.

Both did surveys of opinion in Yorkshire which predictably showed that Yorkshire folk wanted more programmes about Yorkshire, though surprisingly, in view of the Mancunian ethos projected by *Coronation Street* and the Manchester dominance of its new regional magazine, *Scene at 6.30*, only a minority felt that Granada had neglected the 'Broad Acres'. The surveys indicated that the potential ITV audience was a little dim. On average, they spent six hours a day in front of their televisions, but only 40 percent in Telefusion's survey knew that Granada was their weekday contractor. Only 15 percent knew it was ABC at the weekends.

After months of publicity, posturing and muscle flexing the ITA moved towards a merger between the two leading groups. On 9 June 1967, it proposed to offer the contract to the Telefusion bid but with conditions which amounted to a forced merger with the Yorkshire Post Group. This was finalized when Aubrey Singer, Telefusion's programme controller, decided he was safer staying with the BBC and Donald Baverstock, who had been a programme adviser in the Yorkshire Post Group bid, moved over as director of programmes. He brought with him Tony Essex, the producer of *The Great War* series, and the small group of producers who were his disciples, like Liz Kustow, Michael Blakstad and Michael Deakin, as well as great hopes (which were not fulfilled) of bringing his brilliant Tonight team. The deal was sealed, the Telefusion shareholding reduced to make way for more Yorkshire newspapers and the name was changed to Yorkshire Television. Habemus Programme Company (YTV) was born, although there was not yet a building, a staff or any actual programmes. There was less than a year to go.

The regional licence was granted on 11 June 1967, some twelve years after the start-up of ITV. Leeds and Harrogate contended to accommodate the new station but, thank heavens, Leeds, which was more central, stimulating and exciting, won. After a shorter than usual time, planning permission for the building was granted. Leeds Council was eager to have a brilliant new business (or any business if truth be told) on its Kirkstall Road waste land. The chosen site was a weed-covered field where, a few years before, rows of slum terrace houses had sat less than a mile from the city centre (just far enough to make Leeds taxi businesses profitable when TV started). The television centre was to be built where once alphabet streets had stood and Yorkshire TV took the eight acres cleared by the demolition of Otter Street, Peel, Quadrant, Runcorn, Stanhope and Townend Street). All had run down from Cardigan Road to Kirkstall Road but had been demolished in Leeds' great slum clearance campaign. Their inhabitants had moved out to the suburbs leaving a wasteland, some of which remains unused today.

On 5 August 1967, work started to create the first, and certainly the most modern, colour equipped television studios in Europe that would transmit, initially in black and white. It was scheduled to cost £1,800,000 for the building and £2,200,000 for equipment. The foundation stone was laid on 30 November 1967 by Lord Aylstone the new chairman of the ITA and former Labour cabinet minister – Lord Hill having been moved by Harold Wilson to bully the BBC. The building was being erected around the ceremony. No time to stop work.

The Gods, almost certainly delighted to see such a huge development in their home county, did their job and smiled on Yorkshire. Mud and a hard winter's snow and ice could have delayed building but only twenty working days were lost because of weather conditions, although even that was too many on the excessively tight schedule. With men working on three aspects of most sections at the same time and extra bonus payments for speed, by July 1968 three studios were up and 'all but' ready. Unfortunately 'all but' ready covered a multitude of problems. Thousands of miles of wiring were laid and the technical equipment, such as cameras (then costing £24,000 apiece and all made in Britain) installed. Yet much of the building remained unfinished. Dust was everywhere and with the offices last to be completed, most of the staff (by now 360 strong) had to be accommodated in an adjacent disused Burtons trouser factory. Fortunately Burtons were shareholders. So the trouser factory became a seat of television knowledge: tight fitting, uncomfortable, hot in summer and cold in winter. Conditions which might have been marginally acceptable to Leeds garment workers were less so to shivering TV staff coming up from the South to start their new glamorous career in a disused trouser factory which froze in winter, baked in summer.

This was not the only problem. Tony Essex's young team were eager to get going making documentaries to fill the vacant programme spaces lying ahead. The brightest was Antony Thomas, a South African christened 'Crazy Bear' by the film staff, but a star film maker to whom money was no object. Fortunately young YTV had plenty. Thomas began work on a powerful programme on Yorkshire's greatest engineering feat, the North's equivalent of the Trans-Siberian railway, the M62 motorway, then being built across the Pennines. The result was a Yorkshire 'Quo Vadis', a brilliant film produced by a perfectionist who spent a day ensuring that a stripper's brassiere (part of the titivation necessary in ITV's current affairs programmes) fell on to the lens of the cameraman lying on the floor, without revealing too much.

This attempt to titivate and dramatize Yorkshire's toughest engineering project caused public-relations problems when, finding a farmer whose farm was in the middle of what should have been the motorway was refusing to move out, Thomas staged a confrontation by sending in a pretend surveyor, played by an actor, who claimed to need to get on to the farm to measure it for demolition. The ensuring row enlivened the film, but was then exposed as phoney by the *Yorkshire Post*. The even more angry farmer refused to move so the motorway had to be built around his farm which today sits in the middle, accessed by a tunnel as passing trucks disturb the sheep: a monument to Yorkshire's introduction to TV 'conman-ship' and TV's to Yorkshire awkwardness.

Costs rose further when a Rolls-Royce, hired for the programme, was driven over a cliff, some said by a drunken 'grip' who had been ordered to park the vehicle. Others claimed that the director himself wanted a powerful shot of a Rolls-Royce falling to its death and had staged the incident. The truth is not clear but the cost was heavy. Even though YTV had money running out of its ears, it was a very un-Yorkshire gesture to throw great chunks of it over cliffs.

Other crews were also out, at less expense, filming brass bands and Whicker's interviews with well known (in some cases notorious) archetypal Yorkshiremen who had stayed in the county to make a pile of 'brass' instead of heading south. These included Phil Bull, the founder of Portway Press publishers of *Timeform*, a horse-racing form annual and Percy Shaw, the inventor of the 'Cat's Eye' reflective road studs, an idea he had conceived driving home somewhat 'sozzled' to Halifax from The Dolphin, a Queensbury pub where he regularly met his mistress, Rose Linda.

To start a new TV station today would be to invite lorry loads of job applications. In 1968 many did apply, but Donald Baverstock was not one to pick his people from a pile of letters. He preferred those he knew, particularly those educated at Oxford University, home of lost causes and Labour ministers, where Cambridge produced Russian spies and 'Thatcherite' monetarists. Donald was an intellectual snob and worked by his own idiosyncratic methods which miraculously produced a curious collection of very talented people who gelled together under his leadership into one of the best teams in TV production. Yet few of them came from Yorkshire and neither spoke the language nor had any knowledge of their new home. Rather more, though still a minority, had even worked in television. Also there were few women. Only one, Liz Fox, was a presenter, the best in TV until Christa Ackroyd was invented. There were no women on the news staff. Only one woman, Liz Kustow (ex-wife of the more famous Michael) was a TV producer among a technical staff, that was all male which made the language in the studio different to that of today.

Yorkshire was – and still is – a pretty chauvinistic place, though, as I sagely observed at the time, it did have a place reserved for women, called a scullery. I would never of course dare crack that joke these days. Nor would I use the other joke I made at the time, that Yorkshire men viewed a woman's place as being on her back on the kitchen table. Now I repeat these distasteful jokes reluctantly only to illustrate the climate of the time. Yet chauvinism and prejudice, strong as they were, were not the reason for the absence of women. Female journalists, directors and presenters were few and far between and scarcer in Yorkshire than London. The *Yorkshire Post* had employed a few women but the best of them, like Barbara Taylor Bradford, had soon moved on to higher things. So it was difficult to recruit any women for the great adventure of modernizing a chauvinist county where men were men and women, reportedly, glad of it: often.

Of course numerous women were recruited to YTV as secretaries, telephonists and the kind of jobs which keep any organization running. YTV got the cream of this crop because the excited word rang round the Leeds secretarial 'bush telegraph' that YTV was paying up to 25 percent more than local secretarial rates for jobs which were far more glamorous and might even bring contact (of the appropriate type) with the TV stars who were becoming Britain's new priesthood. To the annoyance of other employers YTV got the best available female staff. They in turn became the brightest and certainly the most efficient part of the TV team, contributing a practical efficiency without which *Calendar* would have failed. Some (two) were the daughters of mill owners who always gravitated to jobs in Yorkshire's more respectable companies. Most were clever and enthusiastic working secretaries, telephonists and clerks, who in any sensible world would have run the place, plus a few who were attracted by the glamour and the excitement of working for a television company. The production side only had Enid Love as head of education (which ITV then did). TV, like life, was a man's world.

With no Yorkshire pool of talent to draw on, most recruits came from outside. In 1967, Yorkshire had five universities and ten technical colleges, none of which had media or journalist courses. Today, too late, we have far more media studies students churned out than jobs available. Nor were there any local radio stations as a recruiting ground. The first BBC station, Radio Sheffield, went on air only in July 1968, like us, the second, BBC Radio Leeds, in 1969. Commercial radio did not arrive until the mid-1970s with Hallam (Sheffield) in 1974, Pennine (Bradford) in 1975 and Aire (Leeds, next door to the TV Centre) in 1976. There was a BBC television presence in *Look North* from Leeds, transferred in May from Manchester to a converted chapel in Woodhouse Lane as a spoiler to pre-empt the YTV start up. But it was run on a shoestring budget with minimal staff, low costs and pathetic financing, like a colonial outpost of the BBC 'empire'. It provided competition but no recruiting ground. BBC staff looked up the long ladder to London for promotion and prospects. Until they could climb that they were anxious to hang on to their badly paid jobs and fulfil the BBC's public service remit rather than have fun in the commercial network. This gave *Look North* a public service ethos and a tendency to talk down to people, both characteristics of the BBC which ITV avoided. As for the great Yorkshire diaspora, none seemed willing to return. With no thrusting mass of Yorkshire talent competing to work for the new television company, its recruitment was mainly done in London. Staff had to be brought in from outside and taught where Wetwang and Gomersall were, how to pronounce Appletreewick and what 'giust'best ov order' meant.

YTV had to build, at short notice, a team to provide local and national programmes of a high standard. A basic level of technical competence came from the enforced recruitment of Manchester staff made redundant by the end of ABC's weekend contract but almost all were technicians because that station had no expertise in local programmes or documentaries. These played little part in weekend programming which was dedicated to entertainment rather than educating or informing, things the weekend audience was presumed not to want. Some thirty technicians transferred to YTV, many of them continuing to live in Manchester and driving over the Pennines where the M62 was being built but far from complete. So every day a procession of Ford Cortinas, three wheelers (cheaper for claiming expenses) and older vehicles came over to Leeds, which the drivers said was inferior to the delights of Manchester. They were a genial and good natured lot, though somewhat strike prone because of stoppages caused by the need to drive over. Still, they were a laugh. Filming in Todmorden (convenient for them to go home) about subsiding houses, I found big Roy Buller telling a horrified crowd of old ladies that we were making a film called 'Todmorden, Sin City' about wife swapping, prostitution and drugs in that quiet little border town which was luring sex tourists over from Lancashire.

John Wilford tests staff reactions.

Recruiting other staff was a haphazard process some of it was well done by Tony Essex who brought in an exciting stable of young directors who not only had talent but also something ex-BBC man Donald Baverstock, never quite grasped: a membership card for the Association of Cinema and Television Technicians (ACTT). ITV was a closed union shop. The TV unions, including the National Association of Theatrical & Kine Employees (NATKE) and the Electrical Trade Union (ETU), had a monopoly of recruitment and closed shops which were the source of their industrial strength. New recruits could not work in commercial television unless they had a card but could not get a union card unless they worked in television. It was infuriating, unfair and insane, forcing newcomers like my wife Linda, a trained director from New Zealand, to work for the BBC and join the ACTT there, before they could work on ITV. This dilemma did not face journalists who usually joined the National Union of Journalists (NUJ), as I did, though I certainly was not a trained journalist. All this made poaching essential for technicians, particularly cameramen, though not for journalists or presenters.

*Graham Ironside
gets the news.*

They could be picked up from anywhere, as several were by Sir Geoffrey Cox who recruited John Wilford from ATV in the Midlands. His salary rose from £1,625 to £3,000pa.

Some new staff came down from Aberdeen with Ward Thomas. Mike Bevan, a studio director, who appeared out of his depth in a Calendar studio, was originally there but came to YTV from Southampton. Graham Ironside, a Scottish newsman whose toughness and judgement quickly made him the lynch pin of the newsroom, came directly, as did Charlie Flynn, a brilliant cameraman. Two, Brian Gibson, the director of the Newcastle regional magazine, and Sid Waddell, a producer came from Tyne Tees. Barry Cockcroft, ex-print journalist, came from Granada. Most others were recruited by Donald Baverstock whose selection processes were quixotic. Donald was a television genius, brilliant at making and teaching TV, but as a working-class lad who had got into Oxford he also had an excessive deference for brainpower, a preoccupation with ideas and too great a respect for social superiors whose IQ was usually lower than his. His methods

*John Fairley
deciding whether to
allow another film
on 'Go-Go' girls.*

were illustrated by the recruitment of John Fairley. Educated at a Liverpool grammar school and Oxford, Fairley had had no experience in TV. He had worked in local papers, then the *London Evening Standard* and graduated to the BBC's *Today* programme, presented by the genial Jack de Manio, famous for telling the wrong time in the mornings and for describing an item on the River Niger as 'the land of the nigger'.

Working in the Today office in Broadcasting House, Fairley was surprised by a phone call from a man with a Welsh accent who claimed to be watching him from across the way. It was Donald Baverstock in YTV's Portland Place offices. He invited Fairley to look out of his window and wave, then to come over for interview for a job at YTV he had not applied for. Fairley went, was snapped up and finished his career at YTV as programme director thirty years later.

Other selections were more perverse. One was the recruitment of Jonathan Aitken, scion of the Beaverbrook family, author of several books, already a distinguished journalist and of course not only an Old Etonian but another Oxford

*Michael Partington
– a professional to
his finger tips (not
shown).*

graduate from Christ Church. Jonathan was a rising star in the Conservative Party
which had just selected him as candidate for Thirsk and Malton to succeed Sir
Robin Turton, their cranky maverick MP. Jonathan was keen to add television
presenter to his repertoire of skills but ill advised to do so. He wrote fluently and
well but his television persona was stilted, stiff and uneasy and an Eton educated
intellectual was a somewhat unnatural presence at a Yorkshire tea table. Being a
party candidate should have disbarred him from TV journalism but, undeterred,
Donald made Jonathan the main presenter on *Calendar* and ignored the ITA's
whinging complaints.

The programme suffered the consequences. One was Jonathan's importation of
friends, such as Andrew Kerr, Eithne O'Sullivan and Barbara Twigg. All had worked
with Randolph Churchill on his monumental biography of his father, Winston.
They had just embarked on volume two when, in June 1968, Randolph's body
decided it could no longer take his punishing life style. He died and the team
working at his house found itself unemployed. Jonathan suggested a contract with

Liz Fox:
Heaven's gift
to YTV.

Yorkshire Television. So this group of high-powered historians, led by Andrew (described by Randolph's son, Winston, as 'irredeemably hip,') were recruited for *Calendar,* a populist tea-time magazine aimed at a downmarket Yorkshire audience.

Other recruits came from all over. Many applied. BBC types and other smoothies were quickly rejected. A few were chosen, some after an interview with Donald Baverstock which often consisted of a long soliloquy from him about television. From Granada came Barry Cockcroft, an experienced journalist who had worked on newspapers and on *Scene at 6.30,* then the best of the ITV regional magazines. Barry was brilliant at local items, mostly filmed around Rochdale where he lived, though his travel expenses said further away. He gradually widened his travels to include first the Dales, then Cumbria. Barry knew showbiz and its inhabitants and was a great writer, particularly of green expense claim slips. His masterpiece was a claim I once saw for 'Lunch for 35. Receipt lost'. Others report another claim 'robbed by foot pads' but I cannot vouch for that.

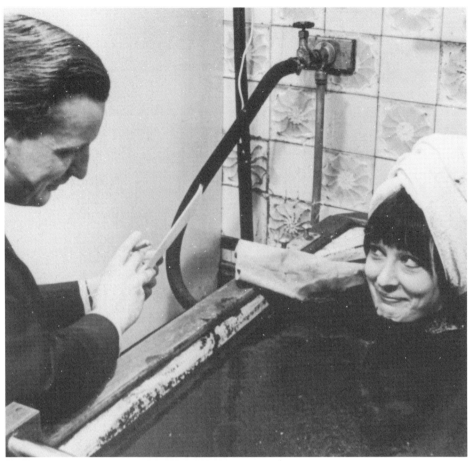

'Can I help you out?'

Barry was an artist with an expertise which embraced the production of beautiful films and fascinating character studies of the individualists he found in the Dales. He was also a deal maker who taught us all how to do our expenses in a system awash with money which he was adept at siphoning off. This was an easier job in YTV than it had been in Granada where he had learned it. His habit, like many in television at that time (it also applied at the BBC), was to live (and eat) off expenses but bank the salary. However, I am not sure he managed his investments well. He regularly gave investment tips and when I was flush with ITV's money I tried two of them, Ernest Scragg and British Leyland. Both went bust within months.

Barry always travelled with *The Good Food Guide* in his glove compartment. A day filming with him started early, preferably somewhere in the Dales or on the moors round the Lancashire/Yorkshire border, convenient for Rochdale. There the film would be made, Barry making boxes with his fingers to envisage the shots. Work finished by lunchtime when we would adjourn to the nearest available five-

Richard Whiteley in TV Heaven.

star hostelry in *The Good Food Guide* (there used to be many on the moors round Halifax). It was a wonderful lifestyle for Barry who never put on weight, but more infuriating for reporters who did and who had to get back to the studio to present that night's programme in a sober and responsible fashion which might have come easily to Reginald Bosanquet but did not to me.

Sid Waddell, our populist genius, was recruited from Cambridge, one of only two *Calendar* members from that university which Donald Baverstock never rated. He came via a start at Granada and a brief career at Tyne Tees Television. The university had not eliminated either his 'Geordie' accent (he was the son of a miner from Easington) or his populist instincts. He was a bubbling source of ideas such as the brilliant *The Indoor League*, precursor of the flood of darts, billiards and booze-fuelled programmes, but also children's programmes such as *The Flaxton Boys* and *Follyfoot*. He was also a writer and in 1969, he published his first novel, *Bedroll Bella* (originally called *Nazi Meat* and so sexy that W.H. Smith refused to sell it), about a pop concert groupie, the first of many more to come. Donald particularly admired Sid and protected him from many of his self-produced follies. His wife did not feel the same and their relationship became more a war than a marriage.

Simon Welfare, married to the daughter of a Scottish Peer, came from the opposite end of the social spectrum straight from Oxford (Donald loved Oxford chaps). Simon wangled an interview with Donald through a daughter of Geoffrey Cox who he had met at an Oxford party. When he told her he was interested in a career in television (as many of Oxford's *jeunesse dorée* then were) she said 'My daddy's starting a new TV station in Yorkshire'. This was the kind of thing that could only happen in Oxford and as a result of it Donald Baverstock invited Simon to the offices of YTV in Portland Place. He recalls 'Donald was in a black mood, asked a question about the school magazine and then, without listening to the answer, threw a huge ring binder across the room. 'Sorry boy' said the director of programmes as it exploded on the floor 'they will keep sending me the corporate plan and I can't abide it. Don't think it's much to do with programme making. Anyway I suppose you can have a job. Get a good degree and I'll see you after your finals.' So I left without ever answering the question, Simon rushed north wearing his new Jaeger suit as soon as finals were over and quickly established his niche as an adaptable producer and journalist, ready to make films or read the news as occasion, or John Wilford, demanded.

From Anglia YTV drew Michael Partington, quickly renamed 'Private Parts', an experienced, indeed immaculate, presenter in the Anglian quasi-BBC mould. As the most experienced presenter in the team, Partington quickly became a mainstay, though his hope was probably to be the presenter rather than one of a group of 'also' announcers surrounding that senior figure. He was not keen to over-extend himself or to go out filming, but was ever ready to help and watch the others, a vital role because we were all far less competent than Michael. The many failures in our initial performances probably made Michael hope that he could inherit the Earth, but he did not. He had a sardonic wit and a total contempt both for Baverstock and the top management, the 'baked bean salesmen': his own work, like his expense claims, was meticulous.

John Wilford came early from ATV in Birmingham to become head of news. A tough, clear-headed, hard newsman redeemed by a manic sense of humour which often comes with serious news jobs, though fortunately this never emerged in bulletins which were always well ordered and effective. This made him increasingly intolerant to the breakdowns, cock-ups and accidents which marred the whole programme in its early days. His instincts were sure but safe; a very good producer, adept at savagely bawling out those who were not. I benefited many times from these short physical instruction courses. The sense lingered longer than the pain.

John McFayden was an extravagant American import. No one was sure how he had got into the company, or the country for that matter but he was recruited to rescue the studio operation which he did, saving it and us in the process, though he received little gratitude. Known as 'McFad the Bad' he was both a studio director and a producer with an expertise on pop groups. He began a steady procession of groups, which included Fleetwood Mac and many other top groups of the day, all passing through Calendar studios. None of them were appreciated by Donald, though they were by us and, I hope, the audience. Some of the groups may have given part of their fee to McFayden who 'lorded' it over them like a 'Master of the Pop Universe', but he gradually emerged as more mad than bad, coming out as a sexually ambiguous cross-dresser. His fate was sealed when he began to appear at parties dressed in a toga and turban and drunk out of his mind. *Calendar* could tolerate eccentricity, but drunken lunacy was another matter.

Liz Fox was recruited directly from 'heaven'. It seems extraordinary looking back that she was the only female presenter in this all male club. In more modern times, this under-representation of women and the total lack of any ethnic representation would have been regarded as major crimes. Back then no-one thought either an issue, though Liz could make up for it by the sheer force and warmth of her personality. She triumphed as a TV natural who did not pretend to be an intellectual but was always fun and became much loved by the Yorkshire TV audience. Yorkshire folk do not laugh much but like someone who does. Liz laughed a lot with a deep, throaty chuckle which was very sexy. Viewers particularly liked her short skirts and the occasional flicker of her knickers.

The natives were seriously under-represented. A Yorkshire TV programme transmitting to 'God's Own County' had few Yorkshiremen on the team. Michael Partington was one, the son of a Harrogate doctor who had been editor of the *Pudsey News*, but it did not show, for Michael had no 'Nah then thee' touch and in fact was rather a bland, smooth, TV-trained type of matinee idol who dominated television. Richard Whiteley, on the other hand, was more Yorkshire. Born in Baildon, educated at Giggleswick, a minor public school (where he had been taught by Russell Harty) Richard had gone to Cambridge where he had been a journalist on Granta and had gone on to start work at ITN. He had only been there a few months when Yorkshire Television began. He immediately applied and was quickly accepted as a respectable native with the skills of a presenter/journalist. That suited him down to the Yorkshire ground because Richard was not only an endearing television performer but a television groupie who loved the medium more than sex, scholarship or even county cricket and worshipped its master performers, Frost,

Michelmore, Dimbleby, Parkinson and others. Indeed, when later on he received an invitation to David Frost's annual party for the TV great, it was as if he was receiving the highest national honour from the Queen. Appearing and adoring were, for Richard, very heaven. His first TV steps were, however, more hesitant: witness his famous question to a farmer at the Lincolnshire Show, 'What kind of cow is this bull?' He asked another, 'I've never heard of a Charolais. What kind of cow is that?' but rapidly grew out of gawky awkwardness to become endearing.

With recruitment, construction and film preparation becoming frenetic, on-air day approached and the last essential part of the regional management team, the newsmen, came in in the shape of John Wilford, appointed earlier and Graham Ironside, his deputy, appointed more recently. A good combination, they were the most professional and best trained of the whole team and began to put together the new operation a month before the start of programmes.

News is a largely independent operation at the heart of any news magazine. It is gathered from a widely-spread network of sources and stringers, so their first job was to drive round the county, more accurately the viewing area, offering goodies, contracts and money to recruit local reporters, stringers, news cameramen and photographers, to build the network of support which any programme needs to reach out into its community. News is a commodity and for sale like any other. The BBC's *Look North*, having started earlier, had got in first, but *Calendar* covered a wider area and had more money to offer than the tightly budgeted BBC. So the YTV newsmen got a better reception and built a better network to provide the core of the programme. They also established the contacts and information channels any programme needs with the police, the emergency services and the prominent industries which dominated the region.

With one week to on-air the production team began to meet in what was known grandly as the 'boardroom' to produce imaginary programmes. Each morning, they gathered around the large table at the north (crutch) end of the trouser factory to come up with programme suggestions and ideas. These were either accepted, in which case the author was sent out to prepare them, or they were rejected. It was a learning process with Donald Baverstock explaining his vision of what made good television, always a brilliant, inspiring exposition but a little more confusing for neophytes who had neither the expertise nor the experience of Donald's Tonight team, all of whom had remained in London.

Rejection meant finding a substitute; selection meant building the story by research and telephone calls. Then the team re-assembled in the afternoon, Donald in the chair, rolling bottles of beer across the table to the team, most of whom, come Friday, were anxious to get away to London. The beer bottles became an insistent drumming. Donald took no notice. The meeting discussed what had worked, what had not stood up and then went home, though most did not have one. All were in awe of their new boss who was viewed – rightly – as a television genius, but also seen as unpredictable, quixotic and sometimes incomprehensible and infuriating as he shot down the more mundane ideas of what the newsmen came to call the 'luvvies'. Newsmen, whose job is simple product marketing, tend not to like intellectuals who are more inventive and imaginative and think up more interesting things. They also mistrust anyone who has not had journalistic training. That is their defence mechanism. It gives them a sense of superiority to the 'luvies' who in turn find newsmen pedantic, unoriginal and uninspired. That is a perennial TV war. I was a 'luvy', though never feeling either lovable or loved.

As the team made their pretend programme items, the race against time reached its deadline. YTV had made enormous efforts, spent huge sums and built a new studio and a new team from scratch. Yet the deadline of 29 July 1968 was impossibly tight, the pressures too great to allow for thorough rehearsal, full preparation and untroubled success. Everything was running a little – if not a month – too late. Studio 2, the smallest in the main new building with all attendant facilities upstairs, was handed over to *Calendar* only the day before the programme went on air. Bad weather had delayed the building programme, losing valuable time on a schedule that was too compressed anyway. Having the studio only a day in advance left no time for familiarization, for testing or for ironing out the bugs or doing full rehearsals. *Calendar* was to be thrown on air on Monday, 29 July. The team was nervous, ill prepared and a bit bemused with some already thinking Donald's northern version of *Tonight* would never be. But they could hardly anticipate the scale of the disaster awaiting. At the original launch of ITV in the 1950s the BBC had run a spoiler to attract audiences away by killing Grace in *The Archers* in a much publicized fire on the same night. In 1968 Yorkshire, no such spoiler was planned by the opposition. As it turned out they did not need to; YTV provided its own spoiler.

NOT SO GRAND OPENING

YORKSHIRE TELEVISION PRODUCTION SCRIPT (Reconstruction because original destroyed)

DATE: Opening Monday 29 July 1968

LOCATION: New YTV Studios, Kirkstall Road, Leeds. Going up like a Temple of Mammon in a weed-covered wilderness where once were terrace houses housing thousands.

CAST: Yorkshire's aristocracy, Katharine Duchess of Kent and Sir Richard Graham (Bart) of Coningsby Hall. Plus: assorted Yorkshire 'gawpers' and 'hob gobs' as unpaid extras. Plus: everyone who was no-one from the four corners of the three Ridings of the 'Greatest County'.

TIME 11.30am

ACTION

ENTER CAMERA LEFT. Enormous Royal Daimler, large enough to carry a football team or the entire Royal Family, but today containing only Katharine Duchess of Kent. It draws up at the new studios. The Duchess is there, not because she is the only member of Royalty Inc., available for a Yorkshire function 200 miles from London, but because she is the most natural, personable Royal and almost a genuine Yorkshire lass, as daughter of Sir William Worsley, former captain of the Yorkshire cricket team and Lord Lieutenant of North Riding. Born and brought up in Hovingham Hall near York and educated at St Margaret's in York, Katharine is as Yorkshire as duchesses ever could be.

The Duchess steps out of Daimler to the cheers and applause of the small crowd gathered in the wilderness where most of them once lived.

Sir Richard Graham of Norton Conyers, Chairman of Yorkshire Television, lopes out to greet the Duchess who turns, waves nicely to the crowd which, being Yorkshire, does not wave back, and enters reception to be greeted by Yorkshire TV's top brass: Ward Thomas, chief executive, respectfully taciturn, Donald Baverstock, programme director, sober and lacking his usual exuberance, Stuart Wilson, creator of the company and deputy managing director, Geoffrey Cox, deputy chairman and David Sumner, general manager. After the Duchess has been presented with a bouquet by Donald's small daughter and a short exchange of pleasantries she is escorted by Sir Richard, adept at walking backwards before Royalty, to a small platform with a table. On this sits a box with a lever, rather like a detonator. There she gives her speech.

'It gives me great pleasure to initiate this first broadcast from Yorkshire Television's new studios in Leeds which will for the first time bring Yorkshire programmes to Yorkshire people and to the network.' She could have gone on to say how marvellous it would be to end the tyranny of TV rule from Manchester and the deluge of propaganda from the idiots over the border and to give the world the opportunity to see how marvellous 'God's Own County' is, but being a lady and a Royal she reads the uninspired collection of platitudes written for her by the company's public relations officer, Alec Todd (Toad to his staff). It is read in her version of Royal RP which is always delivered like an education lesson for the European Student Network (ESN). Sadly a cut glass accent always sounds alien to Yorkshire ears, or indeed to anyone outside the narrow bounds of Britain's upper classes. No subtitles are provided but people seem to understand and applaud on cue. She declares 'Tyke Telly' open, leans forward and presses the lever on the detonator to begin the first ever ITV programmes from Yorkshire made by Yorkshire for Yorkshire. YTV is on air with cricket from Headingley.

All a sham. The detonator was not actually connected to anything. It was there for show to give the Duchess something to do. Nevertheless, as she pressed the lever the first day's programmes began. Not the mindless daytime programming which later became the opiate of the old. Daytime television was then rare. This transmission was Test Match cricket, the opiate of the middle-aged. It started at 11.45am but was interrupted at 1.25pm by the first local programme, a puppet show called *Jimmy Green and his Time Machine* made by Jess Yates who had prepared dozens of programmes ready ahead of time. The Test Match then resumed and went on until network television programmes began at its then regular time of 5.10pm with *The Survival Game*, a quiz about the world's wild life and nothing to do with Leeds's then developing nightlife which eventually made Yorkshire's capital the city of the twenty-four hour rave.

Duty done, the Duchess, whose appearances were more normally restricted to the presentation of the cups at Wimbledon and Wembley, was taken by Sir Richard on a tour of the TV centre which was still being built. He did not know too much about television and rarely watched it. In any case, he lived outside the YTV viewing area at Norton Conyers, a Yorkshire estate which Charlotte Brontë had visited in the previous century and there picked up a local story of family life which gave her the idea for Mrs. Rochester locked in the attic. In each department, Sir Richard introduced the Duchess to people he did not know but whose names were written down for him on cards. They then explained what was going on and what they were doing, insofar as they understood it. This was, after all, the first day the studios had been in full use.

Building work had been suspended for the day. Two studios were incomplete. Dust was everywhere causing the lift to fail with visitors in it. Most of YTV's staff were corralled in the trouser factory across the road, gawping at the brick wall of the new centre for signs of life or Royalty. The 'gawpers' included the *Calendar* team, junior management and non-technical staff, all instructed not to get in the way in case the Duchess or Sir Richard stumbled over them as they picked their way round the wonders of the new centre, breathing in its health giving dust.

As the Test Match coverage ended, the Duchess of Kent disappeared in her Daimler to the applause of the even smaller crowd still waiting outside to see her. The remaining guests gathered to watch YTV's first programme: *Calendar*, the much promoted new regional magazine billed as an opportunity to 'see the region, the country and the wide, wide world through the eyes of Yorkshire Television's team of young producers and commentators'.

Donald Baverstock had held out high hopes of making *Calendar* a Northern *Tonight* where Britain's elite (and the house-trained part of Yorkshire's) would meet and greet as they crossed paths at Leeds (Yeadon) airport or Leeds railway station on the way up to or back from this exciting new programme with its brilliant team of new, young producers, reporters and presenters. Excitement would abound on a programme which would stimulate interest, inform and entertain its excited Yorkshire audience. At the start of *Tonight* in February 1957 the *Radio Times* had boasted that it 'will be Kaleidoscopic but it will not be superficial; it will be entertaining but it will also be intelligent'. Donald saw his regional magazine programme, now christened *Calendar*, as doing much the same job for Yorkshire. High hopes. Exciting prospects, both quickly dashed.

Reality was different as the 'exciting young team' made their debut, heralded by the YTV caption and the station 'ident', a signature tune which was a few bars of Ilkla Moor Baht 'at, expensively re-arranged. In the long history of television disasters this first edition of *Calendar* offers as the greatest, until something even worse comes along. Paradoxically the programme did not go out live but was taped at 6.00pm because on that first day *Calendar* had to go out at 6.30pm, not its usual allotted time of 6.00pm, offering a chance to re-run it live to repair and re-make the disasters. Perversely, Donald Baverstock was not prepared to take the risk of another disaster going out live, despite passionate pleas, particularly from Barry Cockcroft, the only person who had worked on a regional programme. Donald insisted on putting out the tape which has since been mysteriously 'lost' while the scripts have disappeared. So there is now little prospect of it being resurrected in detail, or used as a demonstration of how not to do it on any media course.

Richard Whiteley recalled Jonathan Aitken in full-flow saying 'With the Australians playing for a draw at Headingley, the Russians giving no concessions to the Czechs, the Pope refusing to withdraw his latest encyclical on birth control, it's been a good day for non-events. Here's John Fairley with the news.' Fairley should have winced at this off-putting collection of negatives but probably only gave his usual curt nod and read the news.

Richard then did a report about a girl missing in York. This came up in negative because they had forgotten to reverse the polarity. Simon Welfare takes up the recollections: 'I then did an interview with a beautiful model called Jane Lumb whom Donald had recruited for *Calendar* during a train journey because (a) she was gorgeous and (b) she was from Halifax. The interview was about stainless-steel underwear. Donald, in attempting to instil in a couple of minutes all the skills that it had taken Whicker and the other *Tonight* professionals years to acquire, had advised me to touch Jane's knee during the chat to elicit some points of interesting info. Since I thought it would simply produce a slap in the face I kept my hands to myself, thus probably avoiding a Stuart Hall moment in later life.' Wise man; though wondering whether to obey the boss or avoid the embarrassment of a bit of inappropriate touching caused Simon to sweat. My own instincts would have been to ask Jane to wear the steel underwear for the interview while I sat there with a tin opener. Either way, Jane, who came up from London to appear on a few other items, eventually decided not to join us. Probably we were too unsophisticated for a lovely Yorkshire lass turned cosmopolitan beauty: Great shame.

Simon's account continues: 'Michael Partington, a veteran of ITV, had been demoted (in his eyes) to 2nd newsreader but was caught unawares, mid bulletin, when a story finished early. Richard's other contribution to this catalogue of disasters was a film about a man from Sheffield who, as I recall, was named Joe Albyer and claimed to have the biggest head in Yorkshire. Something that we certainly didn't have after the first night.'

Those who participated remain aghast. Recollections of survivors are scarred and painful. All agree it was a horrendous mess, worse than amateur night at the working men's club, despite an Old Etonian master of ceremonies who did not know what 'Gieusbestov order' meant. Poor presenters shake as they remember incomprehensible signals, films which never appeared, the mysterious blinks, blanks and breaks. People in the control room remember hysterical shouts and orders. One recalls the director leaving his chair to stalk up and down in the gallery wailing 'It's going to be a disaster', only to be told by the production assistant, Juliet Vallans, 'Sit down. It is a disaster.' Another survivor claims that the same PA vainly ordered 'Roll Telecine One' then 'Roll Telecine Two', followed desperately by 'Roll Anything.' Everything rocked, nothing rolled.

It was understandable. The Calendar team had taken over Studio 2, the only one in the new building to be 'completed' (though still not really ready) only the day before. No time for test runs, practice or rehearsals for a team who had not worked together before. No time to ensure that Telecine, captions and the back projection of pictures were available for news bulletins which were delivered standing up like lectures to a class. The result was humiliation for all concerned. It dashed the high hopes built up over the preceding weeks of preparation but the full story cannot now be put together in all its horror. Survivors merely shudder when asked to recall it and prefer to talk about happier days.

So RIP (or pieces) the first ever *Calendar*. Yet it is possible to get a feeling for it from a brilliant description of the following Thursday's programme written for *New Society* by Benedict Nightingale, Northern Theatre correspondent of *The Guardian*.

Nightingale, who felt that YTV had been forced to work to too tight a schedule and should have had more rehearsal and preparation time, chronicled the Thursday programme. It began with a 6.00pm announcement by a young announcer, aged 21 years-old but looking more like a teenager. He announced Calendar's first presenter, Jonathan Aitken, a somewhat urbane presence for rude Yorkshire tea tables. Looking as one of his prospective constituents in Thirsk later told him 'like a rabbit caught in the headlights of an oncoming car', Aitken confidently launched into his script, only to slow and begin to look puzzled.

He was obviously receiving, though not understanding, hand signals from the floor manager waving him to stop. Which he did. Up came the Calendar logo. Its music, a trumpet compilation hijacked from Germany, blasted out. Cut back to Jonathan, looking less comfortable to go into his script for the second time and introduce a rather boring film about Yorkshire MPs and their almost certainly boring holidays. The parliamentary session was just ending. Yorkshire MPs were anxious then, as now, to disguise long and expensive travel plans as time spent devotedly working for their constituencies. Then back to Jonathan to introduce the next item. At which the screen faded to black.

Back to Jonathan again, now recovering confidence as Old Etonians do; this time things worked. An interview with Phyllis Bentley, the Halifax novelist, was followed by the camera staying on Jonathan who stared into it with a developing look of panic to introduce an item on sleep, a condition into which by this time much of the audience had probably lapsed, though those who remained awake could gain little information about sleep from the film because the sound track failed. Next came an item about maggots presented by John Fairley which was well calculated to help the Yorkshire audience enjoy its tea, high, low or maggoty. Next came a film about a pub landlord which was, unfortunately, also incomprehensible because the sound did not synchronize with the image. Signals must have told Jonathan to cut to the news desk: which he did but too soon. This brought a flustered looking newsreader to the screen. This was Michael Partington, a trained and experienced newsreader who read confidently through the news, though at several points reading was all he could do. Promised films never came up.

By this time the control room behind the one-way glass must have been in total panic (again). Control rooms are normally a tightly controlled madhouse. Calendar's was uncontrolled. Survivors remember the producer sitting head in hands, Donald shouting instructions, the production assistant, normally 'Queen' of the control room, counting down and ordering film to roll: which did not happen. Instructions were shouted to the floor manager who gave these to uncomprehending presenters via hand signals because presenters then had no ear pieces. Fortunately, this Thursday programme included a live interview which could be, and duly was, extended to fill in the gaps until a second news bulletin, now read by a less experienced newscaster, became available. Some of the captions appeared in the correct order but the last item on steel making in Sheffield (much of which could not then receive *Calendar*) ended early for some incomprehensible reason, leaving a space at the end too long for Jonathan merely to say goodnight and run from the studio screaming. Nor did he have the gift of quick repartee and improvisation. Nevertheless, he did pad out a long apology for the quality of the programme with a promise to do better next time: it was not fulfilled.

Duncan Dallas: Balliol Man exiled to Leeds.

Thus the opening week was humiliation which did not end with the programme. After each one most of the staff departed, not for the bar, which was the last part of the new building to be completed, but for the Queen Victoria pub across Cardigan Road at the rear of the studio. This was run by Dennis Ramsden who made big profits for a few weeks until the company bar was opened, at which point his new customers all drifted away, leaving Ramsden's diminishing band of locals to themselves to drink his newly acquired stock of exotic drinks. They were much happier that way.

On opening day the presenters and presentable producers were not allowed to drown their sorrows, if not themselves, but had to attend a lavish special reception in the Great Hall at Leeds University. Dutifully most went and were paraded to the front row of the variety show so anyone who was no one in Yorkshire could see their new elite. However, Simon Welfare pointed out that they were not invited to the dinner: 'No one spoke to us and we understood why.' The Great Hall was magnificently decked out for a glittering celebrity dinner but it sagged rather than glittered because the day's TV made it more of a wake. Frankie Vaughan sang, Bob Monkhouse joked but could not cheer people up. The guests mostly went home early and few congratulations were exchanged. The company, its management and staff, dismayed about the first programme, huddled together to discuss it. Top management fell to subdued bickering about the disaster, with blame pointed at Donald Baverstock.

He promised that things would get better. Simon Welfare crept home to the Yorkshire family he was staying with to be told next morning by his host that *Calendar* had been 'bloody rubbish'.

This high-rubbish quotient was maintained by the programme for the rest of the week, with each programme came a catalogue of mistakes, though occasional items were more polished, giving promise of better to come. Indeed things did improve through the week, but not much. Michael Partington did more of the presentation work. More studio interviews allowed more flexibility in timing. Jonathan gradually relaxed. Some of the news bulletins worked with the films and captions appearing on time. Yet still wrong films rolled, correct ones did not, the screen went to black and cameras opened up on presenters gulping like fish or films without sound. Vain shouts of 'roll film' produced only rolling eyes, wriggling of bottoms and no response except control room shouting, studio gulping.

However, one YTV programme redeemed the disaster. This was *Made in Yorkshire* which went out on the first day and stood out like a shining star. It was a thirty-minute documentary made by Tony Essex and his talented team, with Michael Blakstad as producer, Duncan Dallas and Tony Scull as directors, and presented by Michael Parkinson, his Yorkshire accent damped enough to be almost RP. This was a small triumph bringing out everything Yorkshire liked about itself: its beauty, its basics, its strengths and its major figures, all of whom attested their affection for the 'Broad Acres', though mostly from afar because few of them lived there anymore.

All this was cut to music suspiciously like *La Marseillaise* ('aux armes mes Yorkshiremen') to show 'God's Own County' as modernizing, dynamic, go ahead and going through 'an industrial evolution', with new machinery in the mines, new methods in steel production, new styles in textiles, huge new marshalling yards controlled by computer on the railways and a new dynamism soon to be boosted by the most modern, the largest and the best television station in the world, producing a TV output larger than any US television station 'outside Los Angeles or New York' (two enormous exclusions). All this was intercut with statements lauding their own Yorkshire characteristics by famous Yorkshiremen, such as Fred Trueman and Henry Moore, plus images of manic fell runners stumbling up local mountains to illustrate the Yorkshireman's 'undying determination to get to the top first'. It ended with the hymn *Deliver Us from Evil*, a fairly pointed attack on Granada, former ruler of the Yorkshire waves. Parkinson himself worked for Granada not Yorkshire.

This prolonged encomium was rounded off by the 'Top Tyke' himself, a man who had demonstrated Yorkshire guts and Yorkshire determination to get to the top and who now felt himself to be the personification of all those solid Yorkshire virtues. Harold Wilson, the embattled prime minister, for it was he, waved his pipe as he extolled the virtues of the Yorkshire nation; all of which – directness, determination, toughness in adversity, 'knowing what needs to be done', though possibly 'a little too pushy in doing it' – were qualities he himself tried to project as a prime minister embattled by balance of payments problems, strikes, low productivity and the previous year's devaluation of the pound in Yorkshire pockets which had ushered in two years of austerity.

All these brilliant characteristics were coupled in the Yorkshire superman (not Harold, he was now talking for the whole species, though they were characteristics he also claimed for himself) with 'an essential modesty' which made such paragons of 'Tykonian' virtue 'a little underappreciated'. Just like Harold at the time. To round off the film, Parkinson expressed his own hopes that these outstanding Yorkshire characteristics, even Yorkshire's 'bloody mindedness' would be represented in the output to come from the modern dynamic, purposeful production centre he was extolling. It had to be 'very Yorkshire', though he failed to mention that it was 'too Yorkshire' for him because it could not pay him enough to lure him away from Granada. The film made the new station look set for limitless prospects and its productions certain to sweep away the effete programmes of the South which had hitherto dominated the TV screens.

This documentary went out at 9.30pm on the opening day. It was the third locally-made programme that day after *Calendar* and *Jimmy Green and his Time Machine* and stood out like a shining light in a day of disasters; the more so because the promised Yorkshire brilliance had emerged as a heap of Yorkshire rubbish on the first Calendar programme which preceded it. It must have been Parkinson's song of praise, not *Calendar*, which caused one correspondent to write to the *Evening Post* to extend her congratulations to all at the new station, saying it had made her 'proud to be called a Yorkshire lass'. Only Parkinson's programme, or massive bribery, could have evoked such feelings on day one. Nothing else on the opening day's fare could have generated even a glimmer of excitement, let alone such effusive pride.

Made in Yorkshire was a small triumph but the only one of a disastrous week. For an enthusiastic new team the week had been a saddening experience. Morale was low. At the end of the week a delegation led by John Wilford and including Jonathan Aitken went to Donald Baverstock, to insist that the producer of *Calendar*, Brian Gibson, recruited from Tyne Tees (where he had produced their news magazine) was not only incapable of producing the programme Donald wanted but any programme as varied and fast paced as *Calendar* and he should be fired. He was, though he had to linger on like a leper, reading the newspapers for several weeks until the terms of his departure were agreed. 'Well who's going to run the programme then?' Donald demanded. Their answer was 'John Fairley', who had worked in TV for exactly a week.

Friday night brought a reprieve from the agony and a mass tribal exodus which was to be a Friday feature for the next few months until the staff was resettled in Leeds. Cars, motorbikes, Bond Minicars and the company's Jaguars poured out of the car park to go home to Manchester, London or wherever, to allow the new team to spend their weekend shuddering at the thought of the ordeal they had come through. They could look forward to some peace after it because the weekend saw the beginning of an official ITV strike called by the ACTT across the whole country. After five disastrous days on air *Calendar* was off. A fitting finale to the tragic-comic start of what was to be modestly claimed as the greatest regional programme in the world.

CHAPTER FOUR

ENTER AUSTIN

While the first week's disasters unfolded in Leeds I was in Oxford, an official Fellow of Nuffield College, which William Morris of motorcar fame had been conned into endowing. He wanted an engineering college but Oxford's smoothies persuaded him that a post-graduate college for economics and politics would be better and more modern. I was its newest Fellow and fairly bored, not being a 'Bullingdon Boy.'

Oxford is not much interested in anything beyond Kidlington. So neither it nor I knew what was happening in YTV or the TV disaster being created there. Today you can be bored by any regional coverage from anywhere, thanks to digital TV. Not then. Each company had a regional monopoly. Its borders were permeable and erratic but its transmissions could not be seen outside it in those dim and distant two and a half channel days. Oxford never saw *Calendar* transmitted in its far away county. Its Dons knew everything about everywhere but Yorkshire and I sat in Woodstock Road wondering what was happening.

Meanwhile, I continued with the dull and deep potations of college life, occasionally watching ATV, the Midlands' provider. I was probably the only Oxford Fellow to do so. Most were only interested in college gossip and themselves rather than TV, and particularly not 'commercial' TV. I only realized how bad YTV's troubles had been when I read *New Society*'s report on the first week's programmes and thought, sulkily, how much better it could have been if they had hired me, a real Yorkshireman with TV experience. It was a fairly stupid reaction. They had no reason to know that there was a genius to be hired in Oxford and I had never drawn my talents to their attention. But hubris is allowed in Oxford. There is not much else to do.

John Meade.
In Harold Wilson
mode.

It is slightly amazing that an inhibited Yorkshire academic should end up as an exhibitionist TV presenter and part of the team which built *Calendar* into a success but I am not that boastful or I would have entitled this section 'Enter Our Hero, Emerge', or even 'Cometh the Hour Cometh the Man', but I'm not that big-headed and the author of a non-fiction work has certain obligations to truth. As that rare creature, a modest Yorkshireman, product of a county which does not need to 'over-egg' anything, not even its puddings, I am not that boastful. It was all a matter of luck. *Calendar* was a team operation. I was privileged to become part of the team and I arrived just as its fortunes began to pick up. That said, in all humility (something in short supply in Oxford) Yorkshire folk should not be shy about proclaiming a value everyone else is ever ready to ignore. In any case, a certain amount of age and personalization is necessary to sell books. Ask Jordan or whatever her name is this week. So I shall 'big me up' a bit and tell the story of how a naïve Yorkshire swot, who saw himself destined

John Willis.
Learning to type.

for an academic career in the safe shelter of a quiet university (before politics turned academic institutions into forcing houses for the assembly-line production of business 'brains'), directing his life to the more intensive study of less and less, became one of the egomaniac, tight-trousered sex objects we know as television presenters. What took the butterfly out of the hard Yorkshire chrysalis and allowed it to flap around Yorkshire shaking petals (though not pollinating anything)?

The answer is luck. It determined all my career up to the fatal decision to go into politics, at which point it ran out. I'm not a public school chap trained to pursue self-interest, radiate confidence and seize, or better still create, every opportunity for self-advancement so as to rise further than my abilities would entitle me. That public school boost justifies the high fees for Eton, Harrow or Winchester in the top echelon, and even the lower fees for the minor public schools (whose alumni always follow the name of their school with 'It's a public school you know'). Most of these are middle-

Paul Dunstan:
People's Polymath
and apprentice
Yorkshireman.

class 'Dotherich Boys Halls' but all help their alumni to climb further up the slippery pole of life than their abilities might entitle them. I was educated for free under the tutelage of Sir Alec Clegg, the West Riding's education boss. So luck was my engine of advancement, not status.

Fortunately, God favours Yorkshire folk, if only because he is one himself. My first piece of luck was to be born in Yorkshire, an advantage all too few of the world's growing population can claim. I was a true 'Tyke', brought up in a family just like other people, who had never left the county until he was 13 years-old (excluding, of course, visits to Morecambe, which is 'Bradford-by-the-Sea' and so does not count). I was born in Baildon, the same village as Richard Whiteley, though he lived 'at t'top' as John Braine put it, up on the Bank, home of the mill owners, bankers and folk with 'brass' who looked down on we lower middle-class residents of the sprawling Ferniehurst housing estate. I went to Woodbottom Council School, then Bingley

Grammar School (BGS). There I developed my addiction to TV. I first saw it in 1950, when a Baildon dealer erected a huge mast to bring pictures from the newly opened Sutton Coldfield transmitter where it always appeared to be snowing. Then in 1952, Holme Moss brought the BBC to the North. Through that summer I watched test card 'C' for six weeks solid, waiting for something to happen. Which it did not until the Coronation was screened in 1953. By that stage I was at university and gave up watching. In those days of full employment, young people could drift into jobs instead of having to fight and beg them as they do today. This was particularly easy with academic jobs and any academically inclined young person was on a golden high road from sixth form to university to a tenured job as a university lecturer where there was no huge burden of debt.

Most contemporaries from school went into wool or textiles. I did try, half-heartedly, for a job at Baildon Combing, which was smelly, noisy and underpaid. Fortunately, I did not get it or I would have been unemployed twenty years before time. Instead from BGS's twenty-strong sixth form, I won a state scholarship in 1952 and went on to Manchester which made the mistake of assuming I had school scholarship Latin (then a mandatory requirement for an Arts degree) when it was, in fact, the only one of fourteen subjects in which I had failed. Before they could find their mistake, I was there studying first French then History and becoming a perpetual student. I was at university from 1952 to 1959 gathering a BA, an MA (two, one COD) and eventually a DPhil, signifying that I had piled knowledge of early nineteenth century politics higher and deeper.

This brought the next stroke of luck. At the end of my student period at Oxford, I began applying for jobs: teacher training or, better still, university jobs in Canada, Australia and New Zealand (NZ). The professor of history at the University of Otago was at that moment on sabbatical in Oxford, actually in Headington Hill Hall (which Robert Maxwell boasted later was the best council house in Britain). He rang up to meet me, sent Ted Olssen, the senior lecturer in politics who was also on leave at the same time (and the most erratic driver I have ever seen in Oxford), and appointed me on the spot as lecturer in history at the University of Otago, founded in 1869, one hundred years after New Zealand had been discovered by its first great Yorkshireman, Captain Cook. NZ was an alluring prospect: a better Britain in the South Seas. I did not wait for the other jobs, some of which I got, but accepted immediately and went out on a six-week voyage. The greatest stroke of luck I have had.

New Zealand is paradise for the ordinary bloke (i.e. me). Even more beautiful than Yorkshire, a relaxed life-style, a small population (then approaching 3,000,000) and a classless democracy which, being small, was more effective and open and far less class ridden than Britain. I was lecturing in history, but seeing there was very little written about New Zealand politics I began to study that and write books on New Zealand elections: which was another lucky opportunity. In New Zealand you can do pretty much what you want, whereas whatever you study in Britain you are trampling on someone else's field. As 'Lucky Jim' remarked, historians are like a lot of menopausal women all obsessed with their periods. I ranged over a wide territory which was always more interesting.

Other fields opened up because, in a land where anyone can do anything, I began to do regular radio commentaries for the New Zealand Broadcasting Corporation (NZBC). Then in 1962 television reached Dunedin, actually on the night of my

The Calendar *team (minus me – taking the photo). Left to right: Richard, Michael, Jonathan, Peter, Bob, John W., Liz, Simon, Paul.*

inaugural lecture, which consequently attracted an audience of ten. I began to do occasional pieces for television news, gabbling through my memorized text (there was no autocue then) at enormous speed. It was incomprehensible, particularly because of my Yorkshire accent (which many people took for Dutch) but it filled a gap. Then in 1964, when Waldo Maguire, the controller of BBC Northern Ireland, came out to start a news and current affairs department, he employed me to do commentaries and then two regular weekly discussion programmes called *Compass* and *Topic*.

No one in the NZBC's hierarchy knew much about television, in fact the director general described it as 'sound radio with pictures.' So the small group of 'Poms' and 'Aussies', who had been brought in to set it up, could do pretty much what we wanted, which is exactly what we set out to do. NZ needed stirrers and we became good at it. We interviewed the long succession of British politicians sent out to New Zealand to lie by telling Her Majesty's loyal Kiwis that their interests and exports would be fully protected when Britain entered what was then called the Common Market. They all lied and eventually NZ was betrayed, but the research documentation for one of these (Arthur Bottomley) consisted of a badly typed extract from *Who's Who* which told me nothing. I demanded to see the idiot who had done it. We met and eventually married; at least that ensured that she would never do research for me again.

We also interviewed the French Ambassador when that country began nuclear tests in the Pacific. He flatly refused to talk about that subject so I assured him that we were far more interested in French culture and its role in the Pacific Islands. He came, I asked a couple of innocuous questions on those lines, and then demanded to know why France was desecrating the Pacific and ignoring the massive protests everywhere about their tests. He stuttered. The NZBC official in the control room panicked. The lights were cut and the studio went dark. The supervisor came in apologizing profusely for a power failure which, it appeared, had hit only our studio. After some discussion the interview resumed: more innocuous questions, then back to the nuclear tests which this time the Ambassador answered. Unsatisfactorily, of course, but at least he talked about what he had said he would never discuss.

We had similar dealings with the security service when it was discovered that an agent had been attending lectures in Auckland and reporting on students and staff. They did that all the time but as usual this was claimed to be an accident. In New Zealand, the security service is listed in the telephone book but with no name and address. So I rang Major Gilbert, its head, and he agreed to come on. He was surprisingly frank which made his service sound like a kind of divine providence watching over us to protect from communism which he made sound a greater threat to NZ than foot rot in sheep, though personally I never saw any threat at all from the bunch of ageing eccentrics who constituted the left in the country.

All that, plus the issues of the day and serious analysis of the NZ economy and way of life, provided happy viewing. Indeed it was compulsory. There was, as Mrs. Thatcher would say, 'no alternative' to Mitchell, for New Zealand had only one channel and no national link up. Four recordings had to be done of every programme and then flown out to the four main centres. In theory everyone watched, though a study of water consumption in Christchurch indicated that more were glued to *Coronation Street* than current affairs because then there was no water consumption; just a few dripping taps. When I came on people left the room to flush lavatories, fill kettles and take baths while others may well have stayed on the settee for other activities. But most watched.

TVNZ was enormously enjoyable. I lectured in Christchurch for three days a week, flew up to Wellington, then flew back and carried on at the university. I became New Zealand's first 'Teledon', famous to 3,000,000 people, which led me to think it is better to be big with a small audience than small with a big one. I was a 'Kiwi Robin Day' (with a touch of Tommy Cooper because I was also doing comedy programmes). This brought all sorts of opportunities to do elections and by-election programmes and studies of NZ women (a frightening group), done (I cannot remember why) with a Miss NZ in a bikini digging potatoes behind me. The whole exciting experience made me addicted to television. Not watching. I rarely did that now for it was boring, but appearing. I enjoyed working as a team rather than ploughing the lonely academic furrow. I loved the tension and the risk of the studio where life has all the excitement of living on a precipice. To do regular television programmes, particularly live ones, makes the rest of life dull, even boring. A big bug had bitten me.

All of which made for a sad anti-climax when I decided not to accept the chair of politics at Canterbury University which had been offered, but to try my hand in the big pool by coming back to England to accept an official Fellowship at my old college, Nuffield. This left me with nothing to feed my addiction to television. Fame in NZ does not transfer to the UK and demand for commentators on New Zealand politics in Oxford was pretty low. Nor is charisma transferable. Oxford had nothing to produce the same adrenalin and excitement and my Fellowship left me with too little to do. I embarked on a study of the next general election, (expected in 1970) with Oxford's great 'Teledon', David Butler, one of the series of election books he had produced ever since 1950. But where the main enjoyment from my university job had been lecturing, that was ruled out in Oxford by a two-year wait for a lectureship. Tutorials, the Oxford method of teaching, were on a one-to-one basis where a full lecture class had been exciting. The same stale jokes, dead ideas and unlikely suggestions have all to be repeated one-by-one to students in an Oxford system which is retail not wholesale and Oxford brains have to be hand polished, not buffed en masse. Nuffield was a postgraduate college with only fifty-nine students and only one offered for my tutorials. He was much cleverer than I. Indeed, he is now professor of politics at Oxford, a rise to which I made no contribution whatsoever. New Zealand develops 'Jacks of All Trades' and healthy adaptability. Britain's mass society encourages specialization, which traps academics into learning more and more about less and less.

To put it mildly, I was bored, overawed and under-stimulated by Oxford's aridity. Dons thrive on college gossip, clever monographs, some malevolent conversations and passing the port, none of which particularly interested me. So after a year busy doing nothing but travelling up and down to London to interview ministers, who told David Butler and I what they already told *The Sunday Times* the week before (because that paper then did politics rather than the lifestyle and cooking it prefers now), I was ready for change. At that point my luckiest break so far occurred.

David was devoted to getting better coverage of politics and elections on television. He convened a conference of the great and the dud of British television at Nuffield to discuss the coverage of the 1970 election in which he was bound to star. All the top brass of the parties came with the Conservatives led by Willie Whitelaw, as did the big boys from the BBC and ITV, including Robin Day, plus the top team from ITV, Granada (with a Bernstein, I forget which) and Yorkshire represented by Sir Geoffrey Cox, the new deputy chairman. I was there to listen and learn and possibly to tell them how we did the coverage in New Zealand (badly with the party leaders allowed two hour speeches on TV) just in case anyone asked. No one did.

David put his ideas for the election coverage. The party people listened and explained why it could not be done. The Granada people agitated for a more dynamic coverage and we adjourned for dinner. There I had the good fortune to sit next to Geoffrey Cox, founder of *News at Ten* and now setting out to make himself a bob or two in ITV as deputy chairman of YTV, and beter still a New Zealander. We talked about the development of television there and about Yorkshire. He expressed an interest in my Yorkshire accent, which could not have been eliminated by all the elocution teachers in Harrogate. He was more interested in that than in my brilliant contribution to the development of TV in his home country. Perhaps he was starting to think that here was someone who might be understood in Barnsley – at a pinch. Then, as is the annoying habit of Oxford colleges where you get moved just as you have someone interesting to talk to, they reshuffled the seating. We passed the port. I chatted to someone else who probably remembers me as much as I remember him. Not at all.

Next day the great and the good went home, Cox among them. But early the next week, I received a letter from Donald Baverstock of YTV and a man who I had interviewed when he came to New Zealand as part of the world tour the BBC had sent him on to get rid of him when he had been dismissed two years earlier. It was a disappointing interview. Donald had become all defensive and declined to give anything away or criticize the BBC in any way, I assumed because his fare back still had to be paid. Now he issued an invitation. If I was ever in Leeds would I drop in for a chat about their exciting new station?

Would I? I could not get a train that day because David Butler and I were scheduled to interview Harold Wilson on the Saturday for our election book. So I fidgeted and fretted until then and went down to London on the appointed Saturday and interviewed a relaxed but clearly tired Prime Minister while he puffed on his pipe, exuded confidence, and told us that however bad Labour's present poll rating was it would climb again as the election approached. Around him suitcases, golf clubs and holiday gear piled up in the hall of Number 10 ready for his immediate departure to the Scilly Isles.

It was our normal practice at these interviews not to take notes but to write it all down on the train back to Oxford, a humiliating procedure because David could always remember everything word for word while I struggled to get my few thoughts down and usually ended up with illegible notes. No such torture this time. When we left Harold, I made my way to King's Cross and home. My dad picked me up in Bradford and, assuming that no one would be at Kirkstall Road studios to greet me I went home to watch an awful programme from Batley Variety Club which had been filmed as a training exercise and was being put out because Yorkshire, like the whole of ITV, was on strike. The club and Frankie Vaughan, the star, later threatened to sue, claiming that they had been made to look like amateurs on a night at the Rose & Crown. I went to bed; but not to sleep.

On Monday, I caught the Leeds bus from Shipley in front of the Glenroyal Cinema, once my favourite, now a bingo hall. This was the bus my mother had always used to take us on shopping trips to the great metropolis of Leeds, home of Lewis's, Schofields and the excitements of Briggate. Today was even more exciting. I got off after the Kirkstall railway arch, where once crowded terrace housing had been, went into the new building and was directed across the road into a disused trouser factory where Donald Baverstock sat. He did not remember me, his visit to New Zealand, or my interview for the NZBC, but he chatted on about the great opportunity which waited after the strike ended and ended up asking me to come and work with them for the university vacation which had just begun. I agreed immediately and he offered the magnificent sum of £12 a day. Not Robin Day rates but not bad for a vacation job and enough to pay the bus fare to Leeds. Donald did not seem to realize that I would have worked for free if he had asked.

The secretaries were beautiful and multi-skilled.

I accepted and we went through the deserted building, devoid of all ACTT staff, to the poky Calendar office where people sat around pretending to work. They greeted me somewhat coolly but the glamorous secretary slipped me her pin-up photo inscribed 'All this and I can type too'. All prospects were exciting. I went back to Shipley to wait in mounting excitement until the strike was over. My great adventure had started. By another stroke of Mitchell luck it began just at the right time as Yorkshire Television and *Calendar* began to recover from the initial disaster. Fade up the brass band playing Ilkla Moor Baht'at. Even if most of the Calendar team did not know the words.

CHAPTER FIVE

FIGHTING BACK

The strike which took *Calendar* off air ended, as ITV strikes usually did, before Margaret Thatcher destroyed the unions by destroying industry, with the ACTT winning and the companies paying up. So it was, 'Hi Ho Hi Ho' and back to work we went; me to my exciting new summer job, the rest of the team to rebuild hope and save their careers. At the trouser factory the first morning conference began round what had been the cutting table. The team sitting there was enlarged by new recruits brought in one-by-one in the strike and over the next few months. Me, Anne Gibbons who joined as 'Queen PA' in charge of a posse of PAs whose morale had been shattered by the disasters of the first week. A tough lady but charming with it, she brought a new efficiency and authority to the programme and her team. With her in charge in the studio mistakes were much rarer. There were also new recruits to the news and production staff, two of them men of the Midlands, Paul Dunstan and later Bob Warman, both recruited by Wilford from his ATV recruiting nursery. Later Peter Moth, a former congregational church minister then teacher at Gargrave Comprehensive, arrived. All three made a significant and, in Dunstan's case, long-lasting contribution to *Calendar* and to the programmes which came out of our stable. This was the way things now began to work; a lively team where people could fit in, make their contribution but were free to do what they wanted, and other programmes which allowed us all to find our own niche and develop our own strengths. As we all began to do, backed up now by Eliza Seed, team secretary, who was quickly commandeered by John Fairley. She became his own secretary and organizer and, as he grew more powerful, gatekeeper.

With these later additions to the team recruitment was over. It had been haphazard, almost casual, with none of the excessive rigour and intense scrutiny applied today where jobs are scarcer and applicants more numerous. If Donald Baverstock had set out to replicate the cornucopia of talent which had produced *Tonight* and *That Was the Week* he had singularly failed. Those he had chosen were mainly untried – but enthusiastic – beginners but he had picked well and most of them developed into first-rate professionals who gelled together into an impressive team as they began to work well together in harmony. It was almost as if we were in a marriage, joined in sickness (there was not much, people did not want to miss work) and in health, and certainly for richer not poorer (a state unknown in ITV at that time). We began as an embattled team welded by adversity, but now embarked on the most pleasurable of tasks: producing Yorkshire's best programme and Britain's best regional magazine. Call us 'Jammy Bastards', we had grasped a basic truth of television: this industry of egos works as a team or it fails.

It also needs prophets and we had the best available in Donald Baverstock, one of the few real geniuses of an industry which has too many self-appointed genii. Donald was our television tutor: sometimes incomprehensible, most of the time brilliant. The basic principles we all picked up from him were the simple truths of television. 'You're not talking to a camera: You're talking to a person. Ignore the camera and talk to the viewer' was basic and right. 'Get on to a level of conversation with the viewer and make it informal and relaxed, the tone light, even irreverent,' he would say constantly. He could not abide the egomania and vanity that 'presenterial' flesh is heir to ('uphimselfism' they had called it in New Zealand – a painful disease which afflicts politicians too). People obsessed with themselves, are no use in television. The obsession has to be with the viewer and to getting on their level.

We all complied well with Donald's ideal presenter type – intelligent but not intellectual. The kind of person TV needs is someone who can be themselves in any situation ('the boy stood on the burning deck' came to mind). That is to be natural in an unnatural situation, and able to efface themselves and do a decent job watched by millions (we hoped). The presenter is not performing; he is just doing a job which is to be competent and fair.

That job, Donald made clear, is different to that of the producer. The presenter is speaking to the viewer and trying to be honest and balanced. The producer is the viewer with the right to say 'that is wrong'. 'We should not do that' or 'for heaven's sake stop harassing the poor bugger and let him answer.'

Donald was the enemy of specialization: as he put it, we were neither a serious programme nor a light entertainment programme, neither a history nor a politics programme. We were all of them, a Smörgåsbord to tempt the interest of the viewer. What he taught us was that it is essential to get the audience's interest, and hold their attention by giving them what they want and colouring and livening what we gave them to make it interesting because only in that way could television lead them to new thoughts and new interests via diverse paths. This was the importance of the magazine format which *Calendar* exploited to the full because with variety, the mix of the local and the national, the humour and the cultural, of news, entertainment, of music and drama, we could please the audience and hold its attention as it watched. We grew the audience by giving them items they wanted mixed with other items they might not have thought about but which they would watch because it was in the mix. 'Never underestimate the intelligence of the audience.'

Thus spoke the great educator we were blessed with, though those who had been there from the start noticed that though the lessons were continuing they were less frequent and Donald, though he chaired the early meetings when we came back after the strike, said less and interfered less because he had now brought in John Lloyd. I should call him John Lloyd I or the original one because there are so many John Lloyds about. Ours was the producer of *On the Braden Beat* and later its successor, the Esther Rantzen programme, *That's Life!* He had come to tell us how to do it, and as a master of populist television he moved us downmarket from Donald's more intellectual approach. Though he stayed only three weeks his influence lasted far longer because he trained John Fairley for leadership and his advice and training made *Calendar* a far more populist programme and one which Yorkshire people actually wanted to watch and to look forward to rather than one they endured until something better came along. He was not in the business, as Donald sometimes was, of giving them what the producer thought they should see. Doling out television as medicine for the mind was more of a BBC approach.

It disconcerted me because I am by nature a preacher man. John's view was that it is no use preaching at people or giving them what you want but they do not want. On the contrary, the first requirement of good television is to get the eyeballs. You do that by populism. The public does not know what it wants until it gets it but ours wants Yorkshire. So give them what they want, which we did. Yorkshire is a land that keeps on giving because it has lots to offer and Yorkshire being more gritty and natural was rather different to the more intellectual middle-class approach of *Tonight*. We were invariably populist: The best TV is.

At 6.00pm, the audience was eating its tea and generally settling down for the evening's viewing as we came on. Their attention span was short and their interest had to be grabbed.

That meant entertaining, interesting and offering variety. Interest would convey news and information but only if we talked directly, not down to them as journalists and other pedants are ever prone to do. This was not difficult for an academic to understand but very difficult for me to actually do. Academe narrows horizons, television widens them. Lecturers need an exhibitionistic streak but, being academics, tend to go on too long and to assume that what fascinates them interests the wider audience. It is not necessarily so, particularly when the narrow interest is politics and economics. People are more interested in sport and their interest in my specialisms is aroused only by its direct impacts of both on life, work and the pound in their pockets. So politics must be sold as a game, a race, a character study. It is about people, not party point scoring or constitutional 'rhubarb'. All new and exciting to me who thought of it in terms of 'swing', poll ratings, mandates, ideology and all the other paraphernalia politics have been encrusted with.

Lloyd's greatest innovation was a daily 'vox pop' the voice of the people. That made sure that Yorkshire voices and views were heard and also got us out of the studio to hear them and to meet the viewers. I loved 'vox pop' and constantly gravitated to my favourite 'popping' ground at the side of Lewis's. Contrary to my fears, viewers did not hesitate to give their views which were mostly pretty common sense. So 'vox pop' became 'vox Dei', the voice of God, for me. John Lloyd regularly rejected many of the trudging ideas we had developed as the team had sat round playing DIY television in the strike. Out with them went the television tourism which had developed because the Calendar team, in finding out about Yorkshire, were merely proffering what the audience already knew, not giving them a new or interesting view.

All this – the Lloyd doctrine – was not a substantially different view from Donald's hopes to recreate the magazine format of *Tonight* but it moved it down a social notch or two and was very different to the intellectual side of Donald's personality, his interest in ideas. He understood people but he was deferential to status and an academic snob, ever interested in ideas but too ready to assume that top minds convey their own excitement and, moreover, that the big brains embedded in the London 'honey pot' would be ready to come up to Leeds to give real people the benefit of their wisdom. Not only did the big brains not want to come north, they could not have got back if they did come, unless on a soon to be discontinued night sleeper. That more or less cut out the London elite Donald had been used to getting on *Tonight*. We had to breed our own.

Still bruised from his experience at the BBC, Donald wanted a programme which would get national attention and cover national events as *Tonight* had and his introductory opening for the very first *Calendar* had covered the world from the Pope to Czechoslovakia without considering who in Yorkshire wanted to know about either at tea time. We gradually weeded out this intellectual obsession but not before it had one last kick in Calendar's reaction to the Czech revolution which took us back to pontificating; for one night only. Excited by the events in Prague, Donald proposed to devote the whole programme to an issue, which I regarded as largely irrelevant to Yorkshire minds and tea times. The streets of Leeds were hardly thronging with Czechs, bouncing or otherwise. Nevertheless, Donald thought Leeds could throw light on Prague. So Simon was sent out to 'vox pop' Harrogate where people dredged their minds to find reasons for being interested in a far-away country of which they knew nothing and, being Yorkshire, cared less. Jonathan used his wide contacts, in a world where he seemed to know everyone and he had most of their telephone numbers, to invite a former British Ambassador to Moscow. I brought in a Polish student I had worked with at Nuffield who could talk interestingly about communism and the Russian role in Eastern Europe. The two shared an expensive taxi up from Oxford and despite the fact that none of us knew Czechoslovakia or had anything original, or indeed at all, to say about it we launched into a programme devoted to that country.

Czechoslovakia rolled on for the thirty minutes, interrupted not by the sound of tanks and gunfire but by the local news from Gomersall, Heckmondwike and Hull. Then without staying for a drink or a word with Donald, the Ambassador got back into his taxi to go and pontificate somewhere more important and zoomed back to Oxford. We congratulated ourselves. I did not join in the chorus. What could we say about Czechoslovakia that was any use to anyone? I went home to watch *Twenty Four Hours* which was more interesting. It did not have a Yorkshire accent but I have to concede it to the London 'Smart Alecs'; they do know a lot more about things I am not interested in. That was our last attempt to put *Calendar* on the world scene.

Czechoslovakia aside, as Brezhnev might have said to Dubček; under our new guidance and the emerging leadership of John Fairley, a man always willing to learn, *Calendar* began to develop in a Lloyd rather than a Baverstock direction. Jonathan Aitken still presented some programmes with his usual stiffness (he seemed to find difficulty in smiling) but gradually he faded out to do other more important programmes, not however before doing a Jonathan classic with an item for a Yorkshire audience, which already knew it, on the delights of Harry Ramsden's, the largest fish and chip shop in the world and Yorkshire's pride, where my parents had queued for six hours in 1951 when Harry reduced his prices to a penny ha'penny to celebrate 50 years in the business. Jonathan took his friend, Colonel Sammy Lohan, 'Good Food Spy' in the *Evening Standard* with him for lunch and they ordered haddock and chips (which was all that was on the menu. Cod is eaten in the south, not here) and Jonathan asked what wine Lohan would recommend with fish and chips, 'Oh a nice dry white to cut through the grease'. He called over the waitress and ordered a bottle of 1964 Chablis. The waitress did not think so. 'No alcohol: we don't serve alcohol. Do you want tea or coffee?'

Gradually *Calendar* gave me more presentation roles and took more items from me. I was slipping into the main presenter's role and Michael Partington, whose moment should have come, now saw it falling away. With a much smaller audience than *Look North* with its head start, *Calendar* was coming together better and building its audience. The technicians who had come over from ABC had never transmitted news film before but gradually learned how. Even the mistakes which were still being made regularly began to become a bond with the audience as we discovered that a joke and a happy response to them instead of sitting staring at the camera in horror entertained the audience who liked seeing TV personalities fall flat on their faces. So I developed a repertoire of responses and jokes to fill in the gaps rather than sitting staring at the camera, gulping like a fish, which was the standard BBC approach to mistakes. I over-reached myself when I began to call it 'Colander', the programme with the holes. That was too much for the newsroom. Many of the holes were in their bulletins with film that did not roll or photograph captions which did not appear.

Learning was a team effort and an egalitarian process. We were all learning on the job (as Mrs. Thatcher once put it) by mucking in together and doing different jobs to try our hands. Everyone went out on stories with our film crews who were happy to teach, what they regarded as a bunch of ignorant amateurs, the techniques of filming and doing 'Pieces to Camera' (mine were always too long – mini-lectures not terse scene setters) providing 'noddies' to intercut with the interview to disguise the chunks taken out (I was good at that, though I could not always shut up), teach us not to 'cross the line' (a concept I still do not understand). More important, we learned not to overshoot, which I was particularly prone to, so editors did not have to wade through thousands of feet of film to edit 'Quo Vadis' down to a twenty-second item. It was all interesting, exciting and (if we took our own cars – I could not because I did not own one) rewarding because of the mileage allowance paid then, however many cars went. It was an apprenticeship to Britain's most exciting industry.

We wrote our own scripts and edited our own films, often to see our great thoughts massacred by John Wilford who taught me the three words to a second rule of scriptwriting. I would always try for six. He was the best editor in the business and also taught brevity, a strange art for an academic, and writing to the point, again difficult for me because I had always worked on the traditional lecturer basis of tell them what you are going to say, say it, then sum up and repeat what you have said. That worked with bored students but TV was one-shot county. Say it simply and clearly, then shut up and let the film develop it. Unlike most of the others, I had never trained as a journalist and was not a very good one; but I was learning and both Wilford and Ironside were good teachers; no matter how painful their educational technique and however humiliating their critiques.

Preparations complete we all assisted in the studio, taking it in turns to do interviews and read the news. According to Michael Deakin, John Fairley read the news as though he knew more about it than he was prepared to let on. He always began bulletins with a terse nod, John Wilford read them as if lampooning something he did not quite believe, Ironside's Scots accent was less comprehensible without subtitles, so he was quickly excused news reading, Simon always managed to give the most depressing news of mill fires and traffic accidents a jolly air, Richard made it all earnest and Liz was all jolly hockey sticks, while I stumbled and fumbled over scripts. More professionalism came to our rescue when Paul Dunstan joined us from ATV, Wilford's infallible source of supply, in December. He and Partington were dependable and efficient newsreaders and became mainstays of the programme, though that skill relegated them to the news role more than they wanted.

Mistakes were part of the learning process. I made one of many on 5 November, Guy Fawkes Day. Barry Cockcroft had discovered that Nicholas Horton-Fawkes of Farnley Hall, Otley, was a direct descendant of Guy Fawkes. We interviewed Nicholas about his ancestor and got a glowing picture of this most sensible Yorkshireman's plans for constitutional reform via gunpowder. Barry then persuaded Horton-Fawkes to sit on the top of a large bonfire we built, to be interviewed. The interview concluded with me throwing petrol over the fire and lighting it, leaving Horton-Fawkes sitting there as the flames rose around him. He clambered down unscathed, then we drove back to the studios at high speed to ensure that our masterpiece was shown. It was. The result of this flaming indiscretion was a deluge of telephone complaints from angry parents, furious that we had shown their kids how to carry out local versions of an *auto da fé* [act of faith] which could possibly be used on them as parents. They were right of course. We were wrong. We had enjoyed ourselves so much that sense had taken leave of us. Television is not just having fun, John Fairley warned me. For me it was.

The fun rolled on as some of the best brains in the county devoted themselves to preparing and presenting the most idiotic items to a Yorkshire tea-time audience. Andrew Kerr, coming down from the heights of 'Churchilliana', did items such as a film on a house where shrimps came in with the bath water. The presenter, Richard Whiteley, did his piece to camera (P to C we called it, though it was to porcelain in this case), sat on the lavatory (trousers up where mine would have been down) while the tap ran pouring shrimps into the bath. It then cut to an interview with a Water Board official who denied any possibility of shrimps. He then drank glasses of water from a bucket in his car to prove it. It was shrimp-less but did not exactly answer the point, though television is there to puncture the pompous. Another triumph was to make a film about exploding gas ovens, as North Sea [natural] gas came in, to the music of The Rolling Stones playing 'Jumping Jack Flash, it's a Gas Gas Gas'.

Kerr also appeared in an item produced by Sid Waddell who had him sitting on one of the lions outside Leeds Town Hall wearing a military hat and waving a sword to declaim a patriotic speech from Sheridan which demanded that his troops 'let the fountain of their valour spring through each stream of enterprise 'til the full torrent of your foaming wrath o'erwhealm the flats of sunk hostility'. Which flats? Quarry Hill? It produced bemusement. People gawped at Kerr and he waved his sword. The crazed meaningless item went out. Like everything else it was fun. As well as the end of Kerr's brief contract.

Cock-ups could be eliminated on film but not on a live transmission so they remained a studio speciality which demanded a more immediate response. An example came early when Enid Love's education department offered us the use of an elephant they had used for an educational programme – perhaps training people for jobs as elephant minders. We got the elephant at discount rates. It had been brought from a Midlands zoo by road (which allowed me to report that the elephant had done a 'ton' [100mph] on the A1 to get to *Calendar*. Police were clearing the mess).

Which was nothing like the problems it created in the Calendar studio, as we faced the problem of what to do with an elephant on a regional magazine programme? The same day Bradford Police were selling off their police whistles, all 7,000 of them. So we developed the bright idea of Richard and I opening the programme festooned with police whistles. 'Hiya' (the opening I had developed to show a bit of Yorkshire). 'Today saw the end of police whistles in Bradford. It's a great shame. In the old days you could be sure that when a police whistle blew police would come running to help. But what's going to happen now?' At which point I blew the whistle. The elephant was then supposed to romp on to the screen in front of the cameras. Great glee all round. We hoped.

The elephant had other ideas. It was determined to head out of the studio in the opposite direction. All the efforts of four strong stagehands trying to pull it on to the screen were unavailing against its greater strength. To the accompaniment of a heaving, grunting and stomping noise which must have mystified the audience, I desperately handed whistles to Richard suggesting that we should both blow in unison. We did. We blew and blew at some length. Nothing happened. The elephant could not be dragged on stage. So, giving up, I introduced the next item which was a serious round-table discussion chaired by Michael Partington with our trusty Leeds solicitor, Barrington Black, and others now forgotten, debating some heavy issue also forgotten but I am sure important at the time. The discussion began. Richard and I heaved sighs of relief. The elephant changed direction and headed now for the table with the stagehands desperately (and vainly) trying to pull it back.

Reaching the table the elephant began to pee. I do not blame it. I was nearly wetting my own pants, though that would have been less noticeable and certainly less noisy. The elephant peed loudly like a waterfall. The sound was picked up by the microphones round the table as the participants shuffled their chairs away from the stream and the splashes, leaving one microphone pointed directly at the flowing, splashing stream. Total chaos. Here was a decision moment. The director at the controls should have had the sense to give up, show the elephant and let me explain the chaos. The audience must have been wondering what the hell was going on and why a respectable lawyer and others had suddenly decided to do a chair dance round a, by now, half-empty table. Had they discovered a sudden affection for each other? The director was not quick enough. The elephant was never seen (though its fee was not refunded). The audience must have wondered about the water sound and why the studio appeared to be flooded, but they probably assumed it was another *Calendar* cock-up, though more mysterious than usual. You cannot fool the folks. Tell them what is going on.

Cock-ups galore and silliness as well, also a lot of good stuff. We were enjoying ourselves and as the fun went on and the humour built up the audience grew. I discovered the enormous green Joint Industry Committee for Radio Audience Research (JICRAR) reports which recorded audience figures but usually sat around unread. I began to work on them. They made it clear that we had begun badly but were gradually overhauling and soon would be overtaking, even beating, *Look North* despite it having a head start. The figures were not absolutely reliable, ITV audiences were then measured via monitored sets reporting daily which channel the set was on. Working-class ITV households were more likely to leave the set on while they washed dishes, went to the lavatory, gawped into space or indulged in all the other forms of activity which go on in front of a TV set. Middle-class, BBC viewers, being more fastidious and more mean, watched less (or so they said) and switched-off the set when not watching. This depressed BBC figures on JICRAR. The BBC's own surveys were done by diaries. This rated BBC viewing higher and reduced ours. It also produced the strange anomaly that the smaller the audience the higher the programme was listed on the BBC's 'appreciation index' paving the way for *Look North* eventually to be more appreciated than down-market *Calendar*. No matter. The viewing numbers were what counted because that is what the advertisers were buying. Perhaps we were a little biased but so what? In those days you could fool all of the advertisers all of the time because ITV was the only place for them to go. The important fact was that by the week ending 16 March 1969, *Calendar* was reaching 524,000 homes, 29 percent of the total and more than either ITN or *This Week*. Success was assured when Yorkshire fell into line with most of the other commercial companies by scheduling *Crossroads*, then a very popular programme ('Distressingly popular' Lady Plowden said later when she became head of the Independent Broadcasting Authority [IBA]) at 6.30pm so that our own drawing power was boosted as others switched on for Meg Richardson (played by Noele Gordon), her staff and Amy Turtle.

Through these early months the programme developed a daily routine which endured for the rest of its long life. Early meetings had been large and chaotic rather than a regular discipline, becoming more of a rolling seminar with everyone working on *Calendar*, some of Tony Essex's team and Donald Baverstock attending to argue and listen to the teachings of John Lloyd, the master of populist television, with occasional contributions from 'headmaster' Baverstock, to maintain our intellectual credibility (though more usually he ended up by confusing what was still a deferential class learning TV 101). Gradually the meetings became smaller and more purposeful and a new hierarchy emerged with a new leadership. John Fairley was the obvious producer designate and by 1970 he was head of news, then head of news and current affairs. Richard, Liz, Simon and I were the outside reporters, Partington the perfect studio and news presenter, while Aitken drifted out on what became increasingly detached duties. John Wilford and Graham ran the news. But multi-skilling still survived. Fairley and John Wilford still read the news in the studio but less and less often. Unlike the rest of us they were too busy.

The *Calendar* day began with the early man (no need to be sexist about this, we were a largely male crew) coming in at 8.00am to go through the papers, local and national, and draw up a schedule of the most interesting stories of the day. Next in came the newsroom staff to fix local stories proffered from all parts of the region by the local journalists and stringers, several of whom also shot film on their heavy Bolex cameras (producing the inevitable joke that the news was 'a lot of Bolex'). Some of these had already been arranged in advance in the newsroom diary the night before. The details came in on the day with the story dictated over the telephone and sub-edited in Leeds.

The morning meeting took place at 9.30 or 10.00am with the whole available team jostling to offer and get stories so they could go out with one of the full film crews available that day. Those who did not go out, usually Michael Partington, prepared items, wrote scripts, invited guests for interview and smoked foul-smelling cigars. Initially, being nervous of the new medium, some guests were reluctant to appear as if the new (to Yorkshire) medium frightened them, despite the fact that we always paid a fee. Gradually, however, they became more eager. Soon they were almost clamouring to come on. We could have charged them.

Every day *Calendar* had two complete film crews at its disposal in their Range Rovers – cameraman and assistant, sound man and assistant, plus an electrician who drove his own car; as did the reporter. The problem here was costs and logistics. Today all filming is on video. Then it was film shot on Arriflex cameras. Each spool of film lasted only for eleven minutes and cost £800 including processing. So economy was the name of the game. This was awkward for me because I could never shut up and always wanted to shoot more, or again, or to film a new conclusion that I had only just thought of while the cameraman tersely complied or, more usually, looked at his watch. I had tried to turn every small news item into an epic, a magnum opus which would have taken days to edit, indeed on one occasion I was accused of shooting 3,000ft for a film which did not go out. Once exposed the film was taken, usually by the crew, to Humphreys Laboratories down by the station and well away from the studio. Then motorcycle messengers brought it back to the studio and the film editor.

This made logistics a major problem. Today there are microwave-radio links to the studio to get the images back. Whereas then, the final film had to be taken back and Yorkshire had no motorways (when these finally came I made a film as a 'Lollipop Man' helping kids across the M62). We had no mobile telephones so calling in was a problem with so many telephone boxes vandalized. Crews could get lost and regularly did in the Dales. Film could be spoiled in processing. Then when it arrived back to the studio it had to be edited which involved cutting it into strips, matched with the sound, then taping it back together again. Fred Bull, 'the butcher', did the crude rush material, Tudor Lloyd the more sensitive films but we had a good team of editors

'I think it's a camera. Richard Whiteley must be in there somewhere.'

all capable of working under pressure and getting the spools down to transmission on time. Or near enough. All this was teamwork of the highest standard and we all trusted and depended on each other but it was not until the M1 and the M62 were completed and, more important, the company purchased a helicopter in 1973, that things got easier.

By 4.00pm the day's script, always on green paper (news on yellow), was usually ready. The news bulletins, two in each programme, were written. All the film was on two spools, A and B, to run alternatively. The script was then typed on to the autocue which in those days was a large hood above the lens of the camera where a paper roll was reflected by a mirror on to a sloping sheet of glass which could be read from the other side but not seen by the viewers. Some of us stared fixedly at the autocue, the short-sighted peered, the egomaniacs ad-libbed, but not too much for all was carefully timed, particularly the last five seconds, as the film rolled 5,4,3,2,1 came up on screen. The initial autocue was clumsier than it later became. It could tear and stick. These problems were quickly overcome and replaced by variable speeds as the operator slowed or speeded up to keep pace with presenters as newer and as more modern autocues became available.

At first the photographs for the news bulletin were projected on to a screen behind the news reader using back projection operated in the studio from a contraption developed and built by a local businessman who came into the studio each night to operate it himself. Within months it had been replaced by Chroma-key with a blue screen on which the news, film or photographs were shown, as well as flickering on any item of blue in the newsreader's clothing – Little Boy Blue come change your shirt. Captions and titles were all on cards stacked on stands from which some usually managed to fall off on air, producing the wrong face for the right item, or a view of something completely irrelevant to what was being said. In television the maxim is 'if a thing can go wrong it will'. On *Calendar* it usually did.

At 5.00pm all involved went down to the studio for a run through and rehearsal. The rest went home and Andrew Kerr made a point of being home for *The Magic Roundabout* which the rest of us watched waiting in the 'green room'. Everyone except control-room staff crowded into the 'green room' (which was in fact painted yellow) while the studio run through provided an opportunity to check timings for the control-room staff and to read the autocue for the presenters. Guests began to filter in, mostly too early, for television stations, ever nervous, play safe by having people wasting their lives hanging round in 'green rooms' in captivity. No booze in ours (unlike BBC's London programmes) but guests were generously filled with tea and biscuits ready to be ushered in for their two minutes of glory. BBC's current affairs programmes always plied them with drink to make them talk. We offered only tea, though they were allowed to watch *Magic Roundabout* – which was on the BBC. Indeed they had to watch it, so keen were the *Calendar* team on the programme.

Marylyn Webb and Paul Dunstan ready to read the news.

Winding me up for transmission.

'Pray God he won't get it wrong again.'

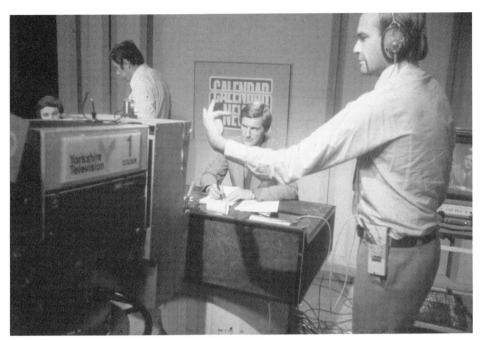

Tom Adam learns to count.

Guests were kept well away from what was being said about them in the film introduction to their item but usually had a rushed few words with their interviewer. I found the custard cream biscuits addictive, with the result that I slowly but remorselessly began to put on weight. Also in the 'green room' were any animals and house-trained pop groups appearing that night, though the wilder variety of both were kept at the other side of the studio behind a rolling door.

At 6.00pm we went on air with the stirring notes of Ilkla Moor in the ident, followed by the blast of *Trompetten und Hosen*, a German piece which still thunders through my head as the witching hour approaches. Back then it kicked us into life with the floor manager in charge of the studio giving us the count downs, followed by throat-cutting signals when the interview was ending. This was a frustrating form of communication. Our first floor manager, Ray, imported from Grampian, was not necessarily the most intelligent person in the studio, but he was all-powerful, being the only person in touch with the control room. He received his instructions through the earpiece. Eventually we presenters got earpieces of our own but until then we were quite out of touch with the control room so it was difficult to disobey the floor manager, though occasionally necessary.

Getting earpieces was not necessarily an improvement since talk from the control room – 'Close up on Camera Two' – 'omni' talkback it was called – punctuated every interview. It was distracting having instructions bawled in through the earpiece while trying to talk and think about something else. Married men may be used to being told off by wives in that way. I got confused by it and was not sure the audience would understand the spasms of worry or annoyance crossing my face. Eventually, we received only selected talkback which made the floor manager redundant but was still off-putting since timings could be very distracting. This put a premium on improvisation, particularly when the programme was coming to its end and there was need either for a terse 'Goodnight', an extempore joke or even a prolonged sermon on some issue of the day, our hopes for tomorrow, the loveliness of the Dales or of Liz Fox, anything (except panegyrics of Harold Wilson) to fill the aching void.

The studio was a crowd spectacular with cameramen and soundmen working and NATKE staff stood around in case the set or the ceiling fell down, electricians hitting lights with long poles, plus reporters and presenters spread round several sets and the autocue operator, all of them marshalled by the floor manager. The crew was mostly male. I was amazed going into a New Zealand studio later to find that women had taken over most of the studio jobs. That was a sign of things to come here, but in my time at Calendar women did not soften or dilute the male monopoly, though I am sure they would have been more efficient (except with elephants) and done a lot less swearing. In fact studios today are almost as silent and reverential as churches, which is frightening to someone whose mind now works only in a din. Strikingly, too, there is no smoking today where our guests could smoke like a mill chimney. I wonder if I would have a case against YTV for lung damage caused by passive smoking?

The floor manager's instructions came from the PA, 'queen' of the control room. She (usually a formidable Scottish battle axe) counted down, issued instructions, rolled film and kept as cool as was possible in the organized chaos that is a control room on a live television programme. Chaos is the charm and the challenge of live television. It tests the wits, builds the excitement and exhausts the nerves. For me it quickly became the aphrodisiac and the attraction of a daily live programme. For thirty minutes life is hyped-up and tense and the presenter lives dangerously on the edge of a precipice. Thought is quickened, everything is heightened, every response tested, producing a greater excitement than is available in any other job, unless perhaps brothel keeping or becoming a lavatory cleaner on cocaine, though I would not know. The thrill is addictive but exhausting: Which is the reason why television stations need bars to let everyone have a drink, wind down and seek therapy. At this stage YTV was without. So we would adjourn to Dennis Ramsden's pub across the road where shaking presenters clutched for reassurance that it had not been a total disaster, that their bit at least had been OK or, on the most desperate occasions, that they had not looked too bad, even if everyone else had failed.

As the team developed its skills we were ready for other ventures. YTV had established offices in Sheffield where the ineffable Arthur Jones presided smoothly, gushing and greasing over celebrities while treating visiting reporters and crews with a polite distaste. I had been thoroughly put off Arthur when John Fairley asked me to go down to Sheffield to represent *Calendar* at the grand opening of the movie *Ice Station Zebra*. I arrived late, stumbled, in the dark, to the VIP seats only to find that when the lights went up that everyone else was in full evening dress. While they fawned on Stuart Hall who had been the regional star only a few months earlier, I asked Arthur Jones what I should do. He said 'Go home matey'. I did and tried always to steer clear of him ever after.

In November 1968, the Hull office was opened with great ceremony and a mass migration of the entire team to stay in the Hull Centre Hotel which reeked of 'pot' for days after. During the days we jostled in a grossly over-crowded office doing as many items from Hull as possible. At 6.00pm we did the programme from a makeshift studio in the hotel. Then after *Calendar* we set out to find something interesting to do in Hull at night. It was a fruitless search.

My own contribution to this 'Hullfest' was a film about the prospects for the Humber Bridge. This had been mooted for decades but was finally offered to Hull by Barbara Castle during the Hull North by-election of 1966, even though each reason for building the bridge had by then been eliminated. The first reason had been to connect Hull to London. Planners killed that by deciding that the connection was to run along the M62 and link-up with the A1 and the M1, carrying traffic first west then south and making a southern route cutting through Lincolnshire via a bridge unnecessary. As this purpose vanished a new one had emerged. The bridge was to be a centrepiece for the development of what was (and remains) Britain's last underdeveloped estuary to link the two Banks [of the Humber], join their population and industry and cultural capital (which Hull insisted was all in Hull) and widen the use of their facilities and labour markets. That dream was killed by the birth-control pill as the population on both Banks ceased to grow at a rate which would have boosted traffic; which led on to the last reason for a bridge: politics. It had been promised by Labour, though the promise was only implemented by the incoming Conservatives in 1970 and not completed until 1979, by which time I was MP for Grimsby. I boycotted the opening ceremony for what was essentially an overpriced, unnecessary, 'white elephant' which still does not pay for itself. Fat lot of good my boycott did. But it gave me a little satisfaction as a revenge for Hull's reaction to my prophetic film.

I tried to make all this clear in my film. I 'vox-popped' Hull in the street; no-one could think of a reason for building the bridge, except the vague possibility of visiting Cleethorpes. Yet they all wanted it. I interviewed Alderman King (we still had Aldermen then) on the site of what eventually became the start of the bridge. He stoutly defended it against my criticisms. Because I was so critical of their pet 'white elephant' my film received a hostile reception from the Hull dignitaries assembled to view it on our opening night in that city. That was compounded by the fact that Tony Essex's script defined Hull as being in the Northeast. Stupidly I had not noticed that and it produced more annoyance, even doubts, about whether YTV knew where the hell Hull was. The attack on the bridge though was tactless, pointless and (as Alec Todd told me) bad public relations. But it was right.

Apart from that the Hull week, while it did not endear that great city to YTV or convert the sizeable section of the population which still watched Anglia (incidentally via Rediffusion), did enable us to do some nice films about fishing and to have a good time, particularly McFayden who discovered an illicit drinking den called the Wellington Club where he holed up for the week. It also inaugurated the pattern of appointing a Hull reporter. Each of us went over for a week at a

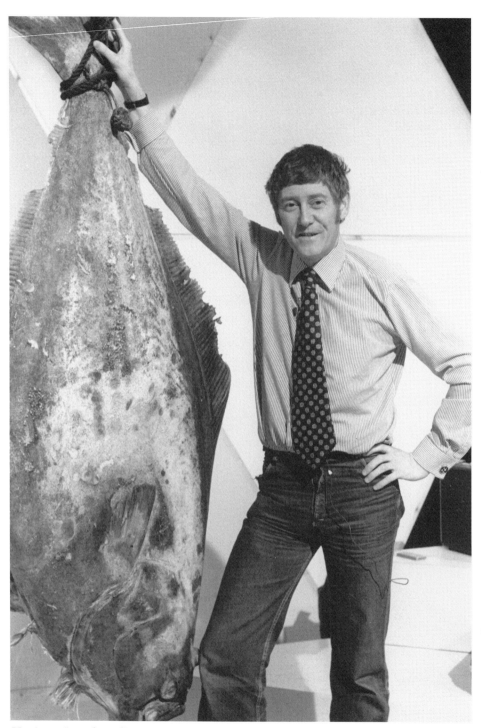

Here's one I caught earlier.

time to stay at the Europa Hotel and send back local stories done each day with the Hull crew, the most amiable, happy and under-employed film crew YTV had. We even ventured occasionally over to the south bank of the Humber where I visited Grimsby for the first time and renewed my acquaintance with Skegness where I had holidayed at Butlin's two decades earlier. None of us discovered much fun in Hull and boredom was exacerbated by the fact that the last train to Leeds, which would get film back to *Calendar* on time, left at lunchtime. That meant a frantic morning's work and an afternoon and evening with nothing much to do in the least exciting of Yorkshire towns. This being before it was designated to become Britain's City of Culture in 2017.

Calendar's *Western Brothers: Bert Gaunt and Lord Farnsbarns. (Top hats from Millets.)*

Sowerby Bridge Broadcasting.   *Sowerby Bridge Broadchasing.*

Activity was frenetic and increased even further at the end of 1968 when (for some reason which no one remembers) six thirty-minute slots on the network suddenly fell vacant. Donald Baverstock grabbed them for Yorkshire's first national documentaries. The benefit was that Jonathan Aitken was taken off of *Calendar* to prepare thirty-minute documentaries. The problem was that we – and he – had little idea what to do. Donald called the series *The Reporters.* Jonathan, who always brimmed with impractical ideas unsuitable for ITV, suggested and reported on three programmes: one on Red Adair, the master of extinguishing oil-well fires, whose talents were then employed in Australia, another on Alice Roosevelt-Longworth, the daughter of President 'Teddy' Roosevelt, who had lingered on in Washington as a mistress of gossip and malevolence: I thought this pretty boring for an ITV programme, but fascinating for the historian. The third was about the captain of the *Queen Elizabeth 2.* This was more interesting, though it revealed Jonathan's scriptwriting deficiency in a piece of commentary: 'The captain is smiling in this shot because...'. It was quickly deleted by Tony Essex. 'Never tell them what they're seeing. They can decide that for themselves.' our maestro explained.

Appropriate touching 1970 style.

After the Charles Atlas Course.

My part in this documentary bonanza was more humble. It was proposed that I should do a programme on Christmas toys (something considered worthy for a D.Phil). This was to go out in December just before Christmas, directed by 'Sneaky' Deaky and featuring all the new toys. We started with the British market then dominated by Triang, with a factory in East London, and Hornby, still making its model railways in Liverpool. We visited both and looked at the new toys, most of which had been devised in a toy 'think tank' in the Lake District. Then we went off to New York to see what was selling at FAO Schwartz, the largest toyshop in the world. Deakin being a dreadful snob decided we were to stay at the Waldorf Astoria, only to find that we had no film crew. The British crew filming Alice Roosevelt-Longworth and led, as we thought, by Patrick Boyle, had not responded to our telephone calls and telegrams. Patrick had registered under his courtesy title of Lord Kilburn as eldest son of the Earl of Glasgow so he never received our messages and no crew appeared. We were forced to hire a hard-bitten New York crew to film a day of toys, thousands of Santas ringing bells by the roadside and over-fed children who did not know what the hell they wanted for Christmas. Exhausted at the end of the day I asked the cameraman what we should do for our evening in

New York. 'Depends,' he said, 'whether you wanna get screwed, blued or tattooed'. None of these appealed. I went back to the Waldorf to bed; a pathetic end to my first-ever visit to the USA.

The series was a failure and never repeated: a setback for Yorkshire Television and for our team. It did not deter. *Calendar* was gaining strength and impetus, becoming more accepted and even popular. We were on our way until, suddenly, in March 1969, after I had burned my boats by resigning from Nuffield College, and throwing in my lot with a three-year contract with Yorkshire, the bubble burst. The impressive new-technologically advanced mast at Emley Moor (this had warning signs not to go near because ice might drop off) collapsed in an unusually bitter cold spell due to the weight of ice that did not drop off.

Richard went out and produced a moving film in the cold and the fog with the great mast lying across the countryside like a huge dead snake. Suddenly, our brilliant programmes could not be seen by anyone except us. Next day the staff, by now 700 of them, gathered in the studio to be addressed by Ward Thomas in his inarticulate way. Ward had been a brave pilot in Bomber Command but he was no Churchill calling for 'blood, sweat and tears' and clearly had no answers to the problem of a television centre with no transmissions. When our floor manager asked deferentially what we, the staff, could do to help and offered a salary cut, Ward's only suggestion was to 'Go easy on the expenses'. Barry Cockcroft choked. The rest of us shuffled. The floor manager was dragged down into the crowd. We left the studio to face a disaster we could do nothing about. There was plenty to say, ideas to develop, programmes to make, excitement to be shared and no one to watch. That night we did the programme. It looked as though it had been filmed down a coalmine but no one saw it so it did not matter.

CHAPTER SIX

SEDUCING YORKSHIRE

Our slow rise to the lead and success was dramatically interrupted by the collapse of the mast in March 1969. At first it looked fatal. No one had ever envisaged the possibility of a brand-new TV station with talented teams and the most modern equipment losing its transmission mast. Disbelief was the initial reaction: 'This can't happen to us.' But it had and realization of the consequences cast a pall of gloom over the whole company. Every mind turned back to the basic issue. Could YTV survive? A particularly worrying prospect because there was nothing the company or its staff could do about it. We were in the hands of the Independent Television Authority, a body which showed few signs of dynamism or inventiveness.

The initial reaction was a crop of ideas, some of them lunatic, about how to get back on air. The most fertile producers of ideas were Jonathan Aitken and Andrew Kerr. Andrew contacted their friend, Ronan O'Reilly, the pirate radio king (the upper-classes are always well connected) who called Ward Thomas to tell him about a method of transmission which had been used in South-east Asia and the US. He suggested an aircraft which would circle round Yorkshire beaming down the signal: *Calendar* by air freight. Jonathan suggested a barrage balloon holding up a transmitter wire to beam the signals down to Yorkshire. But when it came to daft ideas, the team itself could produce more even than the Institute of Economic Affairs working overtime.

Fortunately no one was listening to them. We just got on with our job of making programmes no one could watch, which allows me to say without fear of contradiction that we made some of the best programmes in the world in those weeks. Fortunately the ITA acted more quickly than anyone could have expected. It quickly hired a mobile transmitter from BBC2 (which no one watched) so transmission soon resumed to part

Whitby Fish Market.

of the viewing area. Then another mast was imported from Sweden (a country used to bad winters) and quickly erected. Within weeks we were back on the air. The climb to success resumed. We were on our way, though old habits die hard because despite all the preparation in a Cockcroft documentary which went out as soon as transmission was resumed; Part Two was still being frantically edited as Part One went out.

The programme assumed its basic pattern which never changed much while I was there, though the sets changed regularly. When we started we had been on little platforms round the studio. These were easy to fall off in moments of stress. Mercifully they soon went and tables and easy chairs replaced them with a much more colourful set replacing the grey monstrosity as soon as colour came in. Our news readers no longer delivered their bulletins standing; as if at a pulpit.

Calendar was not turning out to be the Yorkshire version of *Tonight* which Donald had intended. Certainly it was not as intellectually high-powered, but was much closer to the frequency of the Yorkshire audience which made it populist rather than intellectual, for we aimed at and got a larger audience but some degrees lower down the social scale. Nor did it have one main presenter in the role the avuncular Cliff Michelmore had done so well. We worked in a small but busy studio with several presenters, including me, Michael Partington, Richard Whiteley, and later Paul Dunstan and Bob Warman from ATV. On the distaff side until 1970 we had Liz Fox, then later Marylyn Webb who eventually replaced Liz, though not her sexy appeal.

Barry Cockcroft took us to the most exciting places and events.

It all created a busy and active scene with all parts of the set used. Guests were ushered in and out, sometimes tripping over the camera wires which trailed like snakes around the studio. It made for a crowded scene totally unlike the sparse studio settings of today's regional magazines which have either only one presenter, like Peter Levy in *Look North* from Hull, presumably for economy reasons or, in most cases, a mom and pop duo, both preferably young, good looking and all too often beautiful but brainless. Older, experienced presenters cost too much and do not look as good. Only a few older ones and none of the regional figures who were so big in my time have been able to hang on over the years. Both formats are tame compared to *Calendar's* lively crowd scene.

Seducing a whole region may sound a little difficult and look both unnecessary and exhausting but it was our job on *Calendar*. We were the warm up team for the evening's ITV viewing, there to build up the audience from the low point of ITN's news bulletin which went out before us. To do that we had to reach, cover and win, every part of Yorkshire Television's allotted region. Our job was to court it, win its attention and build a relationship. That relationship between a regional magazine and its region is like a marriage. Developing and consummating was the challenge facing all the TV regional magazines, including Yorkshire's. There we competed with the BBC to serve our distinct part of the country. The commercial television stations competed from within their areas. The BBC regions were more like outposts of a London-based empire. We wanted to win, to do better, and personally I was possessed by a kind of

Drumming up the audience.

Shopping before Tesco.

Marching Girls march for Calendar.

fever. I wanted to know everything about Yorkshire, to see or be at everything that was going on, to possess it.

The TV regions were a bit artificial. Ours included most of Yorkshire except the northern parts. It had a distinct identity of its own but was joined to a swathe of the Midlands and the eastern region, reaching down to King's Lynn, both being added by the Belmont transmitter. They had less in common with industrial Yorkshire and its working-class majority. With a less clear-cut identity than Yorkshire and a smaller population these outliers were less well served, even a little neglected, making them more disgruntled or perhaps less well 'gruntled' than our Yorkshire core.

Nevertheless the region turned out to be the best television area to serve. It was too large to be parochial, as the smaller areas of the new local television stations will prove to be, yet small enough to know and understand and to have a common identity and common interests. This was both better and different to the diversity and plurality of a national audience which has to be categorized and treated as sections rather than treated as one as we did in Yorkshire.

Calendar was on the frontline of Yorkshire Television's regional challenge and crucial to YTV's need to put down roots, build viewer loyalty and interest and weld a close relationship with the county that was its home. YTV was Yorkshire's showcase, its servant and the basis of its programme offer to the wider nation, and *Calendar* existed to nurture these roots. For me and for the rest of the Calendar team it was like a courtship. Yorkshire became our central focus, our interest, our obsession. We were learning more and more about it, developing interest in all its aspects, from sport where it always held its own, to history and its industries which had always been neglected in favour of national trends and events.

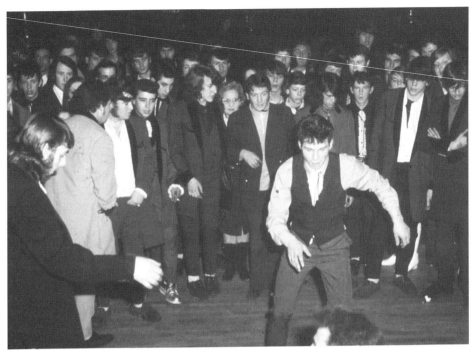

Time out with the Teds: Strictly Don't Come Dancing.

Calendar absorbed, created and shaped our Yorkshire. The team read about it, travelled about it, studied, discovered and devoured it. It was our world and our universe. For all my *Calendar* years, my central interest was learning and reading about Yorkshire and getting to know it better. That process would have been impossible with the nation. That was a unit too large to comprehend or talk to as one. It would have had to be treated in a more specialized way. The process of learning, understanding and covering our viewing area was exhausting but just about manageable. It was also exciting. We managed it because we were at the centre of a spider's web of contacts, stringers, and callers through which information flowed in, while we reporters were constantly out and about travelling round our small universe, learning about it and discovering new aspects every day.

This Yorkshire preoccupation meant that national events and trends, while all important to national television and its programmes, were important to us only so far as they impacted on Yorkshire. The clash of parties, the feverish speculations about who is up, who is down, who will be, who will not, and the endless speculations of political journalism played no part in our programmes. They would have been boring, except when they intruded at election time. Even then we ventilated them only so far as this promise or that policy affected Yorkshire and its industries. We celebrated the differences, ignored the commonalities and generally did our own thing. Wider Britain was background not foreground for our thirty minutes (one forty-eighth) of each weekday.

At the start of *Calendar*, survival and getting a presentable programme on air were more important preoccupations than learning the region and getting to know the people. Then as the teething problems were conquered and *Calendar* took its settled form, the learning process (Yorkshire TV 101) about the 'Broad Acres' and their inhabitants, which eventually led us to mastery and Yorkshire to settled acceptance, became more important. Competition helped here. The fact that two programmes, the BBC and us, were competing for the Yorkshire audience stimulated and improved both, though we should have realized that *Calendar* was bound to win. It had more resources, a larger and more talented team and was devoted to Yorkshire rather than striving for promotion to somewhere else by doing public-service articles and never having fun – until *Nationwide* came along with its skate-boarding ducks.

The programme mix was more varied than *Tonight*'s had been. We were very Yorkshire, and in the case of the news, all Yorkshire. Events in London were too trivial for us and could mostly be relegated to ITN whose 6.45pm news bulletin preceded *Calendar*. Variety was the key and we spread our net pretty widely, covering all sorts of things, from coalmines to acrobats, police methods to politics, music to medicine, which have since been relegated to specialized programmes. No regional programme today reviews books but we did regularly, helped by the fact that publisher's representatives came often, publishers bombarded us with books and a New Zealander, Liz Calder, later the founder of the successful publishers Bloomsbury, was then married to someone in Rochdale. She called in regularly to enthuse us about books (and indeed her) so that the office was often flooded with books she and others were plugging, mostly with a guaranteed appearance by any authors keen enough to come so far north. The books were usually 'borrowed' and disappeared (too often before the interview) one-by-one rather than being taken to the library downstairs, but at least I never found them on re-sale in second-hand bookshops which had happened all the time to books on *Twenty Four Hours*.

We covered films, and not only those like *The Railway Children* or Brontë-based films which featured Yorkshire. We even did cookery, though never on the insane scale it is done today. Just the homely *Country Kitchen*. We were not food faddists. We tried out ideas and strands of programmes which were later taken up by regular series: jokes before Granada's *Comedians*, tricks on an unwary public before Jeremy Beadle, funny sketches before *Monty Python's Flying Circus*, though to be honest we only attempted one and it was disastrous. Our manic moments even produced items which, looking back, seem incomprehensible, like a film about paintings and statues collected by Sir Titus Salt cut to 'Indiana Wants Me. Lord I Can't Go Back There', and another about never-ending road works in Baildon cut to 'Working My Way Back to You Babe'. The mind boggles. But we also did a huge quantity of serious and interesting items. We did history, including several recreations of colliery tragedies, and in 1976 on the 50th anniversary of the General Strike we filled the studio with surviving strikers and miners. The atmosphere was electric. The old hatreds were still real.

In 1976, we also did a series of daily reports on the General Strike. News reporters reported from all over Yorkshire: mines, mills and steelworks on the day's events and Robert Kee presented each day's programme in the studio as if it was happening that day. It was an exciting recreation and particularly interesting because it showed how

Hannah and the Sowerby Fairies.

*Cottingley's
original fairies
1917.*

vast the mining industry in Yorkshire had been and how little the industrial parts of Sheffield had changed in 50 years.

Other historical events which we covered were the shelling of Scarborough and other east-coast ports like Hartlepool and Whitby in December 1914 at the start of the First World War. Then three German battlecruisers caught the British Navy napping, loomed out of the fog and devastated parts of each town, killing 137 people, wounding eighty-six and inflicting heavy damage on hotels like the Grand. They showed that Britannia really did not rule the waves. They actually killed more people (over 100) and did a lot more damage to Hartlepool further north, but while that part of the northeast was in the range of their guns it was not within range of our transmitter. So we did not cover it. Though Hartlepool had fired back, Scarborough had not. Hartlepool's was a better reaction to the German threat than they had made to the French in the Napoleonic war when they had hung a monkey under the impression that it was an French spy.

Another highlight was our film on the formerly famous, now forgotten, Cottingley fairies. Joe Cooper, a Leeds writer, lecturer and expert on the paranormal (he told me I had an aura which he could feel in a kind of appropriate non-touching) came to us with a book he had written about Elsie Wright and her cousin, Frances Griffiths. He was a friend of Harry Patterson, the Leeds writer, who wrote as Jack Higgins and produced *The Eagle Has Landed*, after which he left Leeds for Jersey as a tax exile. Joe introduced us to Harry. In 1917, when Elsie was 16 years-old and Frances nine, they had photographed fairies in the wooded beck behind where they lived in Cottingley, near Bingley. The claim had been eagerly taken up by spiritualists and endorsed in a book by Sir Arthur Conan Doyle.

How the fairies were filmed.

Wilf Lunn's Wonderful Inventions.

Jackie Pallo didn't like the questions.

A Feast of Yorkshire's After Dinner Speakers.

It caused a sensation which went round the world but died down when the girls married and went to live abroad. In the 1970s, they came back and Joe Cooper interviewed them, wrote his book and brought it to us. We took them back up the beck where they described the original sightings which we then reconstructed using my daughter, Hannah, looking at cut-out fairies on black wire to expose it for the confidence trick I took it to be. Elsie and Frances, now pensioners, stuck to their story and continued to deny that they had faked the fairies until, in the 1980s, Frances, nearing death, confessed to Joe Cooper that Elsie had copied the fairies, cut them out, propped them up with hat pins before taking the photographs. Just like our reconstruction. 'I thought it was a joke', she said, 'but everyone else kept it going'. Sadly by that time YTV had lost our film and could not join the rush to reconstruct something we had exposed some years earlier. In any case, films about fairies had a very different meaning by then.

Calendar's basic fare was visiting stars, national or international, artists coming to the clubs, theatres or events all over Yorkshire. They had to be rushed to *Calendar*, and sometimes to or from *Look North* who did fewer interviews, and then on to their place of performance. For me this was the greatest privilege of the job. I met and interviewed lots of major stars of the time, or at least those who were not shackled to the BBC in some way. The most interesting were John Lennon and Yoko Ono, who

Fred Trueman.

Barry Cryer.

Sir Cyril Smith.

Roy Orbison.

I interviewed in London after The Beatles had broken up. They failed to respond to my passionate pleas to reconstitute The Beatles. Indeed, they were bored by them but talked fascinatingly and frankly about anything else I asked. We covered a wide area and the interview (actually two – one for education, one for *Calendar*) could have been seminal. Indeed it could, today, have been endlessly repeated on Sky Arts but YTV lost both. Par for the course with The Beatles because Granada wiped their first ever TV interview in an economy drive to re-use video tape.

The biggest hit for me was Joan Baez, a wonderful, serene, lovely lady, possibly an angel and certainly a joy to interview. I have worshipped her ever since, which is more than I can say for Spike Milligan, who came, answered two questions in perfunctory fashion and then refused to say any more. It unnerved me. I continued to ask un-answered questions but never the crucial two: 'Are you barmy?' and 'Why the hell did you come on the programme if you're not going to talk?' He still got paid. Frankie Howerd was difficult too, though at least he did not touch me up which he did with other male interviewers. The worst, though, was Anita Harris who we interviewed after a so-called kidnap. It was painful because her fabricated story fell apart as she babbled on, making the interview incomprehensible.

Fred Trueman was much more straightforward and became a regular guest. Once he understood that he could not say 'f**k' on air, Fred could always be relied on to entertain. One of the first times he came on was at the start of his brief career as a nightclub entertainer. Unfortunately, the night before he had told several jokes to Donald Baverstock who was so appalled at the prospect of Fred's humour going out to kiddies and causing good Yorkshire folk to choke on their tea that I was instructed that he must not be allowed to tell any jokes on any account: Which sort of removed the point of an interview about his stand-up routine.

Nevertheless Fred appeared, chattered happily about retirement and why he was now going to do the clubs. I kept the conversation going with my suggestions about what he might do, song and dance routines, animal impressions, anything to stay off jokes. Fred kept suggesting that he should tell some of his jokes but I desperately talked on over him. Sadly there was an under-run and time to fill in at the end. This allowed Fred to seize his opportunity. 'Why is Bradford Corporation bricking up the bottom of all the gents toilets?' In the control room the director, who Donald had also bullied, panicked and lost his nerve. The credits whistled up drowning Fred's joke. The screen faded prematurely to black. The punch line of the joke was 'To stop limbo dancers getting in free'; quite funny. So it was afterwards decided that Fred understood the need for clean humour and could be allowed to tell jokes in future. The result was that the next time he came in, his nightclub career now going strong, I invited him to tell a joke, which he did. 'Have you heard the one about the Grand Old Duke of York? You know the one that had ten thousand men.' 'Yes,' I blundered in, trying to show how clever someone with a D.Phil in history could be. 'Well the case comes up next Wednesday.'

The procession of celebrities, comedians, singers (some of whom sang), groups and stars went on. It was a real privilege to chat to so many of the famous, something I had never have done as an Oxford Don, though I doubt if any of my interviewees remember the occasion. Variety and entertainment were, however, only part of our agenda. Yorkshire was the basis of the programme and of our success. The county

Arthur Scargill proud of his old colliery, Woolley, with Ashley Jackson, John Willis and Woolley Deputy.

is interested in itself but not much in the world outside and had been starved of Yorkshireness for far too long. We supplied it in abundance with Yorkshire news, sport, characters, attractions and events and found that Yorkshire folk loved them. The county liked talking to itself about itself. Why not, there are fewer things more interesting. There's 'nowt' so queer as folk and 'nowt' so interesting as Yorkshire folk who were not queer in the popular sense of that word but unusual in degrees ranging from eccentric to crazy. Yorkshire must have more eccentrics per acre than anywhere else. Within that universe we discovered a whole range of new and old characters who the audience loved. They included Bill Bowes, the old Yorkshire cricket great and now cricket correspondent of the *Yorkshire Post*. He could probably have reminisced about W.G. Grace had we not restricted him to going no further back than Len Hutton, Wilf Lunn, the Huddersfield inventor, Ashley Jackson who we helped on his way to becoming Yorkshire's greatest artist, and Terry Durham, poet and artist, who made a beautiful record, with brass band accompaniment about a colliery closure.

     Most important of all we discovered Arthur Scargill who *Calendar* created. He was suggested to us by our Barnsley stringer as the only miners' leader who could string a few coherent sentences together. Being desperate for a miner who could talk, we brought him on regularly and he talked brilliantly about mines and miners. This started Arthur's rise to power because appearing on television helped him to get elected to positions in the union and he rapidly climbed the leadership hierarchy. Militant Marxism took over the NUM which abandoned the canny caution of Joe Gormley. Arthur, in turn, educated us about mining, taking us down several pits, including Woolley where he had worked. All were enormously improved from the last time I had been down a pit in the 1940s. Then I had watched miners lying on their sides hacking narrow seams with picks, a vision which left a lingering nightmare in my mind. On the visits I made with Arthur, I watched miners operating massive cutting machines at the faces which we crawled to. We were always photographed at the end of these trips down Kellingley, Maltby or Woolley and I noticed that Arthur always took the trouble to black up as we came to the surface, though that was not a condition of working at the baronial gothic NUM headquarters in Barnsley where he later held court. By that time he had become so famous and powerful that he did not need us as much as we needed him. Indeed he was becoming 'King Arthur'. We were his pages. He was adept at avoiding us whenever he was in difficulties. When he did come on he always asked about the fee. But he always gave a compelling explanation of his industry and intentions.

Yorkshire abounded in characters, most of them willing to talk at length, for a small fee. Barry Cockcroft was the greatest discoverer of characters. He started on the moors between Rochdale and Halifax where he discovered old guys who could talk happily about the days of cock fighting, illicit stills and the 'double necessaire', a two-seater drop lavatory where couples could hold hands and kiss while shitting. Unfortunately, we never managed to film any of these wonders and some of the interviews were so broad as to be incomprehensible without subtitles. Barry's real treasure house was the Dales. He would disappear, sometimes for weeks, to return with jewels. The uncharitable complained that he was all the while sitting at home in Rochdale, having left a list of pub telephone numbers where he might be found and instructed all of

Liz Fox congratulates the World Knurr and Spell champs.

*Got to chalk
it reet.*

Nipsy in Barnsley.

them to say that 'Barry had just nipped out but would probably be back in half an hour.' That practice was so widespread that I once rang the Spring Rock Inn in Elland about something else and casually asked if they had seen Barry lately. 'No, but he'll be back in half an hour.' He was in fact in the South Pacific with Whicker.

To be on one of Barry's great expeditions to the Dales to film his characters was like being on a royal tour but with better food. I went on one which started with a film on the 'Bainbridge Horn Blower', a tradition which, Barry claimed, had been going on since the Middle Ages with the horn blower going out at sundown every evening to blow his horn and guide shepherds and travellers back to the village before dark. This was evidently a hereditary job. So we were booked into the best hotel in Bainbridge to film the present incumbent. Unfortunately the weather was so bad that it rained all day. The horn blower and some of the crew (but not me) got progressively drunker as we sat in the pub waiting for the rain to stop. When it finally did it was a little dark for filming and the horn blower was too drunk to stand up, let alone blow a note of the traditional call. I did my piece to camera, managed to get a few words from the horn blower, who swayed dangerously then raised the enormous horn and got a few low notes which sounded more like a farts in the rain than a call home. The rain immediately fused the lights.

Next day the disasters continued as we filmed the *Legend of Semerwater*. This was

Even bigger hitters in Elland.

*And wilder up
Cragg Vale.*

in the *Ballad of Semerwater*, a poem by Sir William Watson of whom no one had ever
heard. This tells how the 'mickle town', as it then was, (now it was a field populated
by a few incurious sheep) had refused hospitality to a beggar 'faint for lack of bread'
who was turned away hungry. In revenge he called up a deluge so that the town was
flooded in consequence. So Barry, or 'Cecil B. De Sixteen Mill', as we called him
(sometimes also 'Dino' [de Laurentis]), proposed that I would swim out in the lake
to seek underwater ruins of 'a lost city in Semerwater. Deep asleep til Doom', even
though all of us knew it was not there. Unfortunately, still fell the rain (as Sitwell
might have put it). The wind blew, the lake was choppy, it was cold and the crew was
fed up. The wind stirred the muddy waters so the underwater swimmer could see
nothing, even with powerful floodlights (which we did not have). I donned my wetsuit
and swam. Mostafa Hammuri, the cameraman, donned his and swam towards me
with his especially water-proofed camera. Seeing nothing we collided head-to-head
and my helmet broke his protective lens cover. Filming was abandoned. The ruins of
Semerwater remain undiscovered. I have a shrewd suspicion that they will stay 'asleep
til Doom'. I hope they do.

   Barry's great discovery (before Hannah Hauxwell) was 'Knurr and Spell' or
'Yorkshireman's Golf', so called because there were no fees attached. Played on the
moors around Elland with a variant called 'Nipsy' played round Barnsley, Barry
discovered that the last world championships had been played in 1937 so he decided
to revive them and managed to assemble an extraordinary cast of old, very ornery and

Barry Cockcroft and Fred Trueman running the Knurr and Spell.

extremely thirsty characters to compete for a world cup presented by Joe Kagan, who had been persuaded to sponsor the whole event by Peggy Rushton, his PR lady, and a friend of Barry's. Not only that, we were all of us, crew, presenters and visiting stars like Fred Trueman and Geoff Boycott, presented with Gannex coats, as popularized by Harold Wilson. I still have mine in the hope that it will become fashionable again. These proved invaluable. Not only did Liz Fox look very fetching in Gannex and a miniskirt shorter than the coat, but the appointed day was the coldest ever and mist enveloped the field on the moors above Elland as the 'Knurrs' (or was it the 'Spells'?) disappeared into the distance. My teeth chattered as I tried to make sense of it all. The film was viewed as a great Yorkshire success. Yorkshire had another champion, this time Jack Driver of Elland. We repeated the event, though with a diminished supply of Gannex coats as Harold Wilson made them less popular. We held further games in Elland, Barnsley and out in the Dales, though in each case Barry resisted my view that it should only go out with subtitles. 'Insulting to Yorkshire,' he said. We all recovered from our coughs and colds but the Gannex never came back into fashion.

Yorkshire was a rich seam which we mined vigorously. It produced gems. We interviewed all the Yorkshire greats, too many of whom lived in the South, though we did get James Mason, J.B. Priestley (who was bored) and my hero, John Braine (who did not remember me marching behind him in a CND march in Bradford in 1959 or serving me in Bingley library in the 1950s). We got Joe Cocker by invading his house, hauling him out of bed where he was stoned and dragging him round Sheffield to

The helicopter gave us new views of Selby.

Houses in West Yorkshire.

reminisce, though most of what came over from his radio microphone was his efforts to score. We ended up in a pub where, amazingly, I was recognized and greeted with great enthusiasm but Joe, the megastar who they clearly did not know, was ignored. When I met Joe again several years later, he still remembered me and our interview – with some resentment. We also interviewed everyone who is no one in Yorkshire (because they had stayed home in the county). It all went to show what a prodigious producer of talent Yorkshire is. Nurturing and promoting it was a crucial role for regional television.

In this festival of *Yorkshire for Yorkshire*, we inevitably did Yorkshire sport, in which I took as much interest as in the spread of myxomatosis in Anguilla. Until the day Brian Clough was fired by Leeds United. On that fateful day of infamy, I was the only presenter who had not either gone home early or became incomprehensible in the bar. So when Kevin Sim sold the idea of bringing Clough and Don Revie together in the studio to John Wilford, he took it up immediately and cleared an evening slot for it, I was picked to chair it. I did with some trepidation because I knew so little about either of them or about football. No matter. John Wilford was happy to brief me beforehand and we agreed that I should say and do as little as possible. It was not for me to try to be a star interviewer but to listen to and encourage their interaction. What was said in the interview was fascinating as two very different personalities with different approaches to management traded their dislike of each other. It was historic and has since been made famous by the film, *The Damned United*, though someone better looking than me played me. But Michael

And of the Dales.

Joe Kenyon, Socialist hero who revived the Claimants & Unemployed Workers Union.

Parkinson, who looks much older and now has a lucrative job advertising insurance and funeral costs, was allowed to play himself and presumably received a fee. I did not. People say how marvellous the interview was. In fact it was dead easy. Contrary to rumour, neither Revie nor Clough had been tricked into appearing. Each knew that he was confronting the other. The only haggling beforehand was about the size of the fee, though Revie, who usually preferred to negotiate his fee in the gents' toilet, made an exception as John Wilford shuttled between the boardroom where Revie was and the 'green room' where we had put Clough. Each received the same payment – £400 in cash, not a large sum even then. Keith Macklin, our top sports reporter, was annoyed that I did the interview not him, but as Wilford explained, it was not about football but people.

This is why it was so easy for me because in the studio each disliked the other so much that there was no need for the interviewer to intervene at all. I just sat there and watched the argument unfurl; which it did brilliantly. The telling line 'it's all personal really' given to me in the film was in fact said by Clough. No matter. I was fascinated by the interaction between two great managers, though very much on Clough's side as the more human of the two. The John Humphrys-style harassing interview had not come in yet and would have been disastrous here because it focuses all the attention on the interviewer. As John Wilford regularly argued, the best interviewer should just listen and say 'Really?' occasionally. I was not interesting, but the protagonists were and I enjoyed their interaction without realizing at the time that it was so good. The interview took twenty years to become famous but was the best interview I ever did, though it still awaits the immortalization of being turned into a film like the Frost/Nixon interview. Still it did bring me back from the dead in 2009, though unfortunately it also created the impression that I knew something about football, making people keen to talk to me about it, an enthusiasm they never showed about politics. It also demonstrated the strength of regional TV for Fox, as managing director, was able to authorize it and put it out on the day; that could not happen now.

We built up our own team of predictable and presentable guests: Yorkshire folk who had the gift of the gab and programme suppliers for any matters, from veterinary to criminal or sleazy, which we wanted to deal with. We even used a private detective who worked like a mail-order service. If we wanted a burglar, a prostitute or a car thief he would bring along someone. I interviewed a professional adulteress he produced from the days when divorces were secured by finding the errant partner in bed with someone (anyone would do provided they were of the opposite sex, for in those days the law did not cover lesbianism while homosexuals were usually arrested in lavatories not bed). The private detective would burst in, for a fee, and give evidence of *in flagrante delicto* and more than usually *selecto* because there was no need to prove stains on the bed sheets. Shocked by the incidence of car theft (for this was before the days when cars were programmed to report to the police of their own accord if someone tried to enter) I asked our pet technician to come along to the YTV car park and show us how it was done. He opened every car but found only empty crisp packets and a few dogs. Sadly, John Wilford then refused to carry the item on the grounds that we should not show children how to burgle cars lest they took it up for a living. He was of course right, but I still sulked.

In Joe Kenyon we discovered yet another Yorkshire original, a village Hampden, or more accurately his modern counterpart, a Barnsley Socialist but one of the pure strain who had lived most of his life in that little socialist republic. Starting work as a miner but disabled by an industrial accident, he devoted the rest of his life to preaching, teaching – in Labour colleges – and working as a one-man Citizens Advice Bureau, benefits consultant and agitator. Never one to hide his light under a Barnsley bushel, he came to our attention when he formed the Claimants & Unemployed Workers Union (CUWU), perhaps I should say reformed, for the organization had been powerful and effective under communist leadership before the war but dormant in the 1950s. So Joe's revival was a one-man band projected nationally through the media. Joe wrote for it, designed its posters and advised its members on benefit matters, acting as their representative and defender if they were in Barnsley where his regular visits to the huge new benefits office (the only new development in Barnsley he called it) were greeted with fear and horror by the staff. He was always better informed and armed with facts than they were.

Joe became a regular guest on *Calendar*, both for the discussion programmes like *Calendar Sunday*, and for highlighting difficult cases where beneficiaries had been done-down or cheated by the system. Being on the side of the people we took them up. Duncan Dallas and I filmed cases and tried to get responses from the National Assistance Board which usually paid up rather than argue.

This could, however, lead to difficulties, as it did when Joe told us that the Department of Health & Social Security was spying on single women to see if they were in fact cohabiting with someone, and therefore not entitled to benefit. Officials were, he claimed, spying on these women in the early hours of the morning to see if a male came out of the house. We should expose this monstrous practice. I agreed and we went down to Barnsley with a full crew. This included cameraman, assistant cameraman, soundman and an electrician who was really not required since *son et lumière* would have given the game away even if the crew crowd spectacular did not. At 6.30am we positioned ourselves on the flyover giving a clear view of the house of the woman in question and waited. A film crew of that size is not exactly inconspicuous and is certainly noisy, but we sat silent, watching and waiting like a funeral party waiting for the hearse. We waited; and waited. Nothing happened. At 8.30am we gave up and went down to meet the lady who was just getting up. She did not offer us a cup of tea. 'Try again tomorrow,' said Joe. I doubted that Yorkshire TV would pay the overtime bill for that. We never went back.

Our next venture angered Joe. We were phoned by a clerk in the National Assistance Board who told us that he was paying out benefit to people he knew were working and cheating the system. He would not say that publicly, so we filmed him, voice disguised, face in the dark, as he told his story. Here was the start of the 'Great Scrounger' argument which grew stronger and stronger through the 1970s. I was not convinced because he had no specific cases to give, but many of the public were, including Joe Ashton, newly elected MP for Bassetlaw, a working-class lad and a brilliant populist who could not bear to see social security being ripped off. We interviewed him. That began a long standing relationship, making Joe Ashton a regular Calendar guest who could always be relied on to talk sense. Even if it angered Joe Kenyon.

Joe Kenyon went on from strength to strength. In 1974, the Home Office gave him a job researching unemployment in Batley. They set him up with an office and research support in that town until, predictably, he rebelled against the restrictions, walked out and went back to developing his CUWU with a whole series of demonic posters protesting about the dole. He developed an ingenious plan to fly poor pensioners out to Spain for the winter to take advantage of the cheap accommodation then offered; a brilliantly simple idea, but far too radical for the beleaguered Labour government. I left *Calendar* to be an MP for a Labour Party which he despised and Joe soldiered on, until he died in 1997. Duncan Dallas endowed an annual prize for the best effort to help the poor and needy in Barnsley. There was no shortage of claimants as the welfare bill rose as a result of governments which ran the economy for higher levels of unemployment to fight inflation. That was a folly which Joe exposed in his writings based on a Keynon-Marxist analysis. I thought it overstated insofar as it applied to the Labour government in the 1970s which was doing its best to stop unemployment rising. But when neo-liberalism became an official orthodoxy under Margaret Thatcher and, even worse, and later, George Osborne, Joe's devastating critique was spot on. But sadly, it was too late.

Barrington Black, a campaigning Leeds lawyer and the only Labour man in Harrogate where politics was still a battle between Whigs and Tories, was also a major contributor to the programme. If I were a cynic I would think now that it was a matter of advertising his practice to any criminals in the audience who needed a good lawyer, but since criminals preferred BBC programmes like *Crime Watch* to *Calendar* I am sure that was not the case. Black would regularly send us cases which deserved taking up. We did and it produced several interesting items and several visits to prisons. Other regulars were Phillip Sims, chairman of Pudsey Conservative Association (who invited me to its annual dinner and cruelly sat me next to Edward 'Ted' Heath for my first 'Trappist' experience), Arthur Scargill, Sir Ron Ironmonger, leader of Sheffield and later South Yorkshire Council, and Joe Ashton, but we were constantly on the lookout for Yorkshire talent. Indeed, anyone who could string a few sensible words together.

They included local painter and poet, Terry Durham. Our search for Yorkshire musical talent was precipitated by Sid Waddell's claim that while there was a recognizable Mersey sound, a Newcastle sound with The Animals, and even a Manchester sound, Leeds had produced nothing except flood-warning sirens. I set out to prove him wrong but failed. In the course of the search, however, we did discover a local group formed by Jeff Christie called The Outer Limits. This effort revealed to me the importance of having a producer for each item. Having booked the group I led off a long caravan of cars, vans, the group and our equipment all bringing cameras, microphones and amplifiers, plus our soundmen and their assistants, electricians, grips, PAs and the musicians, a telling contrast with today's lean and mean crewing where things are usually done with one person, often on a short-term contract, doing all those jobs.

As the procession rolled slowly out of YTV, me in the lead, I realized I had not the faintest idea where we were going or what we were going to do. Mercifully we found a derelict site, set up and recorded a number to the great annoyance of the residents in the flats round about. After that I always insisted that 'McFad the Bad' find the groups and direct the items, which meant a succession of tight-trousered, soft-bottomed boy bands. Only Jeff Christie emerged well from the disaster. In 1970 he came to play me his latest record. 'It's good,' I said, 'Nice and bouncy. But it'll never make a hit'; so much for my pop-picking skills: Yellow River reached number one.

The other aspect of our musical interests was our hopes for a great Yorkshire pop festival inspired by the film, *Woodstock*, which made Duncan and I think that such a great experience could have been so much better were it staged in Yorkshire. So in 1969 when we heard of a Yorkshire pop festival to be produced at Krumlin, near Barkisland in the Pennines above Elland in August, we made preparations for a 'Woodstock'-style coverage. We began filming the festival right from the start. It was being organized in a natural bowl in the hills by two Halifax entrepreneurs, Brian Highley, the publican of the Anchor Inn, Milbank, and Derek McEwan. We spent several days filming and

Music in the mud.

Bickershaw floods and fans.

Krumlin Festival from the stage.

interviewing them about their hopes and prospects of hordes of hairy hooligans tramping the hills while a wire fence went up all round the site and the stage was built.

Hopes were high: Pink Floyd, Donovan, Mungo Jerry, Fairport Convention, The Kinks, Elton John, The Humblebums and Pentangle, all the big names were coming but there was a 'Catch 22' situation. Most groups would only come if paid cash in advance. The promoters had no cash until tickets began to sell: which they did not. So came the day but not the groups, only Elton John – then pretty unknown actually – appeared. He was a great success, partly because he passed bottles of brandy out to the audience. By now, though, great holes were appearing in the wire fence and more were coming through the holes than were paying at the gate where, in any case, the 'security staff' was pocketing the money and disappearing off to the pub. I assumed that the police who came in disguised as hippies to catch drug dealers paid for their admissions but they would be the majority of those who did pay – if they did. It began to rain on the Saturday. I took my soaked kids home. The Pennines in August are slightly different to California or Woodstock. Heathcliff might like them, as would Bear Grylls. But teenagers from the towns were a little unprepared and their tents a little flimsy.

We filmed the mounting excitement, the hospitality tent and the few groups who did arrive. I knew nothing about any of them and in my ignorance I did a long interview with a couple purporting to be part of Pink Floyd. At the end I was tipped off that they were not. I had been conned. Pink Floyd never turned up.

Nevertheless the first evening appeared to be a success, as did the second day, Saturday. On the Sunday morning we set off early from Leeds to film the successful climax. I drove ahead, Duncan bringing up in the rear with the film crew, only to

Krumlin before the rain began.

Krumlin after it.
Police search for
drugs and bodies.

find, when I got up on to the moors, a scene reminiscent of Napoleon's retreat from Moscow. Hail and sleet fell (August in Yorkshire). Bedraggled, wet, shivering people were pouring down to Elland with (of course) no buses running Sunday morning. I turned back to find Duncan miles away happily doing interviews with departing kids about their reactions to the festival, none of which included the scene of devastation I had seen. Duncan was always fairly inflexible about his plans but I did manage to persuade him to give up and get to the Krumlin where we filmed the debris, the police looking for bodies (one person had died of hypothermia) and poking round the abandoned tents for drugs. A total disaster: no groups and no proprietors. One had taken what money he could scrape together and disappeared into the night. The other was in hiding. Neither could be interviewed. We had a thirty-minute slot to fill on Monday night but only about fifteen minutes of film; lots covering the preparations, plenty of fence and platform building, but no music.

Yorkshire is better suited to producing a muddy battlefield more like the Somme than Glastonbury and it had worked hard at this, with the added attraction of gales and hail in August rather than days of fun and sun. This disaster was repeated in 1972 (though without snow) at Bickershaw in Lancashire, by which time I was at the BBC. This was organized by Jeremy Beadle who also hoped to make a pile and become famous only to end up with another disaster. This too I filmed as the rain fell, the stage collapsed and the fans were flooded out. We filmed it all, but at least this time we did actually get some music as well as misery.

The North was only redeemed as a pop concert venue a year later when there was a much better organized and successful folk festival at Tupholme Manor, held from 26 to 29 May 1973 in Bardney, Lincolnshire. There, not being Yorkshire, the sun shone, the fences held and the artists turned up. I was able to interview Sonny Terry and Brownie McGhee, James Taylor, Joe Cocker (so stoned he could only just stand up) and other stars. Being a non-pop person I had never heard of most of them, but Duncan had and they all talked brilliantly. We had a thoroughly enjoyable two days, marred only by the crash of metal at night as the young audience tried to get family cars out of an overcrowded car park. Peace and goodwill evaporated in the face of parental wrath and prospective repair bills. Happy days but it was the end of our enthusiasm for Northern pop festivals, if only because there were not any after Bardney. They all migrated south because the North was too risky weather wise. When I became an MP, I had some sympathy for the American jazz star booked to play at the South Bank Jazz Festival in Grimsby. He refused to come north when he found it was the South Bank of the Humber not the Thames. Mud baths and extreme weather are not compatible with good music.

We welcomed all developments and projects, musical, industrial, social or developmental coming to Yorkshire, few though they were. The Yorkshire MPs were not the most vigorous or articulate team of politicians I had ever met and Yorkshire did less well than other regions in terms of government spending, motorways, regional aid or ministerial visits. It received (still does) less public spending per head than London and the South or, come to that, than Scotland, the region most comparable with us. Nevertheless, whenever a minister inaugurated a northern project we were there asking for more: 'Oliver Twist TV'.

The biggest Yorkshire failures were government's unwillingness to help the North. Nothing was done by government about the Kilbrandon proposals for regional devolution. The Conservative government also rejected the Redcliffe-Maud proposals for city regions in favour of a two-tier system of local government which changed Yorkshire's boundaries and abolished the Ridings in favour of two-tier metropolitan counties in South and West Yorkshire. By this stage I had come out of the TV closet as a Yorkshire nationalist. Richard Wainwright, Liberal MP for Colne Valley, and I launched the *Northern Democrat* in which I argued for home rule for Yorkshire on the grounds that small states like New Zealand and Iceland were much more democratic and much better to live in. So, I declared, on the same grounds that Scotland was arguing 'It's Scotland's oil' that we should claim 'It's Yorkshire's gas' and demand a Yorkshire regional government. Richard wanted us to revive the *Council of the North*, being a more cautious Liberal, to cover the whole of the North but neither proposal caused a passionate surge of support. We were ahead of our time (perhaps by 100 years) but it was daring stuff. I never joined the provisional wing of Yorkshire nationalism. Nor did I go round like a 'Tykonian' terrorist painting out the 'H' of Steep Hill signs to translate them into Yorkshire. But I did lead a march from Tadcaster to York to protest against the abolition of Yorkshire. Once at York we came across a small problem. There was no one there to protest to and no interest among the bemused tourists, who always throng to York, about what we were doing. Were we a rehearsal for the *York Mystery Play* or a religious pilgrimage? They looked at us in puzzlement and moved off.

Noticing that none of the dialect words and expressions I had used naturally when I was a kid – words like snicket (passageway), bahn (going), loosing (closing as in 'pictures wor loosin', kalling (chatting), ligger dahn (lie down, regularly said to female dialect speakers) or addle a living (earn a living) were a foreign language to my kids (though not to Danes who understood them quite well), I did a series of *Teach Thissen Tyke* items to teach Yorksher as a foreign language. These brought in contributions from the Dales and from Barnsley, the heart of Yorkshire, where they still thee'd and thou'd.

As interest in Yorkshire dialect developed, we arranged to do a little item in Cardigan Road Primary School with me teaching a Yorkshire language lesson to the bemused kids. It went well. A few even understood what was going on but one turned out to be brilliant. A little girl, part Pakistani with a Pakistani father and a Leeds mother, announced that she could recite *Bite Bigger,* one of the (very few) masterworks by the famous Yorkshire poet and former Chartist, John Hartley, author of *Hartley's Yorkshire Almanac*, an annual publication of poems and humorous anecdotes. In some ways the Almanac was the nineteenth century equivalent of *Calendar*, in others a load of sentimental tosh.

Bravely she stood in front of the class and recited the entire poem, though I shall offer only a Reader's Digest-style condensed summary. Hartley is even more long-winded than me.

It wor raanin an' snawin' and cowd
An 'th' flagstones wur covered wi muck
An th' east wind booath whistled an howel'd
It sanded like nowt but ill luck when two little lads donned i' rags baght stokins or shoes o'ther feet

My first (and last) record and DIY graffiti.

As aw louk'd on, a sed to misen God help folk this weather at's poor
Th'big en sam'd summat up off th grand 'twur a few wizend flaars he'd faand
An they seem'd to ha filled him wi'glee
An he sed "Come on Billy may be we shall find summat else by an by
Sooin th big en agean slipt away an sam'd summat else o'th'muck an he cried aght
"Look here Billy today
Arent we blessed wi' a seet o'good luck
Here's an apple an moost on its saand So he wiped it an rubbed it an then sed Billy
Thee bite off a bit
If that hasn't been lucky thissen
Tha shall share wi me such as aw get
T'others face beemed wi' pleasure all throo
An'he said "Nay tha hasn't taen much
Bite agean an bite bigger nah do
Tuppence wur all tha'brass aw had an'awd ment it for ale when coom home
But aw thowt aw'll goa give it yond lad
He deserves it for what he's been doin "God bless thi do just as that will n'may better
Days speedily come
Tho clam'd an'hauf donn'd mi lad still
Tha'aert a deal nearer heaven nur some.

Calendar. *Five years on. I arrived too late for the photo.*

It was a wonderful moment, at least for me (the reading, not the demonstration of Yorkshire generosity), possibly for a few older dialect speakers in the audience. I made plans to incorporate it in a later item about dialect and Hartley. Unfortunately, the library managed to lose it. Must have been because they had not the foggiest idea what to call it or what it said. We had no facility for subtitles.

The diversion into dialect did have one bonus. It made me a recording artiste. Not a star but at least recorded somewhere other than on Special Branch files. Stuart Wilson, after his brilliant success in getting the Yorkshire TV contract, had been appointed deputy chief executive but not having too much to do, after his success in hunting down and purchasing the number plate YTV1 for the company's Jaguar (which promptly broke down – several times) and YTV2, which was presented to Donald Baverstock who sold it, insisting that the company was Yorkshire Television not YTV.

Stuart Wilson founded YTV's own record label, York Records, which began to record and market hymns, readings and music from *Stars on Sunday,* as well as more secular offerings from Lovelace Watkins, an aspiring sex star and Engelbert Humperdinck replacement with the emphasis on hump rather than 'dinck' in view of his performance in Sheffield where he hired several hotel rooms for his appearance at the Fiesta, put a girl in each and performed from room-to-room after the club closed.

I could not compete there but was nevertheless recruited to make my first (and last) record, *Teach Thissen Tyke* with Bert Gaunt on piano and Redvers Kyle, TV's brilliant 'plum brandy' voiced continuity man. We launched it at Wakefield Working Men's Club (C&IU affiliated) with glamorous salesgirls and finger snapping executives, one of whom came up to me officiously as I was handing records to a girl in a transparent blouse with an incredible uplift bra, demanding to know where the sales point was. I pointed out both of them and handed him the records. Unlike the selling points it flopped badly with 100 sales, slightly fewer than we had given away for publicity. York Records later failed. Presumably my offering was melted down to make Gracie Fields' records which sold more successfully. But at least it was better than the Brontë sisters who only sold two of their first book of poems.

Even our pranks were Yorkshire, if only because they would never have been countenanced in London. I myself excelled at the kind of lunacy which produced the hunt for the disused sorbet mine in Sowerby Bridge, the promotion of Heckmondwike as a tourist hot-spot, the terrible fate of a poor girl trapped on a traffic island on the Leeds Headrow (and naturally wearing only a bikini) who had to be fed by hamburgers thrown from the pavement, so great the flow of traffic, or the consumer test on Yorkshire's best courting spots and parking places for backseat manoeuvrings. Indeed I hang my head with embarrassment when I think how daft and how un-PC we were. But everyone is allowed mistakes. It is just that we made ours on air before a bemused Yorkshire audience, though they were also combined with more purposeful efforts, as when we went out with Brian Jackson to film mothers taking their kids out early in the morning to child-minders. This allowed us to locate and index the network of child-minders who kept Yorkshire going and led, eventually, to compulsory registration.

Yorkshire humour was also pretty successful. We hit a rich seam when we started a regular item on Yorkshire jokes on Fridays. This got in ahead of Granada's more successful *Comedians*. Great minds think alike, but theirs was a more successful series because it was national and used professional comics, most of them from Lancashire which has always bred more comedians than Yorkshire. Our county specializes in prime ministers and mass murderers. Like the *Comedians*, our *Yorkshire Laffs* programme also used the few professional Yorkshire comedians, namely Charlie Williams from Barnsley ('Watch it or I'll come and live next door to you' and 'Enoch Powell told me to go home. I said there isn't a bus back to Barnsley at this time o'neet'). We added Colin Crompton, a Lancastrian, our producer having refused to countenance Bernard Manning for no reason I could understand.

We invited viewers to send in their favourite jokes. We were deluged. Jokes (mostly the same) poured in: filthy, funny, pathetic, none of them subtle or sophisticated. This was Yorkshire after all. They came in quantities enough to keep the show going for years. That was not John Fairley's intention, although we did get several weeks of funny Fridays. When I suggested that it might be fair to call for jokes from Lincolnshire and run a *Lincolnshire Laughs* section, the idea sank without trace. We received less than a dozen jokes, mostly from ex-pat Yorkshiremen living in the second county. Lincolnshire may be good at sausages and plum bread but is useless at humour. It lacks Yorkshire's existential angst.

From the start of the series, I was stopped in the streets by people anxious to tell me yet another joke; most of which I had heard before; several times. I mastered the art of laughing to order, which later proved very useful in politics, though the jokes were less so. From my enormous collection I worked out a taxonomy of Yorkshire jokes which can all be classified as about death, disaster, dog dirt, dialect or (more common now than then) defeat at cricket. The best and most typical is an old bloke walking down a long terrace of houses (which is how the best Yorkshire jokes begin). He comes to the end door and knocks. A weeping woman opens it. 'Jack in?' 'Nay, it's awful. Ee's dead'. Pause. 'Ahm sorry to 'ear that. Did ee say owt about a pot o'paint?' It makes me laugh every time I tell it to myself. The effect on audiences can be less. Which is also true of the variations: 'Can I look at 'im? Eee ee looks well'. 'So ee bloody well should. We've just come back from two weeks i'Bridlington'. Or alternatively 'Ee went down to t'allotment to cut us a cauliflower and fell on 'is knife'. 'Eee. What did yer do?' 'Only thing we could do. We opened a tin o'peas'. Jokes will be the death of me. They were certainly the death of my stage career which was pursued mainly at the Talk of Yorkshire Club, Bradford. The club closed shortly after.

The jokes provided us with several fun Fridays and an attractive part of the *Calendar* mix which was essentially populist. *Calendar* was rising to dominance in Yorkshire because it spoke the language of the people. It did not talk down to them or at them, but with them. It was a programme in conversation with its audience working, thinking and speaking at their level to sustain their interest and present them with news, information, entertainers, jokes and issues which would interest them. These ingredients differed every day but the blend, a matter of judgement by the editor and producers, was consistent and clever. It may look amateurish compared to today's more high-powered television techniques. But it worked, held the attention of a growing audience and took *Calendar* up the ratings ladder.

NON-
COMMERCIAL
BREAK

The growing success of *Calendar* boosted the morale of the team and, less fortunately, the egos of the presenters; particularly me. Television is the great ego expander and even a Buddhist Monk presenting a programme of prayer and meditation on Eastern Tibet TV would not be humble enough not to feel a slight stirring of ego if his programme rose higher in the Tibetan religious ratings. My ego, usually hovering at knee level, was boosted. This led me to make the cardinal mistake of assuming that I was 'God's gift' to television and a master interviewer almost as good as the ex-public school barristers who dominated that profession from London. Indeed perhaps even better. A Yorkshire accent made me sound tough, an excitable temperament made me look more aggressive and a vague niceness defused rows.

Delusions of grandeur; yet difficult for television presenters to avoid, exposed as they are to adulation, adoration and assumptions that they are powerful, even omnipotent. Rather like the Queen. I should have been immune to it all but I was not. Fame is embarrassing but it is also helpful and goes a long way to make life easier. So I succumbed and gradually began to think that my somewhat less than meteoric rise to the top in Yorkshire might be a stepping stone to the national stage. That was a delusion too. As a Yorkshireman, I should have realized that the national TV stage was both different and less important compared to regional television which is the real world. Being me, I did nothing about it as usual. Why should I? I was perfectly happy in Yorkshire and on *Calendar*. But here another of those accidents which guided what I laughingly call 'my career' intervened when Peter Pagnamenta, newly-appointed producer of the BBC's prestige political programme, *24 Hours,* suddenly arrived on my doorstep in Shipley and made me an offer: move to London and present *24 Hours* in its final months as they called it a day for *24 Hours.* Then I could become the lead presenter of its alternative, *Midweek.*

It was an exciting prospect. I dithered about accepting it (as I do over every decision, from going to the lavatory to buying a house). Donald tried hard to persuade me to stay at YTV. As a bribe he offered me a week in London to decide, with tickets to any show I wanted. Misguidedly I chose *Oh Calcutta* for the sex and nudity. It was awful, like a hairy Sunday school picnic. Eventually I decided to go to the BBC which was like a Philosophy, Politics, Economics (PPE) picnic. *Calendar* gave me a big party and a plaque: 'We taught thee Tyke Austin.' I thought it was the other way round.

Off I went: Big mistake. Experience in London did make me a better television presenter and interviewer. It also gave me a deeper knowledge of politics and Britain's political class, that small elite who run things from London and view the rest of the country, my real world, with indifference. Yet it was also a specialization too far, taking me into current affairs, the 'leper colony' of TV. In London, I was working to an audience which was smaller (around 1,000,000 where *Calendar* had regularly reached 2,000,000). It was also more middle-class and certainly more politically interested and involved and a lot less educable being over-opinionated. All very different to the Calendar audience. I had cut-off roots which I treasured and wandered into a strange country where my new language, populism, was not understood.

At least it gave me the opportunity to discover the BBC, its strength and weaknesses. Working for ITV was a pleasure, for the BBC a duty. Working for the corporation is a salutary experience. Everyone who watches it loves it. Everyone who works for it hates it. Most of all it showed me the value of a magazine-format working for a broader but more regional and natural audience, a cross section of society as against a specialized political programme working to Britain's small and introspective political class. I quickly came to see that a local programme like *Calendar* reaching a larger and broader but regional audience was both more interesting and more effective than a prestige national programme like *24 Hours*. It needed twelve months in London to teach me what I should have known already.

Working for ITV was like being on a pirate ship: freer, livelier, more irresponsible and much more fun. You could do more or less what you wanted, go where you wanted and pretty well make your own rules. The rewards were good (now they are abysmal) and the expenses generous. In the BBC, on the other hand, getting expenses is a struggle and they are usually mean because you are not expected to go out anyway. More important, you are part of a vast bureaucracy with layers of faceless bureaucrats above, most of whom you never see, all of whom are disguised not as real people (few human beings work for the corporation) but as acronyms like HOCA, ADG or HLC (which probably stood for Head of Lavatory Cleaning though I never found out). Every day the 'alphabet soup' people meet to make rude, and usually stupid, comments about every programme.

Whenever I found these reports I read them with shock and horror since I was usually described as a Yorkshire bumpkin of uncertain parentage who knew 'nowt' and had forgotten most of it. This abuse was then amplified by the comments of advisory panels of the 'Great and the Dud'. I was particularly struck by the comments of Alice Bacon (Labour) who attacked me bitterly for the rude, nasty and completely unjustified way I had interviewed Sir Keith Joseph (Conservative). She could not have been harder if the interviewer had been a rabid right winger like Sir Keith himself attacking a sweet little lamb with an axe. Of course, this being the BBC, Alice never said anything to my face. Publicly she was my great admirer.

All these vicious comments were poured out behind the backs of presenters who were never defended by the producers. To your face no BBC bureaucrat would ever commit themselves to anything beyond the time of day or the state of the weather. Even there they were fairly cautious about giving anything away unless it could be attributed to their acronym. The other off-putting factor was the BBC current affairs department, then hidden away in what felt like a concrete gun emplacement in Lime Grove which had in fact been a J. Arthur Rank studio but looked like part of the Maginot Line.

Lime Grove behaved like an 'All Souls' in exile in its dingy Shepherd's Bush back street. It was almost entirely manned by clever and intellectually pretentious chaps from public schools, usually minor but some major, like Max Hastings who would sweep in occasionally bringing his dogs and reluctantly do some item on any remote and uninteresting war which happened to be available. This public school dominance made the atmosphere very competitive in a way *Calendar* was not. Britain's public school ethos which had once inculcated 'empire and patriotism' was by now about 'ego and grab'. The schools produced 'self-raising flowers', all confident chaps with a touch of superiority, with neither feeling nor knowledge for (or of) the weak and the ordinary. I am being a little unfair (something I always like to be) to Lime Grove in giving the impression that it was dominated by public school chaps, for most of the management were grammar school products but they spoke an elliptical language all their own which allowed them to look superior while giving nothing away, thus effectively deferring to the chaps. Eccentricity was cherished, normality abhorred. We were there not to talk with the audience but to lecture them with the result that audiences were small. Indeed, by the time I arrived the total national audience of *24 Hours* was smaller than the size of *Calendar* in Yorkshire alone, though much more querulous, intellectual and middle-class. I found myself talking to the political elite not the people. Even the women (and BBC did have the decency to employ more than *Calendar*) were mostly from one of the potting sheds of the English rose, exclusive schools like Roedean or Cheltenham Ladies. As a result the atmosphere was colder and more competitive than happy teamwork on *Calendar*.

I found no kindred spirit to commune with, particularly since all my new colleagues expressed profound contempt for both Yorkshire and New Zealand, the two legs of my own dual loyalties, though of course they had never seen anything of either. The dying programme, *24 Hours*, had several distinguished presenters (plus me) living an elegant lifestyle. I continued to arrive by bicycle at 10.00am in the morning to spend a full day doing nothing because at the BBC the presenter's job was just to present. However elegant, they were puppets not producers. So they drifted in around 5.00pm, ordered a bottle of wine, phoned a few friends in India or Rhodesia, skimmed through the scripts which had been written for them and strolled down to the studio. These distinguished *flaneurs* all dropped away gradually as *24 Hours* died until only Ludovic Kennedy (who later wrote an article complaining that he could not understand a word I said) and I remained.

I then had an interesting summer presenting *Summer Talk* which was produced by Michael Bukht, who claimed to be a descendant of the Moghul emperors. He later emerged as the 'Crafty Cook' and ran Classic FM. Michael's technique was to throw everything against the wall and see what stuck. This produced some exciting results but also some disasters, like the last of the series when he filled the studio with raving homosexuals and lesbians, egomaniacs dressed as clowns and poseurs all shouting at each other so it looked more like a circus brawl than a reasoned TV debate. Bukht typified the lower ranks at Lime Grove. The only real pleasure of my BBC year was the talented team I worked with, most of who, like Bukht, went on to greater success. They included Tom Bower who went on to persecute the great, Michael

Cockerill, producer of fascinating political portraits, and Tiger Townson, son of a newspaper editor and the toughest and best editor I had ever known, who drove himself to an early grave by his punishing schedule of commuting enormous distances both to work and between mistress and wife. He later went on to produce the *Cook Report* for Central but at the BBC he was an inspiration. Working for him was a powerful learning process because his ideas were usually risky but brilliant. For example, he and I concocted an outside broadcast from Kellingley Colliery's Miners' Welfare which allowed the miners to put their case in the 1972 strike. Less successful was his idea of sending five trawler skippers from Hull and Grimsby to Iceland to discuss the 'Cod War' over the extension of Iceland's territorial waters to the 50 miles they were then claiming. A brilliant idea, but he forgot the fact that trawler skippers were a fairly taciturn lot, with Icelandic skippers the most taciturn of all. The British skippers, one of whom was Dick Taylor who had been arrested for illegal fishing, needed a drink to inspire them. Iceland was having its dry days while we were there and I was appointed to bring in several bottles of whisky. As I came out of the terminal I tripped, fell and smashed all the bottles. The whisky ran away down the gutter. Our programme was very flat.

Lime Grove was not a happy place like Kirkstall Road. So when *Midweek* began in September, appearing only three days a week in place of the five I had worked on *24 Hours*, I had had enough. I returned to Yorkshire and took my old job back. There was another excellent reason for coming home. A year in the 'Great Wen' had shown me how awful living in London is. Expensive, overcrowded, heavily pressured, its workers are brought in every day by cattle transport which no decent beast would travel on.

London may be exciting for young people but it is no place for human beings or families. It should not really be in England at all but a separate country, 'Londinium' perhaps. That would leave the rest of us free of its burdens, its inflation, its prices and the propensity of its city and banks to drain the productive parts of the country because London is a cancer sucking youth, talent, money, jobs and everything it can out of the rest of the country. In 1972, that included me but not my family which I kept safe and happy in Sowerby Bridge. From the first I was anxious to escape London, reverse the process and go home to happiness. I had learned a valuable lesson of the 'little fish big pond' type. Not only is Yorkshire a better place to live rather than just exist, but it is better to work for a small company in a smaller region with a real identity than for a vast, pretentious, self-important body in a polity too big and amorphous to comprehend or identify with.

Working for the BBC is like the bland leading the blind. Its political programmes allow 'Clever Dicks' to talk to know-alls about whatever interests them rather than the people. Either way it was not for me. I was a populist talking a different language and hopefully understanding real people. On national TV you speak to a big audience, most of whom you know very little of. On regional TV you speak to friends: the people you went to school with, live next door to, travel on the bus or train with. As Alan Bennett put it, you are part of a family 'like other families'. The people you know and like and who, because familiarity breeds content, come to trust you. I skipped happily back to Leeds and *Calendar*. Robert Frost's traveller took the road less travelled, happily so and concluded that 'knowing how way leads on to way I doubted if I should ever come back'. I had taken the road more travelled. In Britain that always leads to London but, unlike Frost, I had the chance to go back to this better, less travelled, road north. That made all the difference. To me at any rate.

CHAPTER EIGHT

GLORY DAYS

I fitted back easily. It was as if I had never been away. No celebrations (which peeved me because I would have liked a hero's return) no changes. The programme was successful, the audience had not missed me, but fortunately they accepted me back in their taciturn way (this was Yorkshire after all). So did the *Calendar* team. There was very little of the 'Didn't make it down there then?' which I had feared and deserved. The programme was bowling merrily along and doing well along the basic lines it had grown to before I left. I hoped they would have missed me. It was disappointing to find that they had not.

I had come home just in time. *Calendar*'s 'Glory Days' had now arrived with confidence, success and expertise. On occasions we got into the national top ten, not just the regional, and reached 2,500,000 viewers. The audience had grown and we were ahead of *Look North* in the ratings war. Most important of all, Yorkshire seemed to like us because we were cheery, lively and a little daft. Our populist programme offered our teatime viewers a variety of news and interesting items which titivated rather than delved deeply. We chatted to them directly rather than talking down. The programme was nothing like the northern *Tonight* Donald had wanted. It had a unique populist persona all its own which the audience liked and the board was happy with it because it brought in the viewers. Indeed, John Wilford says that as producer he never had a budget limiting what he could do. No board could be happier than that. We had also established a settled routine and looked more professional, with even a little gloss because a succession of freelance directors and nervous PAs had been replaced by Peter Jones, a calm and ever reliable Welshman, and Anne Gibbons, a tough Scot, as 'Queen PA' to keep us in order. In fact we had become almost

Commentary from the air is easy.

But Army training is tough.

Photography classes. Note the Hasselblad.

a grown-up programme. Clearly I had arrived back for the best of times: 'Yorksher's Moment' – *Calendar*'s triumph.

The joy of a daily magazine programme is that you can do what you want. We took every advantage of that opportunity and I spent much of my time in wish fulfilment. For a repressed presenter like me, who had lived the cloistered life of academe, this opened up myriad opportunities for wish fulfilment so I spent my thirties living out the fantasies of my teenage years and doing all the things I had not done as a Don nor as a 'swotty' academic. But they do not really live. Nor had I up to 1968, but suddenly I could live life to excess on *Calendar*. I had lots of wishes to fulfil. I was keen to fly and had every opportunity to fly over Yorkshire on gliders, RAF aircraft, from Tiger Moths to Lightnings or balloons and helicopters, though never on the Ornithopter which a Yorkshire inventor built and dragged to every available air show where it flapped its wings as he ran with it, struggling for take-off but never managed to get off the ground. I wanted to do army training (which knackered me) and to go to sea. I was rowed 100yds out of Runswick Bay, and then took a longer trip on an oil tanker which carried me and the film crew on to Rotterdam when it became too stormy to land us in England. There the film crew, all of us stranded, went off to watch live-sex shows which they found they could pay for by credit card. I stayed in bed seasick and credit card less.

More disastrous was my desire to do a parachute jump, something I regretted as soon as I was in training. Too many films of people enjoying freefall give the impression of people loving jumps from aircraft. In fact it is dangerous and terrifying as I found out too late. The instructor explained the technique of landing, pointing out that I

Fred Trueman campaigns for Equal Opportunities.

How to improve Yorkshire views.

Barry Cockcroft recreates the Playboy Club in Rotherham.

would have to climb out of the aircraft, hang on to the wing strut, then drop. If I was too frightened to let go, he gently explained, he would hit my hands with his walking stick until I dropped. It was too late to drop out (forgive the pun). We flew from Yeadon. Teeth chattering I jumped out, fell, pulled the cord and found myself drifting down slowly (it seemed) at first. It was a wonderful experience, until the fall grew faster and I realized that I was hurtling to earth, discovering as I did so that I could not hear any of the instructions about which chord to pull, which way to fall and how, all being shouted at me from the circling helicopter from which I was being filmed. Too late I realized I was heading for the glass roof of the old Avro factory at Yeadon. I pulled frantically, managed to turn away at the last minute and landed 2ft from the factory, only to have the producer announce 'We missed out most of the jump. You'll have to do it again', which I did. This time I avoided the factory but landed in a cornfield where I made the mistake of pulling in my legs at corn level which I thought was to be the point of impact; it was not. I hit the ground with my bottom not my feet and heard my spinal bones rattle together like a shunting train. It was agonizing. I managed to stand up, do a little (very little) piece to camera to say how marvellous it had been and was carted off to hospital. I had cracked vertebrae and spent weeks lying on a board. Paul Fox came to visit me but unfortunately he chose the day when, after ten days of

How many girls in a Mini.

I've room for one more.

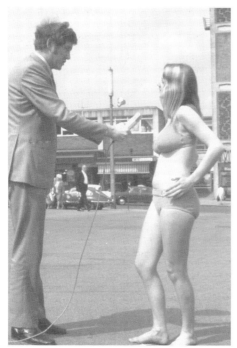

I always did the tough interviews.   *And the jobs no one else would do.*

total constipation, suddenly all was released as he entered the room. I got several letters from solicitors anxious for me to give evidence of the effect of poor training on their crippled clients. I gave none. It was my fault.

The parachuting pain was mine. My other obsession with filming 'Go-Go' girls, dancers, anything female that moved, caused pain and puzzlement but only to embarrassed colleagues, discovering that as a lad who had lived a sheltered Methodist childhood and then become a university swot, I had what they called an obsession (I called it an interest) with girls: girls in bikinis, go-go dancers, girls in saunas, girls moving to music or just girls. It was harmless, a form of delayed reliving of the teenage I had never had because I was swotting at Oxford or in New Zealand which was a decade or more behind the rest of the world. I was catching up on the 'Swinging Sixties'. John Fairley and others assumed they had employed the oldest teenager in the business. They wondered when, even if, I would grow up. I do not think I ever did but I did learn to disguise my obsessions. They carped and criticized while scanning the results obsessively.

I can only hope the audience enjoyed this parade of half-naked girls, making *Calendar* look like the set of a *James Bond* movie, as much as I did. Certainly, Yorkshire TV was offered plenty of visuals with girls in towels sweating in saunas while I rolled in the snow, girls plunging into the sea and out of it, girls testing out bubble baths, and girls piling into a BMC Mini to see how many it could carry; plus me. They were all clad in bikinis (more clothing would have taken up space) while I struggled (fully clothed) to climb in after them. We did not beat the record, we should have used midgets. But it was hell in there, believe me.

Before swimming.

Shark attack.

Get me out of here.

Phew! No more swimming lessons for me.

Historian, Michael Wood, first learns the joys of history.

I was not the only member of the team ready to fill the screen with girls at any available opportunity. Barry used even more when he arranged a deal with an about to be opened club in Rotherham which combined a cabaret stage, a dance floor and a swimming pool. Clearly not a place for full evening dress and Barry decided to promote it by taking along a number of bikini-clad nymphs to dance, swim and show the club to the best advantage, as if it was a Rotherham branch of the Playboy Club. At the end of filming one girl decided to get into the pool with the crew. It was like throwing meat into a pool of piranhas. She was lucky to get out alive and almost clad. I had to follow all that by introducing the cabaret at night but having seen me in action the owner decided that I should not do this in my swimming costume. 'This isn't bloody Moby Dick,' he announced. The more illiterate assumed that 'Moby Dick' was a disease in Barnsley.

Fairley and the rest of the team indulged me in my obsessions. More probably they liked watching the results but felt obliged to excuse their interest by putting the blame on me. They assumed I wanted to be Benny Hill when I grew up, as I eventually did. In any case *The Sun* soon outbid us in the boobs and bums stakes. Paul Fox took a dimmer view of the flesh parade when he became programme director and I date the decline and fall of the flourishing Yorkshire 'Go-Go' industry from his arrival in Leeds. In any case, I was becoming more sober and serious. My wife had kept asking if I had gone mad, but fortunately she worked in Manchester with Stuart Hall, so she did not see much of *Calendar*. Unlike Hall's obsessions, mine were harmless, though it may not look that way in the police pursuit of 1970s TV people for behaving in ways unacceptable today, if that witch hunt ever reaches YTV. I was really compensating for my lost teenage years. The 1950s were a repressed period and in effect I had lived through two lots of 1950s and was doubly repressed by being in New Zealand for most of the 1960s. This put me 10 years behind everyone else on *Calendar*. So really I was only catching up. But I am not sure they believed me.

Even by this late stage we had not seen the end of the production cock-ups and mistakes which at the start had made us so endearing to an audience which never knew what was coming next. The greatest clanger was the day Frank Stagg, the IRA hunger striker, detained in Wakefield Prison, died. He had been on hunger strike for six weeks and *Calendar* had carried the news almost daily, but the fatal night we had planned, without realizing Stagg's condition, a fun programme with a couple of party boosters from Huddersfield who advertised their services as bringing life and fun to any party except a political one. They came along and set up in the studio. The idea was that the programme would end in a burst of fun and craziness cued by my final announcement 'Well it's time to go but…' at which point joy would be unconfined.

We reached the last item. As I readied for my farewell the studio manager, who for some reason had disappeared from the studio, suddenly reappeared to hand me a note 'You must announce at the end that Frank Stagg, the IRA hunger striker, has died in Wakefield Prison.' Unfortunately there was not time to give the same information to our waiting party boosters as I began my final announcement, 'Well it's time to go but first I have to announce the news that Frank Stagg, the IRA hunger striker, has just died in…' I did not complete it. The fatal cue words had been spoken and a custard pie hit me. This serious news was greeted with shouts of joy, cheering and rattles. Streamers flew across the screen, balloons burst and celebratory music and cheering blared while in the control room the producer was desperately shouting 'Take us off air for God's sake'. Upstairs did not respond quickly enough. So I floundered on until the credits rolled, custard pies raining down, cheering continuing. It was thought by some, including me (and hoped by a few) that this might make me an IRA target. Management either saw me as expendable or took the view that though the company was growing with the Trident merger it had not yet reached Northern Ireland and the Yorkshire reaction to the death of the IRA's martyr might not have been noticed. In London, ITN feigned shock and horror. Any poll of the Yorkshire audience would probably have shown them uncomprehending. 'What was that all about?' So what the hell?

Work is a ball when you're having fun. We were. You ride on the crest of a wave, spirits up, adrenalin flowing. Duncan Dallas always argued that we should think through what we were doing and why but in the excitement of a successful TV programme, particularly one as exciting and demanding as ours, you do not. You just do it. But *Calendar* was particularly exciting, not just because of its impetus but because of the opportunity TV provides for wish fulfilment. Being part of the team right at the heart of Yorkshire opened up all sorts of opportunities. Today's television is slicker and more specialized. It is becoming narrowcasting on specialized channels. Programmes are produced by dedicated teams working in specialized areas, be it current affairs, music, drama, arts, travel or the poverty tourism which Channel 4 loves. The teams are isolated in their field. This was never the case on *Calendar*. The joy of working for Yorkshire was that you were never locked into one kind of programme but were able to develop skills and interests in any direction you cared to go. What made it so successful were populism and the sense of fun and the variety and interests it offered every night. It was kept that way because it had all the money it needed and because it was left alone to do its thing, Donald had given up trying to move it upmarket like some Oxford University extension service. He still provided ideas but never interfered. His successor, Paul Fox, trusted Fairley and Wilford's judgement, as Donald had, and just let them get on with things, the main difference being that Fox was more practical and never inclined to suggest that we should get some Oxford Don in. As a result the changes at the top of YTV had no effect on us. Donald went. Paul Fox took his job. Donald was more inspiring and bubbled with ideas. Paul was more solid and more sport and showbiz orientated, but both backed the Wilford/Fairley leadership in case of difficulties, both kept the money flowing and both left us to get on with it.

Thus a nursery of talent was free to do what interested us. We could go off the main diet of Yorkshire news to do interesting items. We could flee the coop altogether, go out to make documentaries, then go back to mainstream *Calendar*. This flexibility offered every opportunity to develop and grow, witness the fact that most of us who were part of the team later went on to concentrate on other areas which interested us. Mike Wood went on to make fascinating history programmes for the BBC but he will not like remembering the costume dramas I pushed him into, John Willis specialized in social issues, Duncan Dallas developed science programmes, Barry Cockcroft made sympathetic studies of Yorkshire's characters and Dales' life, and Sid Waddell developed the coverage of darts and pub games. Richard and I did politics, though perhaps at an amateur level compared to the BBC's specialists. We all grew but we all owed our development to *Calendar* which skilled and encouraged us and provided the springboard from which our talents developed.

This freedom to do anything we wanted took us into industrial history with programmes on some of the major pit tradgedies of the past, others on the railways and canals which had united Yorkshire. Tony Scull had the canal tunnel between Huddersfield and Lancashire re-opened so that I could lay on the roof of the barge, walk on the tunnel ceiling and 'leg' the barge through to the other side. I was so exhausted I refused to 'leg' it back.

When crises happened we were well prepared to respond to them immediately. The day Flixborough blew up – a Saturday – we had a film crew in the vicinity and I was on air in Leeds within an hour to announce the shock. Worse was the Lofthouse Colliery disaster in March 1973. A new face under development ran into uncharted old workings and trapped seven miners when water flooded in. The Yorkshire mining industry rallied magnificently. Rescuers and volunteers poured in for six days, during which I slept in my car at the pit. YTV's outside broadcast provided a national coverage which eclipsed everyone else's. The heroism was all in vain. The miners had drowned instantly. Only one body was ever recovered but the tragic episode demonstrated the greatness and strength of the Yorkshire minig community at its best. Before Margaret Thatcher destroyed both its pride and the industry.

In those days, commercial companies were expected to provide a full round of programming, education, religion, current affairs, regional, drama and entertainment, and YTV had people of great ability in each area: Enid Love in education, Peter Wills, former friend of Joe Orton, in drama, which was the most productive and probably the best department of all, Sid Collins in light entertainment and the great Jess Yates, former cinema organist (the Leeds' Reg Dixon) in children's programmes, then religion. In the early days we saw a lot of Jess, christened the 'Man Monster' by Deakin, but in reality a great entertainer, a lovely bloke and a great showman in the old tradition which had contributed so much to ITV in the 1950s and variety before that. Jess used to drift in and out of *Calendar* telling us about the great days of cinema and theatre, his innumerable showbiz friends and their eccentricities, sexual and social, as well as his views on what audiences wanted.

Jess produced *Junior Showtime*, a kind of 'Primary Schools' Got Talent', using the City Varieties in Leeds, but was soon asked to take on religious programmes, too. We were all impressed by his great idea of *Stars on Sunday*, a showbiz/religious programme which brought stars to the screen to sing hymns (which often belied their lifestyle) and read prayers and excerpts from the Bible. The recruitment of Sir John Gielgud was a classic Jess operation. He came to *Calendar* announcing how much he would like to hire Gielgud to appear on the programme. Deakin warned him how expensive the star would be, but two weeks later Jess came back triumphant. He had hired Gielgud for £5,000 to come up to Yorkshire and read the Bible solidly for two days. This could then be cut up into a few verses on each clip and used every week as the spine of the programme.

Lofthosue Colliery Disaster. Waiting to go down.

As teams of rescuers went down.

Rescue operations went on night and day.

Rescuers came from all over Yorkshire.

It takes a big team to re-open Standedge Tunnel.

Only for narrow boats.

Walking along the roof into Lancashire.

So it went on as a succession of stars, ranging from Gracie Fields to Harry Secombe, Bing Crosby and Shirley Bassey, none of them previously seen as religious leaders, plus the occasional bishop tramped through the studios to avow and embellish their faith. Jess, the 'Man Monster' was quickly renamed 'the Bishop' but was in fact better than any on the actual episcopate. Sadly, unlike them he was defrocked in the greatest scandal since the Borgias had given Rome poisoner Popes. *The News of the World* (Fid. Def) revealed his affair with a young girl from *Junior Showtime*. Hughie Green delivered a further blow by revealing that Jess's daughter, Paula, of whom Jess was so proud, was in fact Green's daughter, the result of an affair between Hughie and Heller Toren, Jess's novelist wife. Disgracefully YTV gave Jess the 'bum's rush' and smuggled him out of the studios in the boot of a car. He retired, embittered and broken, to North Wales.

From the start all the departments ploughed their separate furrows, though several used *Calendar* reporters, as Tony Essex had used Jonathan Aitken and me on *The Reporters*. Tony Scull used me in education with Ann Mallalieu, later a Labour Peer. We jointly presented an educational programme which must have been a disaster because it stopped after one episode. Later Duncan and I did a series on young people leaving school and taking up careers, mainly, in those days, in textiles, like one lovely young girl going to work in Firth's carpet factory in Brighouse. I was lucky, however, to escape the programme on fishing. To save money it was envisaged that the film crew would get on the fishing boat in Hull, sail up the Yorkshire coast doing interviews and filming and be put ashore in Scarborough. The outcome was disastrous because the skipper and the crew came on board drunk and stayed in that state. The only sober crew member was the cook, a Latvian who spoke little English.

Donald was the main inspiration of YTV's general programming. His love for the Dales produced *Gazette*, about a Dales' newspaper, and *Hadleigh*, with Gerald Harper playing an impossibly handsome and wealthy North Riding squire and newspaper owner, nothing like the red faced reality. Then came the programme *Main Chance* about a Leeds lawyer. All of these successful series used professional actors, though I was lucky enough to play Austin Mitchell, a local reporter, in the Scarborough-based soap opera, *Castlehaven*, (which did not last - not my fault) while Sid Waddell conceived the idea for *The Flaxton Boys*, a children's adventure, and wrote for *Follyfoot*, a stable-themed saga about girls and horses. It was becoming clear that Sid was a polymath genius much better suited to production and ideas than to doing pieces to camera in an incomprehensible 'Geordie' accent for *Calendar*. His greatest achievement was the invention and creation of *The Indoor League*, a programme of pub games, from arm wrestling to darts, all presented by Fred Trueman who hoped to become a millionaire out of pool table sales to make up the fortune his first wife had lost him by failing to transmit messages to sell his Poseidon shares before they collapsed. I had only a small part to play but the first day in Leeds's Irish Club was a great success as the club was flooded with glamorous girls and television technicians. I worked the Saturday and arrived back next morning (Sunday) for the second day's filming to find the club closed and deserted. After I had left the day before fighting had broken out between the crew and the regulars, the club had been wrecked, several cameras damaged and the entire programme had to be transferred overnight to the East Leeds Labour Club where Denis Healey arrived to cheer us up, though he would not take any part in

Sid's great invention: The Indoor League. *Arm wrestling.*

Leeds loved it.

Arm Wrestling watched through a glass darkly.

the arm wrestling. The series was a great success which started Sid Waddell off on his career as the 'Dostoevsky of the Dart Board'.

The great strength of *Calendar* was that our team built up a nucleus of skills and specialisms from which presenters and producers could launch out to do more specialized work and longer documentaries, then go back into the pool to resume their normal *Calendar* work. The process stimulated cross fertilization and added interest and opportunity to our lives. Its main beneficiaries were Richard, Paul Dunstan and me working with producers and crews like Frank Pocklington, Charlie Flynn, Mostafa Hammuri, sound recordists such as Terry Ricketts, and producers like Duncan Dallas. We knew them all well because although they were not part of the *Calendar* team they, too, flipped between documentaries, great art and hard news imperatives which gave *Calendar* films a quality few other regional magazines had.

Most of these exciting opportunities came from the science unit headed by Duncan Dallas. This had become a separate unit because Donald Baverstock was told by the IBA to provide the science programmes YTV had promised in its bid. Offered the science vacancy in the ITV schedules he grabbed it with both hands and appointed Duncan, a chemistry graduate and our only scientist, to run it. Duncan recruited a new team of scientists, such as David Taylor, and young enthusiasts with, it seemed to me, an unhealthy preference for Oxford and public school chaps. In the early years before that, however, the network opportunities mainly sprang from *Calendar* itself. My own

Yet more balls from The Indoor League.

documentary debut came with a film about William 'Billy' Holt, the 'J.B. Priestley' of Todmorden, who Duncan rechristened the 'All or Nothing Man'.

Billy Holt had stayed in the town while Priestley had sold out on Yorkshire, preferring to live in some opulence in the sunnier south. This was a betrayal to which all too many of Yorkshire's great, from John Braine to Denis Healey, were prone following the precedent of Robin Hood. Like Priestley, William Holt had been used by the BBC in the war to inspire people to fight by talking to them in their own language, in this case Yorkshire. Being upper-class the BBC assumed a Yorkshire accent was the language of all the 'common people'. Like Priestley, Holt had been a pre-war novelist, though spectacularly unsuccessful compared to the master. Where Priestley was merely suspected by the BBC of being a dangerous Lefty, which became a reason for suspending him from the wonderful series of weekly chats he had begun at the start of the war, Billy Holt, who was used later, had actually been a member of the Communist Party, its northern organizer and a revolutionary so fervent he had been sent to prison for sedition. His main effort in that direction had been long walks on the moors, plotting to build a better world with his friends, and rowdy political rallies in the Town Hall Square, Todmorden where his meetings had been so noisy that his wife regularly complained that sitting in the cinema opposite she had been unable to hear the film sound track of the new 'talkies' because of Billy's loud ranting outside.

William Holt.

With Trigger in Tod.

Back to his old job.

Jim Bullock:
Pit Manager
Extraordinaire.

Billy was a Yorkshire original, one of those awkward, rough diamonds the county used to grow but never polish, in the days before blandness seeped over us from the South. Smoothness was a disability which never affected Billy Holt. Beginning his working life as a weaver in Todmorden before the First World War, he had left to work in Germany where he had been impressed by their efficiency and training. In the war he had risen from the ranks to become an officer but fallen from grace (and a college wall) in the victory celebrations of 1918 which made him lame for life. Undeterred he had returned home to Todmorden to become a Calderdale version of Billy Butlin by starting a holiday camp housed in government surplus tents, at

Barry bribes Gondolas onto St. Mark's Square.

Hardcastle Crags with cold Pennine streams for washing and bathing, earth latrines and hundreds of acres of beautiful woodland to inspire.

Turning next to politics, sedition and writing, none of which supported his family adequately, he had anticipated Amazon Inc. by riding round the Pennine villages selling his own novels from his saddlebag. Some still remembered these sales efforts in the 1960s and it could have been a profitable business if novels like his *Wizard of Whitelaw* or *The Weaver's Knot* had been less awful. Much better were his autobiographical works (six up to 1939) such as *I Was a Prisoner* or *I Haven't Unpacked*, followed by *I Still Haven't Unpacked* after the war.

Author, broadcaster, agitator, our Yorkshire polymath was also an inventor, creating his own 'purn aligned' shuttle which he patented and presented to Pandit Nehru to help India when no one in Britain would buy it. He was a painter of some skill, though his most successful paintings were huge canvases of very phallic mill chimneys worshipped by adoring mill girls at their base.

His greatest triumph came post-Second World War when he saved an old horse headed for the knacker's yard by buying it from a Todmorden Rag & Bone merchant, feeding and training it up and renaming it 'Trigger', a nice 'Roy Rogers' touch. He set off to ride 'Trigger' round Europe. His wife complained that he loved the horse more than her, though his horse was never cited as co-respondent when she divorced him some years later. She constantly complained to us that he had never discussed his departure to ride round Europe, just galloped off, leaving her with a seventeenth century hall, kids and no money, a nice Yorkshire touch. Despite this domestic strain his two books on 'Trigger' in Europe were a great commercial success which saved them from bankruptcy and kept them living in Kilnhurst, their magnificent seventeenth century home which was so expensive they could not afford to furnish it. It provided a beautiful backdrop for our film.

I knew nothing of all this until one day when I was filming with Barry Cockcroft in Todmorden, Billy galloped into our view on his way from Kilnhurst to his favourite pub, the White Hart. Todmorden had long been a 'yo-yo' town because the boundary line between Yorkshire civilization and Lancashire's substitute (the one all hills and moors, the other all mills and whores, Billy said) had originally run straight through the middle, resulting in a frieze above the town hall featuring scenes from the life of both counties, Yorkshire's industry and hard work, and on the other side (I used to joke) scenes of drunken debauchery in Lancashire. This row had recently been re-stirred by the Royal Mail's ridiculous decision to put the town in Lancashire for postal purposes. We were filming public reactions, which were predictably apathetic, until we met Billy. He got down from his horse to rant and rave about his Yorkshire roots, Todmorden's white rose history and the strong defining characteristics of 'Tykonian' supermen, while I nodded and glowed with pride. The Yorkshire characteristics he described were clearly those of Wilson, the 'Yorkshire Superman', who had won most of the prizes in the 1936 Olympics, flown Spitfires in the war and lived to be over 300 years-old, at least, as chronicled in my boyhood reading of the *Wizard*.

Barry knew of Billy from his Granada days. He immediately said 'We must do a film about him.' I agreed, not realizing in my academic innocence that in TV you should keep all ideas secret or they will get stolen, whereas in academe you have got to publish them and shout them from the roof tops to attract attention and mark your territory rather in the way dogs do. On our return to Leeds I told my friend, Duncan Dallas, about this Yorkshire polymath. Duncan promptly swiped the idea from Barry (who was predictably, and rightly, furious) and got an hour-long network documentary, *The All or Nothing Man*, authorized by Donald, with me as reporter and official interpreter.

It was, though I say it myself, a brilliant film, though the rest of the world was slow to acknowledge its virtues, indeed it got hardly any reviews, though it was reshown at the Todmorden Festival in 1982. We filmed Billy riding 'Trigger' up hill and down

Happy Days on Don't Ask Me *with Rob Buckman, Maggie Makepeace and Magnus Pyke.*

Dale, took him back to a weaving shed to demonstrate his old skills as a weaver (which was difficult because most of the sheds had been closed and those that remained dithering on the edge of bankruptcy were reluctant to admit television cameras because of the appalling condition and age of the clapped out machinery). We re-enacted his trial at Todmorden Town Hall and his magnificent speech from the dock in defence. None of it had received much publicity at the time, which goes to show how London-centric the writing of British history and journalism really is. We climbed up the moors to the rock where he had held protest meetings following the precedent of the Chartists who had harangued the textile workers from the same rock over 100 years before, urging reforms, some of which Britain has still not got.

It was a brilliant film. I loved doing it and felt proud to have brought this Yorkshire hero to the attention of the world. It evoked little response outside the 'Broad Acres'. But they were all that mattered.

The sequel was depressing. Billy's wife, fed up with years of being deserted by her randy, disappearing, horse-loving husband, divorced him. Fallen on hard times they had to sell their lovely hall to the Piesse family who made it the headquarters of the Arvon Foundation, organizing schools for writers. Billy was moved to the outhouse

*Sid Waddell on
the Riviera. He
insisted on the
best hotels.*

living above 'Trigger's' stable. There he died within a few years to be commemorated
in a blue plaque and the Todmorden Festival which in 1982 showed the film and
displayed his paintings, which afterwards disappeared from the scene, enormous as
they were. So did his books and writings. It culminated in a wonderful reception at
Kilnhurst where his old friends and descendants of the Cockcroft and Fielden families
(who had made Todmorden great) gathered to pay him the tribute they had refused
him in life, to a loud counterpoint from his wife who continued to denounce Billy
for infidelity, absence, meanness, inconsiderate behaviour and all the other faults we
had ignored in the film. A promised biography from Glyn Hughes never materialized.
Not commercial was the verdict. The dead Billy was to stay dead and from the look
of it poor old Todmorden is going the same way.

Two other 'off-piste' experiences were with 'Sneaky' Deaky. The first in Wales,
Merthyr Tydfil, to be exact, where a mother had raised a child genius pianist who
had attracted the attention of Fanny Waterman in the Leeds Piano Competitions and

showed every sign of being a great star. They lived in an isolated, claustrophobic cottage high on a hill above the desolate city and we filmed him as a genius emerging from the mists of Wales. It was a powerful film, though I am afraid the lad failed to live up to it in his later career. The second Deaky spectacular was more local, the biography of a local pit manager, Jim Bullock, who had not only boosted productivity in the pit but built himself a magnificent house as if he was one of the original coal barons. He had organized the miners into building a stadium and facilities for the pit and the whole village and kept them working hard by standing fake TV cameras around pretending to film them to encourage greater effort. A great character, still 'lording' it in the pit villages, but perhaps more appealing to Yorkshire than the wider audience.

Next in this 'Pass the Presenter' game I went with Barry Cockcroft to make a film about Venice sinking. We arrived there at exactly the right time since the whole town was underwater. Barry, always brilliant at improvisation, hired gondolas to sail us round the flooded St Mark's Square for an impressive opening to a film which took us round palaces, canals, incomprehensible government officials, fundraisers attempting to raise the money to save Venice and literati lamenting its fall. They appeared to have agreed a solution by the end of the film, but five years later more 'Save Venice' films were being produced by other companies. Even today Venice is still sinking, though not quite as fast as Skipsea is eroding as chunks of the divine county are being washed away. None of the new 'Save Venice' crop made reference to our pioneering effort.

The best experience was in the south of France. There Sid researched and Michael Blakstad directed *A Little Place in the Sun* about the developments of new flats, houses and, most dramatic of all, a village built as a 'French Venice' with canal access and moorings for yachts at each house. All this property development came at prices which made me think living in Yorkshire was almost free compared to the Riviera. This was not a film so much as a holiday as we flitted from village to village, restaurant to restaurant, visited ex-pats on their yachts and in their villas and luxuriated in the best hotels in Nice, though their prices were so high that Sid and I had to share a bed. This produced conspiratorial winks when the waiter brought us breakfast in bed next day.

We were lavishly entertained by the developers of *Marina Baie des Anges*, one of the developments we were filming. I got back to find the film being edited by Michael Blakstad with Tony Essex doing his usual trick of coming in early every morning and totally re-jigging what the director had done the day before. To my surprise they confronted me with a dilemma. *Marina Baie des Anges* had been near a motorway though its sound was hardly obtrusive. To make it look less attractive, however, Essex had put on amplified traffic noise over the interviews. Was this acceptable to me? It was not and I could see no reason for it, but I lamely agreed. The film went out and was a great success. Except that the developers threatened to sue and very nearly did. I do not blame them.

The most interesting escapes were with Duncan and the most memorable of these was a film produced by Simon Welfare about R. V. Jones of Aberdeen University who had pioneered the radar which had given warning of German bombing raids and worked as a one-man intelligence service finding out what the German scientists were doing. It was a learning experience for me as we demonstrated how the bombers had come in along radar beams and how these had been detected. We then went on to

Exhausted on the Riviera.

Peter Churchill and Odette Hallowes. Resistance heroes.

Sid samples the Riviera lifestyle.

Charles Flynn samples the Riviera views.

recreate the famous Bruneval raid in which a team of British commandoes had landed, captured the German radar equipment and brought it back to England. Recreating this with Major General John Frost, who had been in command and the survivors from the original force, was fascinating. Equally fascinating was filming the Germans' accommodation where bored guards had put drawings, pin-ups and messages on the walls. All were still as vivid as the day they had been put up.

By now I was a regular presenter in Duncan's burgeoning science department. This needed an entertaining science programme for the early evening and quick thinking Simon Welfare had 'borrowed' from a BBC children's radio programme the idea of *Don't Ask Me* where viewers could ask the questions which the scientists would then answer with demonstrations and experiments. It saved all the pain of thinking up programme ideas and writing scripts and took me on as presenter to play the ignorant layman being educated by Magnus Pyke, who transmitted his thoughts by semaphore, so great was the extent of his hand waving. Indeed, he once got so excited by what he was doing that his false teeth shot out across the studio. With him were David Bellamy, Miriam Stoppard, Mary Archer (occasionally) and Rob Buckman, a brilliant young doctor with a developing future in the media; an exciting science team with me as the dunce.

Don't Ask Me was a studio programme and a very successful one, but I was also presenting Duncan's film documentaries. His next spectacular was filmed in the USA during the bitter winter of early 1977. I went out to New England completely

*Taking B.F.
Skinner back to
his old school in
Susquehanna.
While Peter
Jackson prepares
to shoot.*

underdressed for what was the worst weather in years. Duncan, being a mean Scot, refused to buy me an overcoat or a warm anorak, saying I had to look smart in 6ft of snow. The bastard was only prepared to buy me a cheap raincoat in which I froze to death for four weeks in bitter weather and deep snow. The Charles River in Boston, and even the sea, were frozen, and so was I, ending up giving a good impression of a snow-coated icicle with chattering teeth.

The first film was about B.F. Skinner, the psychologist who developed the theory of conditioning children to set their behaviour. We filmed pigeons at Harvard being conditioned to peck for feed and rats to run a routine. Then we took the aged ascetic back to his birthplace of Susquehanna, a charming but dying town where the steelworks had closed and most of the population had left. The town welcomed us with open arms, though few had heard of Skinner, its most famous son, and he appeared not to like the place. We took him back to his house, his school and then out into the woods which he painted as a far better conditioning for young people who could learn there by adventure rather than watching television and having information and the world handed to them on a plate. Unfortunately, while walking through the woods declaiming this, he disappeared into a huge snow drift and had to be dug out, frozen and teeth chattering too noisily to finish his explanation. It made me think the kids were very sensible staying home to watch TV.

The second film was about Oliver Sacks, the great neurologist, who was at that time building his extraordinary reputation for understanding the workings of the brain. He exemplified this by turning strange cases, like the man who thought his wife was a hat (because she went to his head, I joked. He frowned) into literature. An earlier film had demonstrated Sacks' achievement in treating victims of the 1919 influenza epidemic who had gone into a coma that year but been revived by treatment with the drug L–Dopa which brought back some of them, like medical 'Rip Van Winkles' to a new world where rock had replaced ragtime. These awakenings provided an extraordinary story, though the reality of dazed, bed-bound bodies only semi-coherent was less impressive when we went to visit them.

However, that was not the main focus of our film. That was about Sacks' treatment of Bob, a victim of Tourette Syndrome. Bob was liable not only to convulsive twitches but to *Coprolalia*, a polite way of saying he would shout obscenities from time to time whatever the occasion or the place. Sack's treatment, a mixture of drugs and endless listening, was less impressive than Bob's performance on film, shouting 'fuck' in respectable restaurants to which we had taken him and abandoning the steering wheel of the car he was driving across Brooklyn Bridge to try and climb out of the window, me dragging him back while desperately holding the wheel; a nice lad but impossible to film. Oliver Sacks' analysis of the problem was brilliant but I could see little hope of a cure at the end of the day. So our film, which certainly enhanced Sack's reputation, seemed very unsatisfactory to me. Not so, fortunately, to the critics. What happened to Bob I do not know. He is probably shouting 'fuck' in less expensive restaurants. In New Jersey that might not matter as much as it would in Harrogate. I still wonder, however, because that was my last documentary for Yorkshire, though I did not realize it at the time. Had I done so I might have said the same as Bob!

B.F. Skinner. Just before he fell into the snow drift.

CHAPTER NINE

THE
FAME GAME

In today's television world viewing is spread over a hundred channels, allowing every interest, except perhaps fretwork, to be followed and making it possible to live life in retrospect by watching nothing but the flood of past programmes repeated on daytime TV – though not re-runs of *Calendar*. News freaks can hype themselves up with six news channels. People can follow their interests by watching science, history, art or cultural channels. They can travel the world in an armchair by watching American, French, Russian or Arab news and channels. The audience has more to see. The view becomes atomized and sectional rather than general. All of which makes it difficult to remember the dominance of regional television in the three channel (more properly 2.5) situation of the 1960s and 1970s. Then each channel was a square meal and its regional magazine a Smörgåsbord of tit-bits and hors d'oeuvre.

In that situation, regional magazine programmes were the audience recruiting grounds for BBC and ITV. Each channel vied to ensure that when the television (one to a house in those days and always in the living room) was switched on, it was turned to that channel's regional magazine as husbands, kids and, in Yorkshire (and Lancashire), wives returned home from work. Once switched there it stayed there. Regional magazines were crucial in determining choice because channel loyalty was greater than it is in these days of greater promiscuity in everything, from party allegiance to marriage. So the assumption was that once *Calendar* was switched on that set would stay with ITV the rest of the evening, a loyalty sustained by clever scheduling to ensure that the interest of the audience was held by the inheritance factor, unless something shattered the bond, as it did on Mondays when ITV's requirement to screen

At the head of the parade: Wakefield Miners' Gala.

Joan Bakewell and Ashley Jackson, fellow judges at the Gala.

Filming can be hard work.

current affairs programmes put *World in Action* on at 8.00pm at the same time as *Panorama* on BBC1. The result was that BBC2 achieved its largest audience of the week for cowboys.

This made regional magazines crucial to the success of the channel so ITV companies spent big money and lavished manpower and effort on them. People lived near their work and came home earlier than today. They ate their tea and sat down in front of the television earlier. The audiences were bigger, not as huge as the peak programming period from 7.00 to 10.00pm or for *Coronation Street* and the other soap-operas but always far bigger than today's early audience. They were loyal, too. Most people were either regular Calendar viewers or, with the dutiful middle-class, Look North viewers, preferring a BBC whose regional magazine programme, *Look North*, was duller and more public service and duty orientated. Like the BBC itself. For BBC employees, public service was the path for promotion out of Leeds to London. For us YTV was self-sufficient and *Calendar* provided a career and the base for graduating to network programmes produced by YTV itself.

A small proportion of the audience were promiscuous (which in those days meant only that they were more casual in their viewing habits). Many of them were never sure which channel they were watching so I was regularly told (I saw it as an accusation) that I was on *Look North*. Not quite as bad as not being recognized at all. As our audiences grew this happened less often, though it was some time before I understood that *Calendar*'s audience was growing as much because ITV scheduled *Crossroads* just

Beauty contests are terrifying at times.

*But sometimes
a crowning
achievement.*

'Are you sure you prefer Richard Whiteley?'

before us rather than a recognition of our superiority. The build up waiting for Amy Turtle gave us the larger starting audience than those we got switching on in the hope of seeing more of Liz Fox.

Presenters became regional gods or, at the very least, demi-gods, in their area. National TV figures always treated us with condescension and viewed us as amateurs. But famous in Yorkshire was enough for me. In our viewing areas we were the lords of all creation, monarchs of all we surveyed. Lacking puff pastry write-ups from star-struck print media, with no attendant celeb culture and unknown in London, we were recognized everywhere in the region. We dignified a myriad of minor functions by our presence and were even assumed to have mystical powers, extending to the extent of touching for King's evil, or other purposes in the case of Stuart Hall. We were in demand to open fêtes (some of them worse than death), speak at dinners before the stripper, or entertain crowds just by smiling and waving (more energetically than the Queen). Men (and they were all men until a few women muscled their way in in the 1980s) were invited to judge endless bathing beauty competitions, then far more numerous than now. I was often required to compère them and question the girls about their ambitions, favourite pop stars, and movies, though never their class and politics. The proudest moment was in 1974 when Joan Bakewell, the 'thinking man's crumpet', and I were invited to the annual Miners' Gala in Wakefield. We paraded ahead of unimportant people like MPs and councillors. Then Joan judged the beautiful babies and I judged the 'Coal Queen' while Ashley Jackson judged the paintings.

'It's wonderful to be in ....Wherever this is.'

These regional deities of the 1970s included Mike Neville from Tyne Tees, Bob Greaves (Granada), Stuart Hall (BBC Manchester) and eventually Richard Whiteley and I as the new kids in Yorkshire. Each of us personified their area, graced its functions and entertained its people. The companies viewed us as assets, brand images and symbols. Some wrote books like Stuart Hall's cookery book *Heaven and Hall: a Prodigal Life*, Mike Neville's *Larn Yersel' Geordie* or my *Teach Thissen Tyke* which I tried to publicize by giving my plea to a Bradford Court for a speeding offence in Yorkshire dialect so some poor policeman was obliged to stumble through it. This entertained me and captured headlines but it almost certainly doubled the fine, without doing the same for the sales.

Regional presenters were powerful figures in their area and more powerful then because they were closer to their audience, more local and appearing more regularly than national TV figures, even the stars of soaps like *Coronation Street* or *Emmerdale*. Though those working with these new stars in the firmament to develop and prop-up the image often found them unbearable and occasionally liked to see them humbled and taken down a peg or two, the companies and the BBC liked having them and needed them because of their vital role in bonding the company to its audience. This made them more powerful, sometimes more arrogant, than they should ever have been. They were not only the programme but the company and the area and almost as big in local stature as the historic greats like Fred Trueman or George Best.

That power made presenters money which came in the form of cash and brown envelopes handed over after functions, though never quite as fat as the bundles I have

Coconuts… I've missed.

seen handed to Ken Dodd. But then we were neither as funny nor as brilliant as him. This power could be abused, as Stuart Hall (the 'Ubergroppen Führer' of Manchester's *Look North*) did by turning the Manchester Piccadilly news department of the BBC into his own knocking shop with a 'medical room' which he used as a boudoir in which to entertain groupies, footballers' wives and women he had picked up outside, even a policewoman in uniform resting from her night patrol.

Extroverts do well on television but some have a strand of excess, whether for money, sex or an exhibitionist lifestyle which is their cloven foot or some other part of their anatomy. In Hall's case, sex addiction, which pointed in the wrong direction, as it did with Frank Bough who managed a lifestyle beyond the dreams or cash of humble provincial hacks. We worked harder and had less cash in any case.

This was the fame game. Regional 'gods'; every county should have one. In 1968, Yorkshire did not. The county had to be satisfied with occasional incursions from Lancashire by *Coronation Street* stars. The BBC's head start did not quite work, partly because the corporation was less adept at picking populist presenters. So they ended up with Barry Chambers, better looking than any of us but not as smart, then Michael Cooke recruited from local radio. Until Harry Gration, BBC presenters had no populist flair. The ethos of their programmes was public service dictated from the centre to which many of its most able local presenters, like David Seymour and Jeremy Thompson, got themselves promoted in fairly short order. We were more popular, though the acclaim came mainly from South Yorkshire and I noticed that Barry

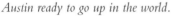

Austin ready to go up in the world.   *Blasting to the top.*

Chambers was always introduced first and put higher on the agenda than we were in Harrogate, a BBC town which I always tried to insult by telling the story of the visitor considering buying a house there and asking 'How about the rates?' to get the reply 'Rates. No rates in Harrogate. A few meece perhaps.' It never got a laugh but then in Harrogate they only smile icily in any case.

Fame created opportunity. Britain in the 1960s was enjoying (or enduring) the first emergence of the celebrity culture which later became so obsessive with the search for fame, or even notoriety, chronicled in *OK!*, *HELLO!* and the 'red top' newspapers. Yorkshire had no *HELLO!* magazine (which would have been called 'Na then' if it had existed) but it already had its heroes, mostly sporting figures like Len Hutton, Fred Trueman or Billy Bremner, all of them important figures of undoubted achievement. In the 1970s, the celebrity culture extended the net more widely to include pop groups, though Yorkshire had few of these until Joe Cocker came along. The top stars also included actors, though all were national figures, but until 1968 no Yorkshire television personalities. YTV then created local figures that stayed local but were unknown outside their own region. I was one.

This was a major part of the revolution YTV brought in, by taking the belated opportunity to create something which had already developed in Manchester, Birmingham and London. *Calendar* created our own DIY, TV celebrities, famous for being famous just because they were on Yorkshire screens every night and, therefore, more important in the public eye than Mayors, Lord Lieutenants, even

MPs. Our standing was region-wide while the authority of all other pretenders to stardom, such as councillors or politicians, was more circumscribed. We were the only stars twinkling county-wide. Better paid and more widely recognized we were clothed in the magic mantle of TV fame and assumed to be powerful and important, so important I even had police, who had stopped me for speeding occasionally, apologize for doing so when they saw who I was. No need even to pull the upper-class trick of 'Don't you know who I am, officer?' Everybody did. And no opportunity to crack the old joke 'My face is my ticket, officer'. 'Then, sir, I must punch it'.

It was exciting, exhilarating, even intimidating. For a naïve student swot who had become a university lecturer and college Fellow and lived a very cloistered existence, carefully protected from the real world in case it tainted the purity of academic truth, fame was a new and strange world. It meant living in a fish bowl and riding a cloud above the levels of the ordinary. Not quite superman but a zone where delusions of grandeur, even of competence, grow. After a few months groupies began to appear as we filmed in the street. Girls tried to wangle their way into the YTV bar. Some brushed languorously against me, though they could have been textile workers checking the quality of the cloth. Singers, comedians, groups and pub acts came to the studio or approached me for auditions, often backing their requests with amazing photographs, tapes or self-made records. Would-be

Skilled work if you can get it.

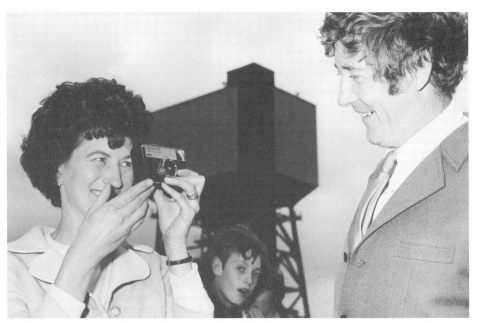

Watch the birdie.

Hand out the cheques.

playwrights and scriptwriters turned up at the studio in such numbers that the receptionist developed her own side-line in reading their offerings, suggesting changes and rewrites and telling people she would take the scripts to the head of drama if they were tightened up, rewritten or changed to Yorkshire locations, all of which she would help with. When I cracked too many jokes about the decline of Bradford Park Avenue – 'What time's the game?' 'When can you get here?' Or 'In Bradford they don't announce team changes to the crowd but crowd changes to the teams'. Or, best of all, 'Two kids were caught climbing the wall at Park Avenue. They were made to go back and watch the game' – angry fans (and Bradford PA cannot have had many) sent the fire brigade round late at night. I woke to find firemen trying to bash my front door down and they insisted on searching the whole house for a fire. They found nothing, not even more red-hot jokes.

Secretaries, telephonists and others brought in relatives in the hope of having their amazing talents recognized. Restaurants invited us to grace their openings for free meals and were never overbooked if we rang up. Peter Stringfellow, having been driven out of Sheffield and come to Leeds, gave us free admission to his clubs, Cinderella and Rockafella's, though Dennis Peace at the In-Time did not, and we had only to ask to be wined, dined and entertained at the big clubs. It was an exciting, ego-enhancing world and we were the new 'Lords of Yorkshire Creation' (Yorkshire style). I was 'world' famous in Yorkshire though, being inhibited by a

Put me down, Austin. I'm not the prize.

*Zut Alors!
Je connais
mes onions!*

Yorkshire non-conformist upbringing, I found it embarrassing and demeaning. Much as I was enjoying it.

Television Presenter was (and still is) one of the best, if not the best, jobs available. It was well paid, certainly well above Yorkshire levels, glamorous, exciting and had all the ingredients anyone could have wanted, along with something no other job, except perhaps monarchy, had: a glamorous aura and an immediate bond with anyone you met. People immediately diagnosed what I called the 'Imoff Syndrome' (Richard Whiteley and I disputed ownership of the joke but he being public school educated, diagnosed the disease as 'himoff'). My version was 'Eee, it's imoff Calendar' (though sometimes it tailed off to 'imoff t'telly'). Those who did not know which programme you were from imagined some distant relationship, some common friends or a bond of military or university service so you had to waste hours convincing them that they did not in fact know you. Always when they bumped into you, people would tell you

Ready Red Ted.

something you may not have known about yourself: 'You're on *Calendar* aren't you?' or 'You're Austin Mitchell' or '…you're taller, smaller, fatter, thinner, older, younger, than you look on telly'.

All this built bonds with the audience. There was a problem establishing credibility in Yorkshire, a county Dimblebys and Michelmores feared to tread and not known for its liking for starry, smiley, glittery extroverts or indeed anyone very much. TV personalities needed to be pretty extrovert. It takes a show-off to do the job, and having loved lecturing I was one. But in Yorkshire, the Yorkshire presenter was talking to his own people and had a shared background and a common experience which no one can have with a national audience because it is more sectional and diverse so presenters talk to their section rather than the whole. The secret of our success was to be one of the folk and never get above them. You could never be 'de haut en bas' or act like a duke over tenants on your estate. The need was to build bridges and establish

Failing the Bucking Bronco auditions.

'For the next hour of my opening speech…'

Missed again.

*Always one
jump ahead.*

I've prepared a few notes for my speech.

something in common, usually Yorkshireness. Once established that produced offers to help to carry bags, to take care of your wife and kids, watch or even wash your car. They would do anything for you: talk about something interesting they had seen on the programme, brush against, more rarely feel you up, or just smile and pass on with an 'I know who you are but I'm not going to let on' expression Yorkshire folk only normally assume with the Queen.

Fame is not a bad deal for a Yorkshireman; it is never having to put one's hand in one's pocket and it certainly made life easy for someone like me who knew so little of the practical problems of the real world. Viewers would help repair your car, come round and paint your portrait (usually badly), take your photograph, tell you about their town, carry your bag or do some small favour they would not normally do for a mere human. Indeed, the offers were so numerous that Barry got the idea of taking me round sculptors and painters to have busts and paintings done and filming the results, a scheme which got no further than having my bust done by Sam Tonkiss, editor of the *Todmorden News* and a self-taught sculptor. I then carried the bust round the town asking people who it was. No one recognized me, at which point the series ended.

For me it was a whole new status. I saw it as more important than the fame of mere London presenters. They were the archbishops of TV. We were parish priests. Not as generously treated but more affectionately viewed. In my year with the BBC, I found that the presenters there got free shirts and suits to wear on air: 'Fred Blogg's Wardrobe Created by Jermaine of Savile Row'. YTV would never have considered captions saying 'Austin Mitchell's Wardrobe Created by Millet's', while 'Richard Whiteley's blazers, created by Fred Farnsbarns,' could have been seen as libellous. Being in Yorkshire we did not get much for free and were not ego-manic enough to ask, being ourselves household goods rather than household gods. Unlike London presenters we were constantly in northern homes, put there by Yorkshire, Granada, Tyne Tees or whichever region we symbolized. It was all too easy to become convinced that you could also do anything you wanted. That became a real test of character. It was failed by me, not because of any of the illegal obsessions which drove some but because I was never particularly gregarious, always uneasy in pubs and quite content with writing and doing other things rather than just reigning and lording as the new 'Princeling of Royalty, Third Division North (Reserves)'.

I had not set out either to be part of this amazing and exhilarating, and at times embarrassing, circus or to live such a privileged lifestyle. Indeed, I had never envisaged these as part of my new television career. My purpose was to enjoy the fun of making programmes on things I wanted to and airing my exhibitionistic ego on the box, not the bedroom. I did not like the lifestyle, preferring to spend my life outside work in my own way rather than doing personal appearances and drumming up viewers. But there was no escaping it. Even my first brush with fame was more or less compulsory. Alec Todd, Yorkshire's PR director, came early on to some arrangement with *Yellow Pages* to help promote its launch in Lincoln. Our programme did not reach Lincoln at that time but Alec decided that only a YTV presenter could do it. He picked me for the date but it was on a day when I had

Austin, Sam Tonkiss, Barry Cockcroft and a severed head. Prizes for guessing who.

just booked my first ever package-tour holiday to Ibiza and was eager to go, never having had such a holiday before. I argued and pleaded. No go. With money no object in those days, YTV flew me back early, leaving Linda, my wife, sulking on her own in the holiday hell that Ibiza was becoming. Not exactly a good omen for marital relationships, but as a Yorkshireman I felt we could not lose all the holiday we had paid for. So she had to stay.

However, I did get five days in Ibiza before the embarrassment of a function in Lincoln where no one knew who I was because they were Anglia viewers. The next step up the ladder of fame was worse. I was invited to open the Horbury Gala. I was driven through the town in an antique car smiling and waving like royalty at the crowds (who actually waved back). Linda was not allowed in the car and the antique vehicle put oil on the snazzy new suit I had bought for the occasion. I had carefully prepared my speech on several pages of notes. When I saw that the crowd did not particularly want to hear it, I cut it down to one page, which might have been appropriate to an Oxford College Gaudy [college feast] but was received with baffled amazement in Horbury. Jokes about the warden of All Souls were followed by comparing Horbury and its neighbour, Ossett (so called, I said, because you had to 'oss'it' to get there) to Yorkshire's Athens and Sparta. I burbled on. The crowd drifted away. Children cried and Linda, filtering through the crowd to gauge reactions, vainly gave me throat cutting signals which I ignored. It was a disaster.

Pushing over pennies is hard work.

Yet as the invitations, phone calls and passionate requests to do this or tell that audience about the wonderful world of television began to roll in there was no resisting it. So I began to accept invitations and soon personal appearances were absorbing an enormous amount of time. I did cooking demonstrations for North-East Gas (which also supplied the jokes, e.g. remembering the 1940s Vera Lynn song 'Whale Meat Again'.) I kicked-off football matches, pushed over piles of pennies (then heavy objects which hurt when they fell on you), judged beauty and baby competitions, was pushed by bed pushers and spoke at functions. The one thing I drew the line at was physical exertion such as the occasional invitation to join coal sack races. I refused them all after my friend, Brian Jackson, died carrying his coal sack in the Elland race. I was happy to make a fool of myself and regularly did, but did not want to kill myself for charity.

Personal appearances did have the attraction that you could use the same jokes over and over again to different audiences. My favourite (much used) was about the oldest inhabitant of Slagsville sent, when he reached his 80th birthday, to Paris by the local Rotary. He came back and announced 'Slagsville's better ner Paris'. At 90 years-old they sent him to New York, again the same reaction. Then he died and passed to the 'other side' where he came to, looked round with wonder and announced 'I've got to say it. Heaven's better ner Slagsville'. At which point a red devil with a trident prodded him saying 'Shut up you old fool. This isn't heaven.'

The Calendar *Football Team. God's gift to cricket.*

It did not always go down well but I liked it. As I did a joke more appropriate to civic occasions about the council deciding to purchase twelve gondolas for the boating lake, only to have an old councillor interject 'That's a waste of money. We should only buy a male and a female and let nature take its course.' I laughed. Sometimes the audience joined me.

Talks were easy because people were interested in what went on behind the scenes and I liked to find out what they thought about the programme. So I spoke to endless women's groups, dinners, even to political parties, even at times to Conservatives. Liberals never paid, and dinners I liked less. Unfortunately, you had to be funny and I am not a natural comedian. I can mess up any joke. Yet there was a whole array of service, professional and promotional groups desperate to find speakers. They would pay up to the dizzying sum of £25, often in cash (but don't tell the Revenue). Nothing then reached Blair levels or I might by now have been the owner of Chatsworth. After Horbury the fêtes became more enjoyable; once my speech was over. So I did them too, though they were usually on a Saturday afternoon and Linda was always unwilling to go and face a whole series of questions about 'What's he really like?' which she felt she could not answer truthfully. Thank heavens.

In the early days of *Calendar* we witnessed glimpses of the bigger fame game played by the big stars. On one early occasion, I was invited to play not second

Sign a few autographs before the game (they'll not want them after it).

fiddle but eighteenth to Violet Carson, who played hatched-faced Ena Sharples on *Coronation Street*. She had come over from Manchester to Leeds to open a television dealership. This she did with a curt and unfunny speech and I was allowed (so far as I remember) to press the 'on' button on one of the sets. Violet appeared very disgruntled (as she did most of the time – I guess she just had that kind of face). The chap Granada had sent over with her (something YTV never did, in fact we never got so much as a Metrocard to support us) explained that it was probably because she had not been able to take a television home with her. Evidently when Pat Phoenix opened supermarkets she had become notorious for saying 'I'll just inaugurate your wonderful shop' then wheeling her trolley round and filling it with smoked salmon (caviar not being available, for this was before Waitrose) and every expensive dish she could find, tipping the whole lot into the boot of her car and driving off. This, the Granada driver explained, was a little difficult to do with television sets.

Such was my learning process of the pains of greatness. The invitations, dribbling in at first, had become a flood by late 1969 as I was invited to speak at dinners of bankers, accountants, junior chambers, at village fêtes, Women's Institutes (none of those, I noticed, went to Liz Fox) and every imaginable function. Yorkshire Television would not help. Indeed, they made the situation worse by passing on

Last surviving Lollipop man on the M62.

invitations which had gone to them. These all piled up on my desk, along with letters from viewers about how lovely (a few said awful) I was, complementing, insulting, asking whether I was related to them or, in a few cases, complaining that because I had been struggling with my twins screaming and running round, I had ignored their greetings in Marks & Spencer in Bradford or anywhere where kids could run riot. I was incapable of dealing with all this. Academics do not get much mail because no one is interested. I spent most of my days out of the office filming or chasing 'Go-Go' girls round the county disguised as a caveman. So the piles of un-answered mail grew until John Wilford announced that I would not be allowed to appear on *Calendar* until the desk was cleared. This is the most dire threat that can ever be made to a TV presenter, depriving them of their ego-boosting appearances on TV. My lovely secretary, Chris Wilkinson, and I cleared the desk in two days.

One thing Chris did not need to sort out was the one form of personal appearance organized by the programme, specifically by John Wilford and his wife Meryl. This was the Calendar football team (we never challenged at cricket because of the prevailing rule that no one born outside the county could play cricket

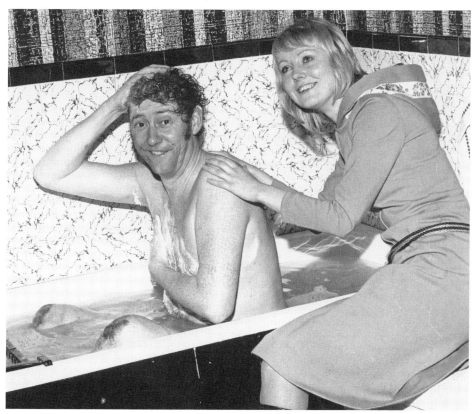

There were compensations for coming off early.

for it). We were a formidable football squad because some of the hairier men in *Calendar* could actually play football and we usually managed to draw in two retired members of Barnsley FC who were real stars. Richard and I were not. I was regularly dragooned in but the experience was humiliating. As I romped on to the field with the team there were loud and enthusiastic cries of 'Good old Austin' or 'Go for it Austin'. But as I lumbered around, miskicked, tripped up and lost the ball each time I could not manage to avoid it, the cries turned nasty, to end up, after perhaps fifteen minutes, as 'Gerrimoff', 'Gie up Austin' and 'Gerrome'. I was happy to go off, exhausted and rubbing some mud over my face ready for the inevitable shot in the bath, usually with a girl in a bikini, brought along by a photographer (the girl I mean, not the bikini). I guess I was not ever going to make it as a footballer. Not even for Bradford Park Avenue Reserves (relevant joke: Don Revie advised Bradford to practice by putting eleven dustbins on the pitch. Two weeks later he rang up to ask how the practice had gone and was tersely told 't'dustbins won 3–0').

Personal appearances were a way of building up the audience and encouraging people to watch *Calendar*. YTV did nothing to help and Alec Todd regarded this kind of PR as beneath his dignity, but others soon stepped in to fill the gap, in one case disastrously. Barry Godfrey, the son of the leader of Sowerby Bridge Council, which was (at that time at least) proud of me as the most (and only) famous person to live in Sowerby Bridge, for this was before Shirley Crabtree became famous as a wrestler, appointed himself, without bothering to ask me, as my agent and went round making bookings which he did not bother to tell me about either. One night I was sitting at home at 9.00pm, drink taken, as the Scots say, when he rang frantically from West Vale School, 'Can you come down here? (two miles away) I've told them you'll do a personal appearance at the parents evening.' I was furious knowing nothing of the date or the occasion, but he continued to shout down the telephone that there were a few people left waiting for me, even if most had gone home. On another occasion I received a telephone call, not from Barry but from the Nutcliffe Tavern in Hebden Bridge. Barry had told them I would do a personal appearance and push over a pile of pennies built up over the years. I could not and did not. These non-appearing personal appearances were pretty annoying to me and to the people whose functions I was supposed to be at, but fortunately Barry eventually stopped – or rather was stopped – by his own personal appearance in court, then prison, for impersonating a striking miner and purloining contributions collected to support the strike.

More important was the man who billed himself as Yorkshire's greatest impresario, Carl Gresham: 'The Gresh', a great man with an even bigger ego and an archetypal Yorkshireman. Carl was in love with television. His great aim was to appear on it himself and he regularly devised programme ideas, chat shows and items, none of which were ever commissioned. Failing that, he was happy to arrange personal appearances anywhere for we lesser stars, indeed everyone who had ever been on TV. He started in showbiz as press officer for Batley Variety Club, vigorously promoting Jayne Mansfield's visit there as a double attraction, the first 'two for'. He then set up his own agency. He began by booking stars to open stores and perform at functions, then persuading us to have them on *Calendar* to publicize the occasion. His first big catch was Alexandra Bastedo. She was followed by a succession of semi-famous personalities. He then turned his wiles to us and began to book *Emmerdale* and *Calendar* stars, starting with Frazer Hines, for less important functions. The first time he booked me as a minor star in his firmament of much bigger stars was to open a fête in West Yorkshire. It was a total disaster. Not many people attended the pathetic little fête. It rained without ceasing. There was not much to do beyond going round spending my own money buying wet sweets from sodden stalls. Both Linda and I were wet and bedraggled and desperate to go home and dry out, but Carl insisted that his fee (in this case £30) must be paid. So the poor organizers had to count it out of their pathetic receipts in sixpences and shillings. I said 'Forget it, I don't need the money, let's go home'. Carl insisted that a contract was a contract and had to be honoured. So we sat in the car in the rain and eventually a small bag of silver and coppers was handed over and we drove off. I have never felt so guilty in my life. It was the kind of humiliation grander figures managed to avoid. Magnus Pyke always had the good sense to insist on payment in advance and whenever I appeared with Ken Dodd I saw that he usually received a thick brown packet of money while I was lucky to get a free lager.

The Gresh Guests On Yorkshire TV's........
Frankie Howerd Strikes Again in 1981

You never know who's on the show with you? Anne Rice appeared - Later to change her name to Anneka Rice - well what about that !!!

The Gresh. Yorkshire's greatest. But can you understand it?

Carl built up from there. Soon we were all being bombarded with 'Gresh Style' cards, calendars, circulars, Christmas cards and bumph, much of it suggesting ideas and programmes on which Carl could appear, but most detailing his stable of famous people whose appearances he could command. This included a long list of the famous, from me to Morecambe and Wise, though Tony Blackburn complained that his brochure carried Carl's name more times and more prominently than his. Still, Richard and I were on it early and Carl persuaded me to open a refurbished Woolworths store in Beverley which went splendidly, leading to a major coup when he produced stars to open thirty-seven Woolworths on the same day. He also arranged for me to present cheques at Bingo halls where I was usually asked to call the first few numbers, though I rapidly learned that it is difficult to get the lingo right and impossible to give it at the speed of delivery the customers demanded so they could not wait for me to disappear so they could pursue their game obsessively, some with up to half a dozen cards at once, for many of the players were faster than any PC. I had to circulate round and encourage them but once the game had started I was not only superfluous to requirements but a bloody nuisance to the fanatic players. Indeed I am still not sure why Bingo proprietors were keen to pay good money to television stars, particularly those like me who brought a worried brow and an inability to count rather than the glamour they expected.

Still, their demand was universal. In the year I worked in London on *Twenty Four Hours*, I bumped into the former manager of a Leeds Bingo hall. He was eager that I should come along to his new appointment as manager of a London Bingo hall to sprinkle some of my stardust over the eager punters. I had to explain gently that they were Londoners and, therefore, so underprivileged they would not know who the hell this itinerant 'Tyke' was and in any case though I was still on television I was now on a late-night current affairs programme which no one watched and they would never have seen. I couldn't convince him and he walked off saying I should come and see how it goes.

Carl was always great fun and has chronicled his life in *The Gresh: a Lifetime in Show-biz*. He was good for a laugh, though it could be at, as well as with, him as he ceased to be Carl Gresham to become 'The Gresh', the one and only, a friend to all on television, bubbling with new ideas about getting himself on to the programme, which Fairley and Wilford monotonously vetoed. Eventually he got himself a radio programme, first on Pennine, then on Aire, and finally on Community Radio where he still officiates.

Carl wanted to be a television star. I was one already. I may have been Third Division North rather than national but I was not bothered about that. Yorkshire was all that mattered. I was not particularly bothered but being a star was certainly far better than being a lonely academic hewing through the library jungle to carve out a little clearing all his own and rule over it unchallenged, whether it was resurrecting dead figures from history or defending against all comers a little-known area of history as I had done when I wrote about British politics from 1812 to 1830, a brilliant preparation for becoming a Labour MP after 1979. I had not set out to be a star, just to do the most interesting job I had ever come across. Yet being one made life a lot easier as people discovered we had something in common, namely liking me on TV.

I was more important than Yorkshire's MPs (which annoyed the MPs), more powerful than their councillors (ditto) and probably better at curing their illnesses than their doctors, though all I had to prescribe was 'Enjoy Yourself' (always difficult in Yorkshire) or 'Keep Watching' ritual incentives (like a Papal blessing which probably did more for TV personalities in London than in a Yorkshire which was less easily impressed). The famous in London did find it easier to get into over-priced restaurants while I still had to queue at Harry Ramsden's. They may have been admitted to clubs no one in their right minds would want to join but though I was embarrassed to be lauded I was usually disappointed when I was not. Fame could have encouraged the 'tall poppy syndrome', an egalitarian instinct to knock big heads off, as the Australians do, but surprisingly it did not in Yorkshire, perhaps because the county's new television personalities were no threat to anyone, and certainly not to their daughters, but mainly, I hope, because we were people of the people.

So I became one of the new 'Masters of the Regional Universe', several rungs down the ladder of stardom because Yorkshire was less respectful, more egalitarian and more hard-headed than fickle southerners. There was the same 'gawp' factor but mainly to pick holes and point out that the king had no clothes, or the wrong tailor, or bad breath. Respect may have been accorded to reputed 'brass' but I could not go around with a sign saying that I was paid five times more than the average miner but ten times less than Robin Day, and unlike some I was not keen to show how important I was by the kind of car I drove. I stuck to cheaper models. In the case of one, a Morris Marina, I left the delivery coating of protective wax on it for over a year to be able to sell it as pristine. That must have caused great disappointment at functions when I rolled up in a Burton's suit and a mucky Marina, but I was still assumed to be important, though perhaps a Yorkshire eccentric.

I achieved the benefits of fame while eschewing it and there was one other great advantage to my television job. It was a platform for doing other things and opening up other opportunities, and as a compulsive activist, always happy doing two jobs at once, I began to write occasional articles for periodicals like *New Society* and a book for New Zealand which sold well. I also played a leading role in setting up Pennine Radio in Bradford which in 1975 beat the flabby favourite for the contract by offering itself as a community radio distributing dividends to a community trust and catering for the large Asian community by offering programmes and presenters in Urdu and Hindi. I was the putative programme director of the station but dropped out when my parachuting injuries disabled me in the launch period. Nevertheless, I picked the presenters by listening to the thousands of tapes they had sent in. From these I picked one triumph, Peter Levy, and a marvellous madman, Julius K. Scragg, but by the time Pennine went on air I found that Yorkshire Television had doubts about my continuing as a presenter while doing another job in Bradford.

I reduced my commitment to that of a presenter doing programmes there. These included a folk music programme which the 'folkies' rejected because it ended up wall-to-wall Bob Dylan, phone-ins which inarticulate Bradfordians never phoned and a Yorkshire programme called *Tops and Noils*, the meaning of which Bradfordians were slowly forgetting. I loved phone-ins, not because they are the voice of the people, because the people who call in are all abnormal in motivation, ideology or simple lunacy, but because they are good at getting popular views on issues and an exciting test of the presenter's wits. I also left one *damnosa hereditas* to what became, no thanks to me, a very successful station. To accommodate the Asian programmes we abruptly stopped the pop and music programming at 7.00pm and handed over to *Meeting Place* with Pakistani and Bangladeshi presenters all chosen by me. This killed the local pop audience which never came back when *Meeting Place* ended at 9.00pm. It also laid us open to minor rackets. One presenter used the slot to promote his own musical agency, and another threatened shopkeepers who would not advertise by slipping in occasional messages not to buy Mohamed's bananas because he had not bought advertising time. The IBA said it was monitoring all this. I doubt it. If it was audited at all it was by auditors who were either stone deaf or spoke Urdu and Hindi only enough to be able to recognize well-known swear words but not to understand anything beyond that. I am pretty sure *Meeting Place* was not a 'swearfest', though some of our presenters were 'cheeky chappies'. Personally, I did not mind that as long as we got rid of flagrant abuses.

These other activities: writing, radio, the round of speeches and public appearances which were still grinding on, satisfied my love of activity and added to the interest of my basic job as *Calendar* presenter, though that should have been exciting enough for anyone. My problem has always been a continuous restless desire to be doing something and an inability to sit back, rest and just enjoy life, work, wine and women. Having nothing to do always makes me feel guilty and restless. So I always take on too much. Friends hoped that age and wisdom would slow me down. They never did.

On any sensible stocktaking of the type (which I never made because I was not a public school, 'self-raising flower' making daily calculations on my progress up life's ladder to the ultimate goal of becoming a 'Man of Destiny Grade One') I should have been the happiest man. Not quite the 'King'. One was Freddie Trueman, the other Geoffrey Boycott (we had a dual monarchy) but I was certainly the 'Clown Prince', with Richard as heir apparent. My throne on *Calendar* was burnishing more brightly all the time. It was secure unless I took to drink, did a Simon Dee chucking it all in, or became an amateur Stuart Hall, none of which was likely. One thing I'm not, is daft.

My position on the pantheon was secure. Unless the building itself fell down, which was not likely for something built in 1968, ITV was still rich and Yorkshire was among the most successful companies in the network. My ability to do network programmes also seemed secure with the rise of Duncan Dallas's science department and Barry Cockcroft's ability to turn the Dales into a television wonderland. The future, which I never thought about very much anyway because the present was so exciting, seemed secure. I had very occasional twinges of the presenter's angst, worrying about the security of their position, eying potential challengers and worrying if the powers that be still love them. TV performers are as successful as their last programme. If that flops they fret and always wonder what a contested divorce, a blabbing mistress or an inappropriate touch thirty years ago might do to their career. Is it time to get out and retire, run a bookshop, spend their accumulated pile of money or devote their lives and brains to the lucrative after-dinner speaking circuit organized by London agencies who would not dream of approaching anyone from Yorkshire. No one loves an ego when it is old. Unless it's called Dimbleby. I was not old but it did not worry me, nor did presenter's angst. Presenters are perennially insecure; they're on their own, totally dependent on their own skills. Being a 'Master of the Universe' is not a secure job. But it seemed to be so by me, absorbed as I was in my little whirl of activity; fame was not my spur. Yet it was nice to have it and it certainly oiled the wheels of life. I did not care about getting on, I just wanted to enjoy myself and I was. The only thing to mar this was a touch of Yorkshire conditioning which inculcates a sense of duty. Was it right to focus on enjoying yourself, having fun and doing what you wanted? What higher purpose did this serve? Should I not do something better, more worthwhile?

SEX ON
THE TELLY

Not on the TV set, too uncomfortable. Nor on the screen, that was not permitted in my time, though it now has whole channels dedicated to nothing else. I mean sex at YTV. Philip Larkin tells us that sexual intercourse began in 1963, some five years before YTV. He probably meant that it reached the North in that year when he was living a melancholy masturbatory life in Hull, though he is almost certainly wrong. Yorkshire then had a population of 5,000,000 so there must have been some sexual intercourse before that fateful year, even though southerners might dismiss it as nasty, brutish and short. We must assume that Larkin meant that sexual intercourse first became a public obsession, as distinct from a private practice, in the year of the Profumo Affair, Christine Keeler and the extensive study of the whorls on his pubic hair to identify the headless man photographed pleasuring the Duchess of Argyll.

That obsession originated in London rather than the land of chapels, chills and charabancs; there sex was an obsession. In Yorkshire it was more of a hobby, like having an allotment, but since then it has heightened and spread over the land to be highly dramatized in 2013 by prosecutions of famous gropers, fondlers, paedophiles and sexual athletes who, after the revelations about Jimmy Savile's amazingly sordid career, became the object of more prosecutions and hostility than homosexuals had ever been. It began to look from lurid media coverage and the allegations brought in court against Dave Lee Travis, the retired 'hairy cornflake', and William Roache, who had managed fifty years on *Coronation Street*, as though all the regional television stations, *Look North* in Manchester (home of Stuart Hall), Yorkshire stations (playground of Jimmy Savile) and Granada

I'm in there somewhere.

(William Roache) were hotbeds of sex, wandering hands and predatory perverts. Autre fois autre touch-ups, as they said in court.

Savile was a fairly regular Calendar guest and talked regularly about 'birds'. On one occasion when I was filming with him in the Mecca, (where he had been manager early in the 1960s), while the teenage girls danced round their handbags piled on the floor, he would tell what I took to be tall tales about how he had 'had' so many of them when he was manager. He was sex obsessed but it looked to me as the kind of boastfulness of someone who is not getting enough and certainly is not as active as he would like to be. So I discounted the lot. Certainly no one knew or thought he was a predator preying on girls much younger than the pubescent pop fans in the dance hall. Anyway he was keener on working for the BBC and *Top of the Pops* than ITV or *Calendar*. We had no pop programme. He would have been incomprehensible as a Calendar reporter. We just stopped using him.

Undoubtedly, though, sex was in the atmosphere everywhere, even the Calder Valley, so it was inevitably part of *Calendar*, though far from obsessive. It is part of life, even in Brontë land. Yet it was never an obsession and we were a tea-time programme remember. *Calendar* was never the kind of hotbed of sex revealed

*Ah, I've found
a pen.*

in recent court cases. Many petals have been shaken-off Yorkshire roses but few
by us. The girls (perhaps I should say ladies, but I did not then) working there
as secretaries and production assistants were the cream of the Yorkshire crop,
including a couple of the mill owners' daughter breed who moved into every
respectable organization in the county. Better pay had attracted better workers
and though they were attractive and, in many cases, positively beautiful, they were
Yorkshire and not to be meddled with unless for serious purposes of domestic
bliss. One glamour puss did indeed disappear with a famous television personality
when he demanded a date with her as a condition of appearance. Indeed, he
later set her up in a flat in London, but I realized how stern the rest were when
I made the mistake of hiring a stripper, along with a traditional jazz band for the
Calendar Christmas party at Heppy's fish and chip restaurant in Wakefield. The
chill reception that got from the girls told me that this was neither a universal
preference nor a wise move on my part. So I pretended that the coolness was
because they disliked traditional jazz and the stripper just happened to be passing
and was dropping her clothes off before heading for the laundrette.

Always sensitive, though usually belatedly, to changing atmospheres I even
stopped using sexist jokes, such as 'We've reserved a special place for women in

Yorkshire. It's called a scullery.' Women did not laugh at it. But, in any case, few knew what a scullery was now mangles and scrub tubs were not part of anyone's life any longer.

Our open plan office was not a hotbed of touching, groping, feeling and fondling and there was little sign of consenting sexual relations (though a couple of failed marriages) among YTV staff and one groper in the science department who later perfected his 'skills' at the BBC. Always more professional. My own wife believed (as she has done in every job I have ever worked in, and particularly now in Parliament) that 'They're all at it' but they were not so far as I could see. One journalist claimed to have slept with most of the office staff but retribution quickly followed when his wife laid siege to the studio and refused to go away unless he was disciplined. It was a tempting environment. Cindy had the longest long legs I ever saw and I managed to do a film which featured nothing else, cut to the Gainsbourg song *Je t'aime… Moi non plus.* Few saw any connection and neither, to confess, did I but they were nice to look at. Everything brightened when hot pants and mini-skirts arrived, but it was left to Simon and me to wear them in a Calendar item dancing in our male hot pants. That brought in neither any sexual suggestions nor hot pants round the office. I was, however, somewhat stunned when Chris, my secretary, arrived one morning bra-less in a see-through blouse. I stayed in all day answering the mail which had piled up on my desk and arrived early next day eager to carry on the work. Sadly the bra-less experiment was over, never to be repeated. I went out filming.

Most of the journalists, researchers and producers were newly married, a state which is not conducive to promiscuity as a lifestyle, unless for celebrities in the sun. Few marriages broke up; only two did in my recollection: I'm not a close observer of sexual habits so only Richard, who knew who was sleeping with whom and probably where and when, could confirm or deny that observation. There were few overt signs for my unobservant eyes, though Liz Fox regularly and loudly recounted the efforts of Jonathan Aitken to break down the door of her humble lodging late at night declaiming his desire for her and demanding entry, presumably not just to the flat. But then Jonathan was a public school chap. They not only had the *jus primae noctis* but a different view of women as yet another prize in life's race. Indeed Cyril Connolly, described his fellow chaps as permanent adolescents: 'The experiences undergone by boys at the great public schools are so intense as to dominate their lives and arrest their development.' Not so, those of us who had been brought up in co-educational schools. We were in awe of the inaccessible. My view was that public school chaps brought up in an all-male environment see women as objects to be used, road tested and, if suitable, married, but the products of co-education are more inhibited. In any case, Yorkshire was a pretty male chauvinist place where men were men and (I joked) women were glad of it. Freddy Trueman's jocular greeting 'I don't suppose there's any chance of a fuck?' never got any response. Apart from loud laughter from me at what I took to be a funny joke.

This was not a touchy feely, 'kissy-kissy' age; that crept up from London only later in the century and still feels very un-Yorkshire and no substitute for an appreciative pat on the bum. In those days men and women lived in two separate

Advanced Anatomy studies class at Hunslet College of Musical Knowledge.

Don't tell the neighbours. They'll all want one.

worlds and were not competing for roles so contact was less and more perfunctory. Each left the other to get on with it, i.e. their job not sex, and touchers and gropers were quickly sussed out as a nuisance, particularly those who regarded a hand up a skirt as a form of affectionate greeting. Everyone knew who the gropers, touchers and feelers were and women either avoided or tolerated them while warning each other. I do not think many, even any, such warnings were given at YTV.

I have never worked with such an attractive set of co-workers but, as General de Gaulle remarked, 'Chie', (or anything else), 'en lit' is always a messy mistake whether in France or Yorkshire. One star did shack up with a lovely girl but after a couple of years he left to further his career, leaving her hurt and pained at home. It is never a good idea. Fans may be another matter and I confess to being constantly amazed at the endeavours of the groupies who besiege television stars. It was not that the stars assaulted the fans, though Jimmy Savile may have had to, being both mad and ugly. More amazingly, the groupies threw themselves at the stars as if we had some kind of sexual magic and our touch cured 'King's Evil' or any passing sexual itch. For someone so inhibited as to be in awe of women, believing that sex was a prize to be worked, wheedled, waited, wooed, even married for, it was amazing to have it thrust upon us like samples of fabulous pink Camay soap.

I was a mite too old and certainly too inhibited by a non-conformist upbringing to become prey to all this, though on occasions, when surrounded by a crowd clamouring for autographs, hands would display a close interest in the texture of my trousers and their contents. On one occasion, a hand went right down into them which was a little embarrassing. Most of the time life was too pressured to take advantage of all this. 'Sorry. Must go. I'm interviewing the Archbishop of York,' was my conventional excuse. We were not models of virtue, who was in that sexy but unsophisticated age? – but this is not the confessional, I was not an MP and there is no point in giving retrospective hostages to fortune, or Rupert Murdoch.

I will admit, however (if only because it was glaringly obvious) to a propensity to filming dancers, 'Go-Go' girls (then abounding in Leeds), bathing beauties, models and any available beautiful women prepared to endure the Yorkshire moors, clearance sites, rubbish dumps or used-car lots in a state of undress for musical films, humorous items, or any of the thousand available excuses, like re-enactments of caveman days or medieval banquets, which sprang to clever minds like mine, such as holidaying in a bikini in Hull city centre, chasing in leopard skins across Ilkley Moor as a slice of prehistoric life or consumer testing courting spots on Ilkla Moor Baht'at clobber. All the symptoms of a second teenage of someone who had never had a first.

When a clearly fallacious news item claimed that a northern stripper was to appear before Prince Charles it seemed a little unlikely but we leapt (more honestly, I did) at the opportunity to see what the prince was to be exposed to. So we filmed the poor woman on a car crusher while her husband clasped my arm and kept murmuring 'What lovely tits'. Then we took her back to the studio

Tassels before twirling.

to strip live on the programme. Sadly, Fairley in the control room lost his nerve and switched the lights off before a bra had fallen. We did a consumer test on Yorkshire's courting spots, most of which were very uncomfortable and all of them were much underused now that so many people had cars. I filmed several 'Go-Go' girls in the scenes of urban 'grot' which abounded in Leeds and I got one particularly brilliant 'Go-Go' girl from Bradford to dance on a lifting platform in Hull docks. This had the unfortunate effect of bringing the entire docks to a standstill. It produced complaints from Walter Cunningham, the dockers' leader, and from the docks' management. That clipped my wings for some time. I decided that a more grown up approach to industrial relations was necessary and I could not help noticing that when *Calendar* introduced its own beauty competition (Miss YTV) I was given no role in it.

The final break in this sex obsession was when I was sent (yes, it was not my choice and I did not discover the story) to the tatty 148 Club on Chapeltown Road, Leeds. Someone, 'McFad the Bad' I think, had gone there to see Britain's bustiest tassel-twirler at work. It was decided that I was the best man to film this epoch-making phenomenon but the entire team felt it necessary to come with me. By boosting demand for tassels we could have saved the declining Yorkshire textile industry. Reluctantly I set out with a full crew, including electricians who insisted on paying meticulous attention to lighting the stage and grips who might have been necessary if she had fallen over because of unbalanced weight distribution.

The big-hearted stripper had been got out of bed too soon to be fully-aware of what was going on, but she duly gave of her magnificent best while I crawled on the floor to keep out of shot to take photographs, or watch, eyes rolling wildly. Proudly I hurtled back with my epoch-making film. Fairley condemned it as sordid. Others cackled. My floor crawling photography had appeared in shot and my rolling eyes as I followed the trajectory of the tassels produced derision. The general atmosphere was hostile. The film did go out but was widely condemned and years later, when I had become chair of the Parliamentary All Party Media Group, Charles Allen, then managing director of Granada which had taken over Yorkshire by that stage, brought a copy with him to the Commons and threatened to show this walk down 'Mammary Lane' to the assembled MPs and Peers unless I promised him support for his plans. I did and he did not. He gave me the video but I discovered later that it was not the only copy he had produced. By then *Calendar* was run by women and it was widely distributed to them to show them how awful it had been in the bad old days. Anyway, at the time that film was the end of any effort to become Yorkshire's Paul Raymonde. Unable to stand all the ridicule and humiliation I had been subjected to, I turned my attention to politics where, of course, sex plays no part and would be totally inappropriate. That is except for Conservative MPs. I was never going to be one of them.

My obsessions were not forgotten. They were taken by the production team as an indication that I was a late developer (true) who was reliving the 1950s which the rest of our staff had got out of their systems. They took a snooty position (while watching the output). I regarded it all as harmless fun, though I do not know whether it produced any boost to the audience figures, apart from a few 'nudge-nudge-wink-wink' gestures at me in toilets at the various clubs then flourishing all over Yorkshire. Nor do I think it did any harm; except to my reputation. Nevertheless, Mary Whitehouse was girding up her loins against the deluge of breasts, bums, orgasms and bouncing bodies pouring out of television screens, and our producers began to feel that too much of it might cause mass indigestion for Yorkshire's tea-time audience. It was no worse than they were soon getting in *The Sun* and not one nipple appeared on *Calendar*, but it was no longer felt appropriate that so much female flesh should appear on our happy, wholesome, family programme. Now it does not appear at all. No wonder viewing figures for regional magazines are down.

CHAPTER ELEVEN

POLITICS

YTV changed Yorkshire by plugging it into swinging Britain, and vice versa, a process which benefited them more than us. It stimulated change and boosted the new economy of admass and consumerism. A 'Brave New Britain' had been promised in 1964 with Harold Wilson using the 'White Heat of Technology' to modernize the nation. We saw ourselves not as modernizing Yorkshire but as livening it up. A political revolution was not part of our ambition, though we did want to bring the excitements of Yorkshire's life, industry and ideas to the nation from our new television station and to emancipate the county from both London and Manchester. This would energize a somewhat staid and conservative area. A political revolution of the type that was then in the air in London, Paris and Berlin was not part of our aspiration, though some of the excitement was. The year 1968 was the time of great revolt but ITV was never a revolutionary organization, so for us it was the excitement of change and building the new.

Politics was far from our minds. Jonathan Aitken was, inevitably, Conservative, indeed the adopted candidate for Thirsk and Malton. Richard, ever equable, was I would guess a Liberal, though he had never admitted to that or any other aberration. I was Labour, though a *sotto voce* [unannounced] party member and hardly active. Fairley had voted for all three parties. I hardly knew the views of the rest, though I do not think any taint of Scottish Nationalism had been smuggled in from Aberdeen. Nationalism does not travel well. Management were all Conservative, part of the group conformity of business, though this showed only in the fact that they were always keener to meet Conservative leaders, particularly Mrs. Thatcher when she took over in 1975, rather than Labour big fish who were, in my view, far

Pathetic Picket pursues parity.

more interesting. Only one director, James Hanson, who came in belatedly, took any position on the Common Market, the great issue of 1974-5. He was anti and so was I. The rest bleated for Europe.

Most of the staff was new to the North, producing suspicions about strange offcumdens [newcomers]. Duncan Dallas was a supporter of the Socialist Workers Party (though he kept very quiet about it). He had also taken part in the American Civil Rights movement in the earlier 1960s and had even been arrested, though he escaped prison when the prison chaplain, a Balliol man, found that Duncan, too, had been at that congested arboreal slum. Somehow word of Duncan's political propensities had reached management and he was called in soon after his arrival by Alec Todd, public relations manager and formerly public relations officer for the Conservative Party and ICI, to be told that he, Todd, knew Dallas was Socialist Workers Party (SWP) and he would be keeping his toad-like eye on him; Dallas should not think that he could get up to anything political. Duncan left amazed but not abashed. He was not a natural revolutionary and I am pretty sure that if the revolution had in fact come Duncan would be stood on the sidelines wondering if the time was right and whether the camera angles were correct.

The only other 'Lefties' were a few Communists in the ETU, run by party members. until Eric Hammond broke their hold (without making that union any less 'bolshie'). They ensured that the ETU was a constant source of trouble and strikes but always

'Yes I support the strike if it keeps you off the air.'

about money, never ideology. David Sumner, YTV's general manager, claimed that their strikes were usually for trivial reasons. Indeed he said that on one occasion they had even called a work-to-rule but decided that the reason for it was a secret so he could not be told but would have to guess. They did not support other strikes. When we NUJ members went on strike for parity with the BBC, ETU members were as vicious as anyone in driving their cars at our pathetic picket line as we waved our sad hand-painted signs (which my children later re-wrote as – We demand Parity with *Planet of the Apes*). The electricians loved to see journalists jump and showed neither solidarity nor scruples about crossing other people's picket lines.

Political activity, even debate, within the company was effectively non-existent, but this did not stop suspicion. The Chief Constable of West Yorkshire, Ronald Gregory, was constantly enquiring about what the politics of our presenters were. Whenever he came in he would ask me what kind of Labour man I was. Was I a 'Gaitskellite'? Or a supporter of Harold Wilson? I wondered how he knew I was a party member at all. I did not go around broadcasting the fact. I was in fact the last surviving 'Gaitskellite', agreeing with my hero, Hugh, on revisionism and opposition to Europe. When I explained this at length his eyes glazed over. He really wanted a quick, simple plea of guilty or not guilty, though the mention of Gaitskell, clearly a good guy in police files because he was dead and his wife was a director of YTV, seemed to placate him.

If only he had shown the same assiduity in the pursuit of the 'Yorkshire Ripper'. I suppose looking back on it that he was concerned about our propensity to give air time to Arthur Scargill and to use Vic Allen, a Communist economics lecturer at Leeds University, but the police move in a mysterious way and we shall never know until the files are opened. Which they never will be.

Whether my responses to the chief constable satisfied the security service is an open question. Cathy Massiter, who deserted MI6 in the early 1980s, revealed that Harry Newton, a Leeds 'Leftie' of indeterminate red hue, whom I had invited regularly to political discussion programmes as a voice of the Left, was in fact an agent for the service. Presumably, therefore, he was reporting on our sympathies and activities. Since these were all harmless he must have had a difficult time discovering any subversives in our tightly-knit little circle of monetarily motivated men and women. Both Harry's friend, Tony Scull, and I were amazed when he was revealed as an agent but by that time he was dead so we could not ask him. I doubt whether GCHQ's TV appreciation index will ever be revealed. However, if you have nothing to hide you have nothing to fear, as William Hague would say.

The political impact of YTV depended essentially on our programmes. I thought then, and still think now, that politics is an essential part of the mix of any responsible television coverage. Today, the TV networks do their best to avoid politics as an audience loser and an unwanted bore. In my view political programmes are a duty. Every TV station should have some, even if it meant administering medicine to an audience which does not want it, just like my mother forcing the horrible 'Fenning's Fever Cure' on me. As a pompous prig of a lecturer, I could never understand why people were not as interested in politics as I was. Only when I entered politics did I begin to understand that the sad reality is that people are more interested in sport, sex, drinking themselves stupid and a thousand other ways of passing time, though when I went to work in the BBC's current affairs department I understood how boring politics can be. I there devised the 'S Test' which posits that when a political programme comes on, people Sit up, say 'Shit' and Switch over. Politics and current affairs lose up to 50 percent of the audience they inherit.

Fortunately the ITA mandated a certain amount of political coverage with a duty, since diluted, to local politics, a magazine programme like *Calendar* isn't as 'S' liable. People will sit out a brief item on politics waiting for something more interesting to come next. Indeed, they may well be interested in political issues in their area or on issues which interest them. So we did politics on *Calendar* – something they do not dare do now. Having taught politics in various universities I hoped that it could be made interesting. Even if the audience did not particularly like it, getting to know about politics was good for them. TV politics are like medicine: should be taken on mental health grounds. If they do not like it, it was because BBC current affairs is produced by PPE graduates for PPE undergraduates. We were different. I enjoyed it and hoped, naïvely, that populism, a more attacking stance than the corporation would allow and interviews where the interviewee is allowed to say something, plus local interest, could make politics interesting.

We were not afraid of doing politics or of putting politicians of all three parties, good, bad or indifferent, on at tea time to shout at each other for a small fee. Nowadays local magazine programmes run a hundred miles from politics, assuming that it is boring and an audience loser (which it is). We did not feel that to be the case. Sensibly, Britain was ruled by Yorkshire folk in the good old days so we had serious figures like Denis Healey and the big city bosses, all of whom were happy to come on to reach their electors. Politics is part of life's rich mixture. So I began to agitate for a political programme as well as *Calendar*.

Not that YTV was pushed into doing it. Their real reason was that the ITA required them to do politics. ITV wanted to cultivate politicians and required contractors to put local politicians on to win goodwill for commercial TV by giving minor notables an opportunity and a small bribe to do what should have been a matter of duty and responsibility. This led to some of the most boring programmes ever screened. At Oxford, I had fallen asleep watching *Midland Member* on Friday nights where Reg Harcourt interviewed local MPs in a manner that can only be compared to putting pennies into juke boxes in the hope of getting some sound emissions, if not any intellectual life. Every company had similar programmes, all high on the boredom index and all put out at a time no one would be watching, though many were drunk, on and off screen.

We could be different; even better. But the company would not pay overtime for an audience loser like politics. So we put it out on Sunday and recorded it on Friday when most MPs (though certainly not all, for in those days the pressure to visit the place they represented was less) were back in their constituencies after a week in Westminster. The programme went out on Sunday lunchtime as if live, on the assumption that nothing will happen in Yorkshire between Friday and Sunday (though sometimes it did – the Flixborough explosion for example). The original title was *Yorkshire Matters*. By pointing out that this meant that 'God's Own County' exuded septic puss we got it changed to *Calendar Sunday*.

In my ignorance of the real world I had assumed that local MPs and councillors would be eager to appear. Some were. Shooting off their mouths for money seemed a good idea to most. Indeed the story of the MP, telephoned and asked to appear, agreed eagerly, then asked how much the fee was, to be told £15 (we were very generous in those days) was true. Today MPs do not get paid when they submit to the humiliation of being torn apart on television but then so eager was one MP that his cheque for £15 arrived in the post next day. A few, however, were loath to appear at all, though in most cases they were well advised not to. We had some 'lunkheads' as MPs in Yorkshire in both parties. Indeed, the ex-miner MP who had the largest majority in the country never appeared at all. He could not speak and was hanging on only to avoid a by-election. Another was an alcoholic who would regularly promise to appear but only turned up once and was incoherent.

There were some problem MPs. Dennis Skinner was difficult. On his first visit to *Calendar* he refused to take his trench coat off in the studio. He rarely came and always needed heavy persuasion, a lot of telephone therapy and a taxi from Bolsover before he would come on *Calendar Sunday*. If he arrived to find a picket line (a not uncommon occurrence with our 'red' electricians) he would turn the taxi round and go home. So did Arthur Scargill when he became a regular. As a result we were lumbered on several occasions with a very one-sided (Tory) panel which 'lefties' then saw as discrimination.

If Skinner did get inside the studio he would not come to the lunch provided upstairs in the boardroom, or drink the booze lavishly available there on Fridays (sometimes a whole glass of wine) to fire the politicians up. The food was better than we got in the canteen – and free to the MPs and to we impoverished hirelings working on the programme that day. However Dennis, a sea green incorruptible who would never eat the sandwiches at Labour's National Executive meetings because he had not paid for them, would insist on eating in the canteen with the workers and paying for it himself. When we eventually persuaded him to come up to the boardroom after his lunch to have a coffee, he insisted on pushing sixpence across to Sir Richard Graham to pay for it. Sir Richard, who seemed so old I always expected bits to fall off him, pushed it back. Skinner pushed it back to him and it finished up uncollected on the dining room table. The waitresses must have thought they had got an unusually generous tip that day.

Sir Richard's presence was unusual as directors did not turn up to the Friday lunches too often. They were not interested in politics, though Conservative ministers were deemed to be 'non-political' so they would turn out to greet particularly important ones and positively fawned on Mrs. Thatcher. Donald Baverstock came more regularly and stirred things up by telling the MPs what they should say and think, most of this coming as a revelation to them. Indeed with 'drink taken' Donald could be positively rude and abusive to them. But that apart, the lunches were usually pleasant, social occasions, probably because the company gathered there, did not scintillate, despite the wine to fire up the guests. The conversation was not exactly high-table stuff but still enjoyable, except for one held after I had become an MP at the start of the 1979 election campaign. A galaxy of Parliamentary talent, now including me, gathered with a full attendance of directors. In the course of the discussion I expressed the view that American interns (and I had taken mine with me) were very useful aides for MPs, provided one could get the right qualifications. Margaret Jackson, then MP for Lincoln, observed loudly 'Come off it, Austin, we all know what qualifications you asked for, at which Richard, who knew too, asked with a beatific expression 'What was that Austin?' 'Big tits,' Margaret tersely replied. My intern, the daughter of an Archdeacon who had indeed both qualifications, choked. I blushed. Richard sniggered. Silence fell.

Dennis Skinner's technique was bullying. He had the trick of launching into an apparently uncontrollable rage. It was frightening and intimidating. The only way of coping with it, I found, was to sit there until the storm passed, which it always did. On one occasion he came on to *Calendar Sunday* to discuss education with others, including Sir Alec Clegg, former director of education for the West Riding and a man I revered, being one of Clegg's children – those who had benefitted from his enlightened control of education. When Sir Alec arrived upstairs Dennis terrorized the great man. Told that Clegg had been overseas to advise other countries, Dennis loudly demanded 'Who paid for that? Did the ratepayers have to pay for you gallivanting round the world?' adding 'I'll be asking a Parliamentary question about this.' Sir Alec was stunned into silence. When we got into the studio he had little to say beyond 'I agree with Dennis Skinner.'

Other MPs brought more excitement. It was always good to interview Denis Healey who usually had a programme to himself. Denis would offer gems like 'As I said to Henry' (Kissinger of course) or his assessments (low) of the IQ of President Ford or (high) Jimmy Carter. We all clustered round, eager to hear the views of the great. Much the same was true of Peter Tapsell, the best chancellor of the exchequer the Conservatives never had. He was (reluctantly) hijacked into our area when Yorkshire took the Belmont mast over the protests of the Hull and Lincolnshire MPs. Tapsell, who earned his non-parliamentary thousands as a stockbroker, was always more generous in his advice on stocks and shares than with the parliamentary gossip we were keen to hear. Usually it was "buy Krugerrands" whenever Labour was in, not the Keynesian economics I hoped for. I don't think any of us could have afforded to take his advice but Tapsell posed a problem. Horncastle is a long taxi ride away from Leeds. He would only come if he could be brought in the company helicopter. We agreed to do this several times until the managing director's wife decided that the helicopter was better employed on Fridays taking her to Harrods to shop. No helicopter. No Tapsell. So when he later retired from Parliament and quashed rumours that his seat would be taken by Boris Johnson by saying 'Boris wouldn't come here, there's no TV studio within a hundred miles,' I knew exactly what he meant.

Viewing figures for *Calendar Sunday* were low. But so were costs. The lunches were entertaining and gave us an inside view of what was going on in the political scene. So whatever the audience thought of the programme, and of politics, we loved doing it. Leeds is not exactly at the centre of the political universe but we felt a lot closer to the great beast of power and up to date with the gossip when the politicians came and let their hair down at Friday's lunch. It was not the most exciting of programmes because the area had no Ciceros (and still has none), no Demostheneses and no Obamas among its elected representatives. At that time it had few women either. In any case, our interviewing technique had more in common with putting the pennies in and hoping the record would play than with the forensic skills of a Paxman or the horrible harassing of a Humphrys. A Yorkshire audience would not have liked it either. Yorkshire is a Labour county. We were friends talking to friends.

We achieved good debates on specific issues and occasionally we brought in greater numbers to take part and put their own questions. Among the memorable ones was John Prescott's plan, developed with local workers and unions, to save the Imperial Typewriters factory in Hull. Then his efforts in the 'Cod War' to get some compromise which would at the very least have kept us fishing there had the greedy owners not vetoed it. It was the only sensible development in that fall out. John and the 'Cod War' provided good programmes, particularly when Jonas Arneson, Icelandic poet and former People's Party (Communist) MP, came down from Iceland to put their view. We were a voice of sense in that era of entrenched stupidity.

If all else failed there was always the guarantee that Marcus Fox and Bob Cryer would come and wrestle in mud on any issue. Bob dismissed Marcus as an 'intellectual lightweight'. Marcus thought Bob a raving 'Lefty'. But they always generated a lively discussion because each had a total contempt for the other, and it showed. They were among the smartest and most articulate of our region's dull posse of parliamentarians. Many of the others were inarticulate brute votes, there to serve their constituencies or earn their retirement from their union, particularly the NUM. In those days, careerists and men of destiny preferred the convenience of London and southern seats, leaving the rest of the country to the solid, stolid and unexciting. In Britain genius does not travel North.

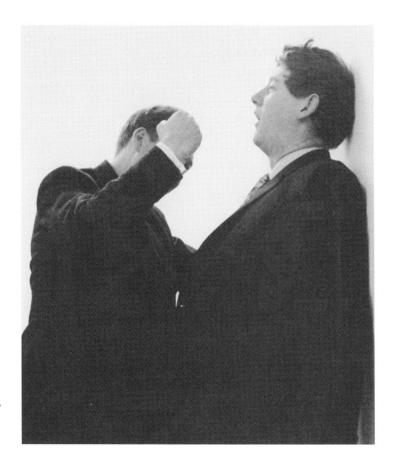

Inappropriate touching. Wilford style. Just because I messed up an interview!

Politics may have been more of a duty than a pleasure for the audience and more educational than exciting, but our coverage provided the region with a chance to hear the 'weltanschauung' of Dennis Skinner, the wisdom of Barnaby Drayson, the barmy-ness of Sir Robin Turton and his Cavalier son or the practical wisdom of Joe Ashton. For the first time MPs had to speak to the region and their electors outside elections: I am sure that the MPs too were all the better for it. It allowed constituents to form impressions of their local MP not otherwise available and led to a new generation of much smarter MPs in place of what had previously been a trade union dumping ground. We certainly enjoyed it and what's the use of producing TV programmes you do not enjoy doing? That's for the BBC. Unfortunately, though, one effect was to make me more addicted to politics. They became a notifiable disease rather than another exciting (to me) bit of fun. That infection eventually proved fatal. Much healthier to be addicted to TV, as Richard was, than to politics.

We were pretty impartial. Not all that difficult, for though I was Labour and smelled it, most MPs were so inarticulate that I could neither interrupt nor question what they were saying, because it was so far from academic political science that it was better to just sit and listen while they read from memorised party fact sheets, drying up if interrupted. Rave on! We were there to give them the opportunity to say what they wanted to say, however stupid, not to bully them into saying what we wanted. If it was pure rubbish, that was up to them.

This did not stop us raising populist issues, though these were not available in the quantity they are today when people hate and distrust MPs, find politics sordid and are convinced that 'they're all crooks' or 'they're all in it for themselves'. Both claims are utter balls. Anyone out for themselves goes into other occupations, such as banking or burglary. Then MPs were respected, however stupid and ours became keener to appear on television so they could attack each other. They preferred that to being harassed by BBC 'smart Alecs'.

One populist issue we exploited was the decision of the Conservative government to start paying councillors an attendance allowance. These were published. So it was easy to work out who was getting what and tell the world. Yet when we began to do that it produced a furious reaction from indignant councillors as if revealing their expenses was a kind of lese-majesty (never an omnipresent characteristic in Yorkshire). We were telling the world what they thought it didn't have a right to know. The result was a flood of indignant and angry calls which of course incited us to do more. I should, as a result, have been sympathetic to The Daily Telegraph's revelation in 2009 of MPs' expenses which singled me out for spending £1.50 on Fox's biscuits, buying a bottle of whisky and being overpaid on my mortgage (the bank's fault not mine). Explaining that my wife was an alcoholic and Fox's biscuits grew brain power did me no good. I felt just like the councillors I had hounded thirty years earlier. The truth is that MPs and councillors should be paid larger salaries but British hypocrisy requires us to pretend that elected MPs and councillors are providing their services free for love of the job and should be allowed to maintain a discreet silence unless they get too greedy. No matter how small the sums the actual figures only upset people, particularly pensioners and anyone on lower wages; although paradoxically they do not seem to mind ludicrous executive salaries and bonuses in the private sector.

Publishing their incomes made us unpopular among the councillor class. But they still needed us. We were their only channel of communication with their constituents, as was demonstrated when the IBA (as the ITA had now become) decided in 1969 to transfer the Belmont transmitter, from which Anglia had previously served Lincolnshire and the east coast right up to Hull and beyond to Yorkshire. The result was an immediate explosion of anger from local yokels and farmers in Lincolnshire but a much more cunning reaction from their MPs. They had enjoyed being on Yorkshire Television as well as on Anglia, even though few of their constituents could see the result. Preferring two cherries to bite rather than just one they clamoured, not to stop the transfer, as their constituents wanted, but to allow Anglia to continue to cover them as well as Yorkshire. The revolt was nominally led by Tony Crosland, MP for Grimsby, who as a minister worked behind the scenes because he could not appear or speak on it. They went in a deputation to the IBA and arranged a debate in the Commons, though it was all for show. The transfer of Belmont went ahead. The Yorkshire viewing area was enlarged to include everything down to King's Lynn. Constituents were satisfied that the MPs had done their best. The MPs got more coverage from Yorkshire, anxious to make amends for its imperial urges while several of them continued to appear on Anglia which did not have enough MPs to draw on. The moral I drew was that they liked us and the opportunities we provided to politics and them.

We did not treat politics with the same high seriousness as *Panorama* and *Twenty Four Hours*. They had more in common with embalming. But people watched us. Nor were we Oxbridge know-alls anxious to demonstrate that they knew more about how to run the country, the economy and foreign policy than the hapless politicians actually doing the job. In any case, most of the time we were talking about Yorkshire where the issues weren't as heavy as those of the bigger nation state, just more interesting. Nor did we have the backing of researchers to delve and dig out dirt (always hinted at, rarely used). We did not have a film library or an adequate clipping library to allow us to contrast what they were saying today with the different things they'd been saying five years ago. YTV had no newspaper library to inform interviewers, presumably all the old papers were sold to fish and chip shops. All these services were magnificent at the BBC. You had only to give a name or an issue and a bulging file would arrive in minutes, a practice sadly abandoned when John Birt reorganized the corporation and made programmes pay for library services, with the result that they stopped using them. All the clippings had to be junked, sold off or scrapped in one of Birt's less well-known crimes against history.

Compared to all that, we were bumbling amateurs, too harassed and overworked to be fully-informed and too busy to think it through like a game of chess. Where we did gain, however, was in ability to be more direct, in a friendly way, and to ask the tough questions because we were on better terms with our local MPs. I once worked out the perfect rules for the interview game which is in fact loaded in favour of the interviewee and against any revelation of truth or a sudden realisation of that 'My God, you're right, I've got it all wrong,' moment. My new rules started with the deprival of information, a technique which I had seen constantly used on *Twenty Four Hours* where the interviewer was kept up in the studio rehearsing while the interviewee sat downstairs in a crowded room awash with booze (in the hope that the drink will loosen tongue and coherence). When he anxiously asks 'What are we going to talk about?' he is plied with misinformation by researchers who know nothing but suggest enough lines of questioning to confuse, even terrify. In that state, he is ushered up to the studio to meet the interviewer who is then free to launch off on some totally unexpected tack and ask questions the researchers have promised he would not.

Not quite our style. We were usually too busy to prepare properly and had no-one to do research or plan questions. This was DIY politics. As interviewers we had to act as hosts as well as interrogators, a job I sometimes did badly. A councillor was brought a hundred miles from Lincolnshire for one programme. I did the interview and never asked him a single question. A furious John Wilford took me gently by the throat to ask what the hell I was doing, I explained that I had talked to the councillor before and found him very boring. So he was sent back the hundred miles in his taxi never having said a word. Wilford punched me. Hard. As interviewers we had to rehearse while they sat in the green room (actually painted yellow) contemplating eternity (or *The Magic Roundabout*). There was no booze, just lashings of custard creams and a few Penguin biscuits.

Our interviewees were often nervous and new to TV. So it would have been cruel and unnecessary to harass them like a Humphrys or to withhold information they

Dick Taverne fights his by-election. Lincoln.

needed or try to trip them up. You were a friend coaxing information, not a superior being. Best therefore to point them in the right direction so they did not fill the slot by pouring out their life story. Yorkshire folk do not talk much but when they do it is difficult to shut them up if they are talking about themselves. We had to deprive them of the opportunity to do that so we could get a word in about the problem we were concerned with. Therefore we usually told them the questions – a mistake with clever buggers like Ken Woolmer, then Labour leader of Leeds Council, who would ask for the questions, announce that they were very interesting and then in the studio deny the facts on which they were based. 'Why is the council doing this ridiculous thing?' 'We aren't'; collapse of one 'custard-creamed' interviewer.

A second technique was the pool of silence so nervous interviewees (and many were in those early days) felt forced to throw words into it. They were compelled to say something, anything, to avoid just sitting there like Trappist monks. Another technique was to ask a question then just sit and wait for some kind of reply to rumble out. This could then be interrupted by accusations about avoiding the issue.

Third, a technique to be used only on those who were uncooperative, hostile or clearly had something to hide was concealed physical violence. The interviewer had

Rapture at the result.

Candidate's wake-up call.

to sit there, leg over knee swinging gently to show he was still alive while the tide of words flowed from interviewees who could not shut up. The interviewer should let the words flow, then, when the camera was clearly on the interviewee, preferably head and shoulders, swing a quick kick at his genitals. This trick was one I never had to use, unlike the other two, though one politician who shall be nameless did try to bop me. My fault I think because my line of questioning was wrong, but inexcusable, if not exactly un-Yorkshire. Usually, though, our technique of interviewing was friendlier and less aggressive, more aimed at eliciting information rather than showing how clever the interviewer was. The best technique, Wilford was fond of saying, was to get people talking, then occasionally say 'Really?' or 'That's interesting' to keep them going. This simplicity caused the big guns, like Llew Gardner, Mike Scott or the Dimblebys, to regard us as regional hicks well below their league. Indeed, at the 1976 Labour Party Conference I managed to persuade Denis Healey to do an interview about his speech and the International Monetary Fund (IMF) terms and conditions. The big league guys promptly muscled in, took it over and pushed me out. A Third Division North player was clearly not fit to play with the First Division elite.

The only time I was admitted to the big league was at the 1975 Liberal Party Conference which was held in Scarborough. At 9.00pm on the Friday night Graham Ironside rang and ordered me over to Scarborough. The ITN team were all bored stiff by the Liberals and had decided to rush off back to London and leave the Saturday coverage to us. Alone and unaided I did it. It was somewhat bleary as I had been kept awake all night at the Grand Hotel by the crashing of glasses falling from young Liberal parties upstairs. I not only had to do the conference and announce speakers I did not know, but also run round persuading anyone I could find to do interviews. Fortunately Peter Hain, then a Liberal, was ever ready to appear and speak on anything, just as he is today as a Labour man. His views now are slightly different but, being over 60 years-old no-one now wants to hear them anymore because they are interested only in the views of young neophytes who can recite the party line having learned it by heart as an essential condition of promotion. But, boy, did I want them then. Everything he said, however boring, was received with gibbering gratitude by me as sole primary representative of the national media with the fate of the Liberal Party in my hands.

In the 1960s when he was a government minister we had interviewed Dick Taverne but not often because he talked several frequencies above the reception range of the average audience. In the 1970s, however, he emerged as a Labour rebel in conflict with his Lincoln constituency party over the Common Market. He was an enthusiastic advocate of market membership which was becoming almost a new religion. On this and other matters he clashed with both his local party and his agent, Leo Beckett, custodian of the anti-market majority. Granada's *World in Action* stole a march over us when it filmed the crucial meeting of the local party which decided on the issue. It voted against Europe. Taverne, more Burke than 'birk', resigned his seat and forced a by-election.

This was one of the most exciting political events which I watched unfurl. I was amazed at the hostility to Labour in the town, a feeling which I thought was largely due to dislike of the trade unions. I was surprised at the incompetence of the Conservatives who selected Jonathan Guinness, a maverick intellectual, who suggested in private chats to journalists that he would be happy to issue razor blades to murderers in prison so that they could save the state money and trouble by DIY deaths. I was amazed too at the pettiness of the official Labour candidate, John Dilks, who ran a defensive, petty-fogging campaign which elicited neither excitement nor interest while Dennis Skinner roamed the council estates demanding that residents take down Conservative posters and telling them that if they had put them up in Clay Cross they would lose the tenancy.

The surge of non-Liberal liberalism and naïve idealism from middle Lincoln was difficult to understand but became an extraordinary new phenomenon. It pitted Dick Taverne, standing as the young 'Lochinvar', against the Labour machine which had got him elected in the first place. Taverne, a natural idealist, though consistently impractical and wrongheaded as idealists are, became a romantic figure, a 'David' powerfully attacking the 'Goliath' party which had selected and supported him for ten years. Taverne won. The surge of excitement at his street meeting afterwards was one of the most emotional events I have ever filmed. It showed the North can stage 'epics' as well as the South.

Here for the first time in Britain was wave politics. Most electors are conditioned to support one side or the other. But those loyalties were weakening and could be swept away in a wave of excitement generated by the media. This was a foretaste of the great Social Democratic Party (SDP) surge of the early 1980s and of the 'Cleggmania' of 2010. It was also a foretaste of what was to happen to all these surges for the wave broke, Taverne's democrats faded. He lost Lincoln and his supporters lost the council in 1974, thus pioneering the downward slide of the SDP and the Liberal Democrats which was to come later. The wave could not be sustained and the whole process showed that a third force was doomed to failure unless one of the two majors split and allowed it to break through to majority status. At the time I could not understand why such a surge of naïve idealism could banish old allegiances and real self-interest, but I gradually began to understand that here was a new politics. It was evanescent, but soon was to become a pattern which the United Kingdom Independence Party (UKIP) is now following.

We later used Dick Taverne in a powerful documentary which went out nationally on Clay Cross. There the local council was defying the efforts of the Heath administration to put up council house rents. Clay Cross was an unregenerate Labour Party of the old school: solid, stubborn, socialist and dominated by the large Skinner family, led by Dennis, the MP for neighbouring Bolsover. His father and most of his brothers worked for the council in various ways, or were councillors. They dominated the town like, opponents said, a local Mafia. Certainly Skinners en masse are an intimidating sight and far too socialist to be persuaded to 'Wilsonian' compromises. Taverne put the case for the government and obedience, David Skinner the case for resistance. I attempted to moderate and the film provided an extraordinary insight into the mood and morals of a small and sharply divided mining community, caught up in a brave power struggle with the national government, which eventually crushed it. Several councillors were sent to jail. It was a meaty issue and my film and an article I wrote for *The Political Quarterly* captured national attention, particularly from Labour modernizers who viewed resistance as folly and did not want the pre-war victories of Limehouse and other London boroughs to be repeated in the 1970s. This was not the lesson I had hoped to teach.

Clay Cross Council in session.

On *Calendar* we interviewed both the big boys and the lesser lights. One of the first was George Brown who came just a few days after I had arrived. George was my hero. In 1963, I had deluged the few Labour MPs I knew with telegrams urging them to vote for him rather than the 'Man Monster', Harold Wilson, when Gaitskell died. I had attended a very moving meeting of Leeds Fabian Society at the Metropole in December 1963 just before I returned to New Zealand where George had given a sober but compelling forecast of the problems facing the Labour government we all hoped to see in 1964. I was delighted to be chosen to do his first interview with YTV and proud as we walked together from the trouser factory to Studio 2. The men working on the scaffolding round the building stopped work and gave a loud cheer, 'Good old George.' That was a sad contrast with his last visit to YTV in the 1970s when he was too drunk to speak and had to clutch the wall as he staggered along the corridor to go home. People avoided him and turned their eyes away, a heart-breaking fall.

Barbara Castle, product of Bradford Girls' Grammar School, though she sat for Blackburn over in alien territory, appeared a lot. On one occasion we decided to do what we supposed would be a happy reunion between old friends, Barbara and Vic Feather, Secretary General to the TUC, who also came from Bradford where he had worked at the Co-op. The idea was to bring them together in a Bradford Labour Club where they could reminisce happily about great days in Bradford and the rise

*Dennis Skinner
leading the revolt.*

of Labour. But it was not as successful as we had hoped. Conversation was stilted and reminiscences brief. Only later did we discover that the two did not get on. Each distrusted and disliked the other.

Barbara was a stickler for appearances. She ran us quite a dance in 1970, when we arranged to interview her at the start of the election campaign in Blackburn after an open-air meeting in which her hair blew all over the place. We filmed it but then she flatly refused to be interviewed. 'Got to get her hair done first,' husband Ted explained. So we agreed to 'do' her the next weekend in Hull after a Saturday night meeting. This went on and on like a Ken Dodd show so that she reached us in the Station Hotel only after midnight, well into overtime hours. The interview began hastily, aiming to finish quickly, but in the middle of the first question Ted stalked in front of the camera; 'Stop. I can see your knickers' he ordered. We stopped. Skirt and knickers were adjusted. We resumed and did what was finally a very successful interview, though I never even saw Barbara's knickers.

Denis Healey was the most accommodating and helpful of our local MPs, coming regularly at times chosen by him rather than us, and always dropping us little titbits of government gossip. Tony Crosland came rather less but when he was foreign secretary he came to talk about the 'Cod War'. John Prescott helpfully supplied me with hostile questions for our last interview with him in November 1976. Crosland was relaxed and chatty but did not look well. He was dead in six weeks.

Conservatives were less forthcoming and it would be honest to say that I was less keen on interviewing them. They had fewer senior figures in Yorkshire, though Sir Keith Joseph could occasionally be persuaded to come. He always brought with him a brown check scarf which seemed to be his equivalent of Linus's blanket as he sat twisting and untwisting it round his hand during every interview. Eventually we managed to persuade him to appear without it in an interview which, I have to admit, was less successful because he still insisted on swinging his chair round and turning away from the camera at the end of the interview, so the credits which were supposed to roll over a shot of him in fact featured only the back of his chair. No wonder some called him 'The Mad Monk' though we would never dare.

Conservative leaders occasionally came too. I interviewed Edward 'Ted' Heath in the gallery of St George's Hall in Bradford during his February 1974 election campaign. He was tired, though (unusually) talkative and reflective but it was a sad interview because my overwhelming impression was that here was a man with the kiss of death on him. He seemed to me to have realized that he was not going to win, was resigned to defeat and becoming philosophical about it. It was very moving. I always respected Heath afterwards, but in 1974 this insight meant that I knew better than the polls when a defeat no-one had expected actually happened.

When Mrs. Thatcher became leader she agreed to come on *Calendar* but hesitated about whether I should be allowed to interview her rather than Richard who was keen to do the job and much less suspicious than she found me. Finally, she agreed that I should do it on the grounds that it was my wife, Linda, who had shot the *World in Action* film *Why I Want to Be Leader by Margaret Thatcher* which, many said, had made her leader in the first place. She came on and talked freely to me, though always in that 'I'm so sorry your dog has died' tone which she was inclined to use whenever she talked down to people. Clearly, I was not sound. The next time I had any contact was when she came to Grimsby to speak against me as a candidate. It was an enormous help.

In any natural order there is a Yorkshireman in his proper place at the top of the tree as prime minister, like Asquith or Wilson, or as chancellor. Harold Wilson was a pretty regular visitor, particularly in his second term when he appeared to have more time for us and was more relaxed (as well as better as a prime minister) than in his first. He came to sum up on the referendum campaign in 1975. As Harold chatted to the directors, all anxious to tell him how to run the country, Mary Wilson revealed to me that she and Harold had gone into the referendum polling booth as a united couple, smiling and waving at the press. He had voted to stay in. She had voted to come out. Having cancelled each other out, they both re-emerged smiling and waving: One couple.

The one field of politics we did not do well was local. The big Yorkshire cities were then ruled by city bosses, Sir Ron Ironmonger in Sheffield, Sir Frank Marshall in Leeds, Leo Schultz in Hull and (non-politician) Howard Moore, the chief executive in Bradford. Most of them agreed to appear regularly and Sir Ron Ironmonger was always particularly good. But while Anthony Sampson and the media dissected power

Poetry for the pickets: Miners strike 1974.

and how it worked at the centre, local power was more concentrated and more opaque. Local stringers may have known the inside stories but would not expose them. We would have needed a huge team of researchers to know what was really going on in those Masonic networks of petty corruption which characterise local government, particularly in the police and planning departments. Scandals emerged, such as the Poulson affair. They were not unearthed by us but exposed by Poulson's bankruptcy and researched by *Private Eye* and the Bradford *Telegraph & Argus* whose reporter, Raymond Fitzwalter, went on to Granada not YTV. We should have investigated the widespread bribery which led northern cities to opt for high-rise flats, the incidence of which provided a rough guide to the degree of corruption: the more tower blocks the more corrupt the town. Similarly, we were too uncritical of police incompetence in the 'Yorkshire Ripper' search, although Paul Dunstan dealt with it afterwards in a network documentary and a studio discussion. Later on we never exposed the police culpability for the Hillsborough tragedy. Can't win 'em all. But we should have won some and we did not. We did, however, campaign strongly against the growing centralisation as central government took money and powers from local authorities. We defended the 'Socialist Republic' of South Yorkshire and tried to do justice to the Clay Cross rebellion on council house rents.

    We also attempted to go behind the scenes to show how politics work. We were one of the first stations to film a selection, that of the Labour candidate for Goole. It turned out to be a bit of a farce because the local party was so dazzled by the arrival of TV that they failed to realize that the winner, Edward Marshall, who claimed political experience because he had fought Grimsby in 1966, had actually stood then as a Liberal. We did, however, develop good election coverage, local and national, even without the expertise of David Butler, Anthony King or Bob McKenzie; the 'teledons' and pundits would not come north to pontificate. So we grew our own in Bradford University where Michel Le Lohé and his student, David Cowling (who later became the BBC's election analyst) provided excellent expert analysis which was better, as well as less long-winded, than the BBC's.

Our very first election programme was on the 1969 council elections. I covered the results from a tiny and very overheated continuity studio upstairs. Messengers crawled in below the one camera to pass notes about party gains (mainly Conservative) and losses (all Labour) as Labour was swept from office, even in Grimsby. It was a better way of losing weight than informing the electorate.

Come 1970, we were doing it better and now had a whole studio for two days. We were also better prepared and began to use a panel of ex-MPs and passing peers because we could not use actual candidates unless we also brought all their rivals in. By 1974, we were doing election outside broadcasts from all over the region with particularly exciting ones at Harry Ramsden's, at the Pump Room in Harrogate (much more genteel), at York University and also from the constituencies where party representatives (not the candidates for that constituency) appeared with a local audience to discuss the issues. At each we issued a dramatic warning that anyone who was a candidate for that constituency must leave immediately and could not appear under pain of death, disqualification or emasculation. The programme began, the questions poured in. The discussion was heated and a man who had come in late asked a question. It was a successful programme until we discovered that the questioner who had come in late and missed the warning was in fact the Liberal candidate for Scarborough: Consternation. By rights, the programme would have to be cancelled and re-recorded without the intrusive Liberal. We decided to keep quiet. The programme went out. No one protested or even commented. Liberal candidates were not very well known in those pre-Clegg days.

Our lively coverage continued in slightly reduced form for the second 1974 election and for the local elections but we had to devise a different form of coverage for the 1975 referendum on membership of the Common Market. We had studio discussions on *Calendar Sunday* but mainly relied on campaign meetings, the biggest of which was held in Pudsey and featured a spectacular combination of Enoch Powell, Tony Benn and Jack Jones all speaking from the same platform without making physical contact with each other. It was a spectacular meeting but the audience seemed to me much more on the Right than sympathetic to the Labour speakers. I made the crew, who wanted to go home once they had got extracts from the main speeches, stay to the bitter end. My sympathies, which were easy to conceal because no-one really understood what was going on, were entirely on the outside which I voted for. As it turned out I was clearly right but the national vote was heavily against me. In politics, as I later learned as a practising MP, to be right is to be wrong. No-one wants to acknowledge that you could be right if you are arguing against the flabby consensus and there is no credit in boasting of it. That's the great difference between television and politics. On television it is great to be right. Indeed you always are. You can be clear, challenging and effective. In politics you are a pariah, however right your argument.

Which brings me to Harold Wilson, whose skill in holding Labour together and winning elections transformed him from my hate object of 1963, when I had urged every MP I knew to both vote for George Brown as leader, into a kind of hero ten years later. Mainly, I suppose, because the Conservative government which succeeded him was so bad but also because he was doing his best through the seventies to hold together the post-war settlement of welfare, Keynes and full employment, which I thought was the basis of a good society. In his book, written after he had stood down, he rated me as his second favourite interviewer. Unfortunately I came after Robin Day. But it was still a higher commendation than I had ever had before, though it might reflect the fact that by then Harold was working for YTV in a series called *A Prime Minister or Prime Ministers*. It was a disappointment.

Our final triumph with Harold was to persuade him to do a full-length interview in November 1975 just after his return from a European Council meeting in Rambouillet. He was relaxed, happy to reminisce and I was well prepared to guide him over his career and premierships. It was, though I say it myself, a very good interview. Even Paul Fox liked it. It went out in November 1975, when suddenly in March 1976 came the surprise announcement of his retirement. This hit us like a bolt from the red that morning but, quick thinking as ever, John Fairley and John Wilford rallied the network and got them to put out my interview. It went out just as if Harold was giving his farewell interview exclusively to me and Yorkshire Television. No one knew different and it was not clear from the interview itself. A triumph, one of those things which are always nice for a poor presenter.

It is puzzling now to compare this happy history of effective and, I hope, interesting coverage of politics with the picture the current affairs mafia in London, the later history books and most Conservatives paint of the period in retrospect. My Calendar years are portrayed as a British nadir, the collapse of governability. Britain, it is claimed, was being crippled by strikes, low productivity and union power. Both governments struggled with trade-union reform. In each case their proposals were destroyed by trade-union power. The dominant question became 'Was Britain governable?' and the Conservatives fought the 1974 election using the slogan 'Who governs?' The electorate firmly decided that they did not. So depressing was the picture that I never realized until these later histories emerged from the pens of historians like Dominic Sandbrook and admirers of Mrs. Thatcher, the socialism slayer, that we had been living through such a depressing, chaotic decade of decline and disintegration from 1968 to 1977. On the programme it did not seem that way: If only, because it was not. Perhaps the strife made for a more lively coverage in which we did our best to cover the issues but they never felt like fundamental threats to the state, the government or anything else. It was a happy time whatever it seemed to be to those headless chickens, current affairs groupies and doom mongers in the London media, all of whom run around excitably at any fear for the establishment. To us the record was one of industrial disputes over basic issues like pay and conditions but neither incipient revolution nor the collapse of society as we knew it. It all seemed like what it really was: a struggle for a better life for the people.

The real damage was done later. When it came it was welcomed by the London punditocracy as a new dawn, but in fact it was Margaret Thatcher's enthusiastic destruction of unions and Britain's basic industries on the assumption that phoenixes rise from ashes so the more ash created the better Britain's prospects. But the worse, Yorkshire's. We disappeared under most of the ash. But that came later. We did not realize that the stresses and strains we chronicled in the 1970s would be the prelude to a counter revolution and an excuse for Margaret Thatcher to shatter the post-war settlement by breaking the unions, accelerating globalization and installing neo-liberal monetarist economics as the guiding ideology of government. All this had a deeper and harsher impact on Yorkshire and the North generally. The basking whale was harpooned and skinned.

All that was to come, although in the excitement of the 1970s, we never realized what lay ahead and the strains of the time certainly did not justify it. Our coverage then was neither pro-Labour nor pro-Conservative but populist, meaning that it was on the side of the people, our viewers. The media are not there to preach but to explain. We were a politically mixed team ever ready to attack either party, even the saintly Liberals, with equal glee, but always people orientated. TV is inherently — and rightly — Populist. It communicates with a mass audience. To do that it must be humanistic and sympathetic. Yorkshire's was predominantly a manual-worker audience as an industrial area. We talked with the audience, not down to it. Nor did we preach to it. Both these approaches could be left to the socially-superior BBC. Inevitably we were on the side of the miners. Like most people we sympathized with their case. It was a strong one in the two strikes of the 1970s when they had fallen behind. Doubts came later in the 1980s when Arthur clumsily put himself in the position of seeming to want a strike to take on a government which had made powerful preparations and was prepared to use the whole machinery of the state, the police and the security services against them.

There was less sympathy for the dockers, partly because their restrictive practices were more noticeable, mainly because Walter Cunningham, their leader in Hull, was not the most sympathetic of characters and did not put his case well. Arthur Scargill always took great trouble to argue his and was brilliant at doing so. Moreover, he took trouble to help us and familiarize us with the industry and its problems. He was a friend, though one whose mind ran on the Marxist track of an inflexible ideology.

By contrast the textile workers in wool and cotton were too rarely on the frontline so they did not get the sympathy or support they deserved from us. They were badly paid, though Jack Peel, the general secretary of the National Union of Dyers & Bleachers, was an effective and articulate advocate of their case until he was hauled off to gather dust in Brussels by Roy Jenkins. That was good for Europe though he was sidelined and badly treated there, but it was a sad loss for Bradford. His workforce were exploited and underpaid but, being female and Asian, they attracted far less sympathy than the miners, a stupid mistake on our part.

It was not our job to put the case for any of these unions. We did not, but they were well able to put it for themselves and, as with every issue, the portrayal of suffering, of the camaraderie of picket lines, the sufferings of the families and the feelings of the workers, miners and even the poetry of a 'miner poet' (Geddit?) we discovered was more effective than any abstract arguments. It was certainly more telling than the be-suited spokespeople mobilized by ministers and employers. This was not a political position but a simple fact that workers are human, their concerns simple and understandable and widely supported in their community even when they turned to violence. The other side was the suits, usually pompous and employed PR people. Whose side would you be on? Not a question that needed an answer in Yorkshire.

Party politics were different. No taking sides there. None was necessary given the willingness of MPs to come in. Labour had more ability in its Yorkshire ranks than the Conservatives, if only because it had more MPs to pick from. But when in power, which Labour was for most of this period, its top people were more difficult to get. So the weight of Denis Healey, Merlyn Rees or Eric Varley was less frequently deployed and debate fell back on Bob Cryer, usually evenly matched with Marcus Fox, or on Kevin McNamara against Giles Shaw. We rarely had to go down to the level of some of the less able (but longstanding) Labour men whose job was to vote not think, or the rural Conservatives who regarded wrestling in mud for a £15 fee as beneath their dignity.

I cannot claim that we developed the new and far more interesting approach to politics I had always hoped for. Politics is a minority sport with interest less than gardening or angling and certainly less than sport. It does not motivate most people. Yet responsible television stations should feature it as a matter of public education and television's duty to inform. We did more than that. We put it on a populist level, took up real issues and avoided the endless speculation. I was allowed to follow my political interests (but not my partisanship) in a way that certainly cannot happen now. This ran up against a conditioned apathy but still succeeded better than most TV politics, largely because on Calendar politics were interspersed with all the other interests we brought to the screen and never pursued to the extent of boring and alienating. Our political programme was short, lively and did not go out in peak time. Where possible we treated MPs as characters, which is why we featured Cyril Smith from over the border and made a lot of use of Joan Hall (Keighley), Wilf Proudfoot (Scarborough) and Joe Ashton (Bassetlaw), the liveliest of a fairly wooden bunch.

The aim was not to force politics down the throats of the people but to draw the impact of politics on their lives to their attention and provide through *Calendar Sunday* and our election coverage the opportunity to Yorkshire's political class to air their views and debate the issues. We did more of both than ITV attempts today. It was right to do so because parties and their people are both essential for a healthy local democracy. Politics is part of life. I hope we managed to enliven it enough to fulfill these purposes. The real problem was not that we gave politics a proper place which it has since lost but the effect on me. My own interest in politics was growing. It's a minority sport but an obsessively interesting one. As I did more, it began to absorb more and more of my attention and effort. Politics is addictive and I was being hooked. A dangerous infatuation was developing. I should have realized that I was becoming so involved, a feeling so deep that I would want to play the game rather than just arranging the bouts and doing the commentary.

THE END OF
THE AFFAIR

What killed my nine-year idyll? It was politics 'wot dun it'. One minute I was happily writing the script for our two American films, settling back into *Calendar* and helping prepare for the advent of Britain's first ever breakfast television news, *Calendar Breakfast*. The next, only five weeks later, I was pushing through a horde of press photographers at St Stephen's entrance to the House of Commons as the new MP for Grimsby (renamed Great Grimsby after I had represented it for two years) to take my seat in Parliament. Suddenly and entirely unexpectedly, *Calendar* and I went our separate ways, me to politics and what turned out to be a long rear-guard action, *Calendar* to new heights of success; without me.

What looked like a terrible mistake was a chapter of accidents. I had never planned a political career. Indeed, I had specifically rejected one in New Zealand where I had declined to stand for Dunedin Central, a safe Labour seat where I was chair of the only Labour branch in a Labour constituency which became vacant in 1963. I had sought selection in Sowerby where I lived a decade later but I did not fancy facing again the character assassination, lies and intrigue which characterize Labour's processes of candidate selection. I was happier watching the great game of politics than getting into the mud to play it. Why bother being humiliated, traduced and abused to take a salary cut?

Yet my interest in politics was growing, I was irredeemably Labour and when the foreign secretary, Tony Crosland, MP for Grimsby, died in January 1977 and I learned of the death (symbolically in Jared's Coffin House in Nantucket) I had wondered idly about standing but immediately realized that with Labour deep in one of its regular nadirs, only Fred Trueman could hold the seat, and he was more likely to stand for

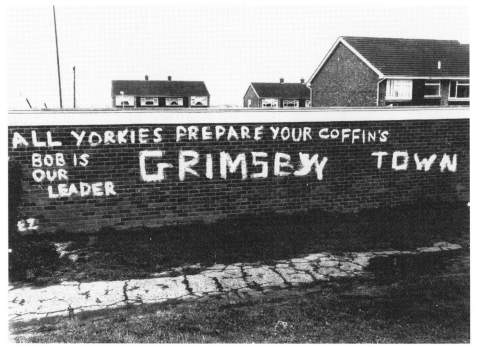

Welcome to Grimsby.

the 'Genghis Khan' party than Labour. So I put it out of my mind and took refuge in my usual resort of doing nothing. Unbeknown to me, however, Joe Ashton, MP for Bassetlaw, regular contributor to *Calendar* and a friend, took the opposite course. He put my name forward to the hierarchy and promoted the idea to the regional organiser, who in turn suggested it to a 'Grimsby Party' already deluged with hundreds of 'kamikaze' applicants.

I knew nothing of all this until I received two phone calls. The first was a message left by Chris, my secretary, 'Ring Reg Org' at a Nottingham number. I did, to find they had no Reg Org working there but they did have Labour's regional organizer and he wanted to talk to me. 'Was I interested in standing for Grimsby?' I hedged my bets. 'Maybe,' 'Well you'd better get your name in, there's six hundred applicants.' I did nothing. Next was a call from Grimsby from Jack Franklin, chairman of the Grimsby party, who clearly had neither heard of me nor seen me on television. He suggested that I should put my name in. I should have seen all this as the symptoms of increasing desperation. Instead I agreed to put my name forward.

It was not a considered decision. I did not see it as a step in my destiny (I was not a public school chap) or a stage in my non-existent life plan. The train was leaving the station. I was on the platform. Should I jump on and catch it or stay on the platform enjoying life? I did not think it through. I jumped. Even if I was selected I assumed that I would probably lose the seat, given Labour's poll ratings, then plumbing depths which needed Jacques Cousteau to study them. It would be experience and probably at the general election which must come soon. I would win the seat back. So I put my name in and went to Grimsby, undeterred by the welcoming 'Death to all Yorkies' and 'Yorkies Prepare Your Coffins' graffiti on the road in 3ft high letters. I spoke at a few branch meetings, taking trouble this time to make it clear that I was against Common Market membership having been damaged in Sowerby by rumours that I was not just pro but Euro-barmy. This was something of a mistake because while the Sowerby party had been strongly anti, the Grimsby party was pro EU. It remains so even after decades of me.

I got on to the shortlist to be called, along with five other hopefuls, to the selection meeting held appropriately on 1 April 1977. This was rather like the auditions for *Junior Showtime* which I had watched Jess Yates do years before. We spoke and answered questions, then waited downstairs in the town hall while my wife Linda (the only wife to turn up) went for fish and chips. She came back with six packets to find the other five had all cleared off to their next selection. I had won. I spent a restless un-sleeping night feeling like a re-enactment of my disastrous parachute jump, falling, falling, at increasing speed: To what? The next day, I met the press and stole a joke from Jimmy Carter: 'My name is Austin Mitchell and I'm running for Parliament.' They yawned. On the Monday, I went back to Yorkshire Television to pack up and collect my P45. Paul Fox bade me farewell, though he clearly thought I would be back. Others wished me luck. No one thought I had much prospect of winning and most assumed I would be back in a month with my tail between my legs asking for my job back to keep me going until the general election due in 1979. It was not an exciting prospect because I knew that I would no longer be able to do the political programmes I enjoyed. Television does not like partisans; unless of course they are raving right wingers.

The campaign was a four-week outward bound course and terrifyingly short. We took a flat over a Cleethorpes fish and chip shop which gave us the benefit of smelling local, but I was terrified. On the second day, I rang the chief whip and asked him to postpone the election date. He laughed uproariously: 'I've just moved the bloody Writ. Good luck.' I needed that because the anti-Yorkshire feeling had not abated. The long fishing rivalry between Hull (which Grimsby fishermen said caught 'shit fish') and Grimsby (which caught quality) had produced an anti-Yorkshire feeling which the Conservatives exploited by bringing in ladies from Harrogate in Wallace Arnold coaches to warn 'Grimbarians' about rabid 'Tykes'. Some even added the rumour that my wife (a third-generation New Zealander) was Arthur Scargill's sister.

We fought a good campaign, helped by sympathetic coverage by Yorkshire TV newscrews (who said they were anxious to get rid of me). On polling day, 28 April, the ITN exit poll said I had lost. The Conservatives were clearly doing well on the ballot count, and the news coming from the safe Labour seat of Ashfield, whose by-election was held the same night, was that they were winning there. I was dragged into the media room by David Rose of ITN to make a concession.

Suddenly John Wilford, who had been watching the count more closely than I, came in and started giving me throat cutting signs to shut up. Linda crept up behind and put it more clearly: 'Shut up you fool. You're moving ahead.' I had won with a majority of 760 (Crosland's had been over 8,000). I went out on the town hall balcony (later condemned as unsafe) and shouted at the small crowd across the road: We won it for Jim. I do not suppose they realized the effort we had made for him and when two of the crowd were arrested later it turned out that they were there to cheer for Stanton, the SWP candidate. We adjourned to the Labour Party rooms and sang the 'Red Flag' which a few remembered, and then, incongruously, Ilkla Moor Baht 'at, which I thought was a bit ill-advised, particularly later when another huge graffiti 'Yorkies Prepare Your Coffins' appeared on walls along the road.

Still, I had won. I was Grimsby's MP. Some critics immediately put the contrast between Grimsby and Ashfield down to the glamour of TV, inferring that 'Grimbarians' were daft enough or simple minded and would vote for a 'plastic puppet'. This was an insult and totally untrue. Being from television had certainly been a help because it made it easy to establish my name and face in a short campaign and meant that electors were coming towards me in recognition rather than wondering who this lunatic proffering leaflets was, but votes are still determined on whether they like a candidate or not and what they think of the party, and Grimsby as a low-wage town had benefitted more than most from the £6 pay policy and did not burn with hostility to Labour. This had become clear from an opinion poll carried out by Bob Worcester of MORI before I had even been selected. That poll was the reason why, all unbeknown to me, Percy Clark, Labour's head of publicity, had been able to assure Labour MPs in London that the party would win the Grimsby election it was supposed to lose but lose Ashfield which it was supposed to win.

No time for rejoicing (and no inclination, I was too dazed). I was in. Five days after the election I took my seat, the first sign that the tide had turned for Labour, to a warm greeting from Jim Callaghan, the prime minister, the life of whose government I had helped to extend. I had left television, jumped on the train which turned out to be anything but a gravy train, and moved off to a new future. The transition could be seen as another – the last – stroke of the Mitchell luck; it was not. Entry into politics was not only the loss of all the excitements and fun of television but the end of lucky breaks. It was a transition to a new career which began in triumph but ended in a long drawn-out failure because I came in at 44 years-old, rather too old to be a rising meteor, just as the electoral tide turned against us and brought eighteen years in opposition at a time when the road to promotion was blocked with the large number of powerful men and better women from Labour's great period: Healey, Hattersley, Shore, Castle, Smith. Had I thought about it and had any choice I should have picked a better time to come in, say 1945, and a better age, say 18 years-old, which seems to be the median age for promotion today.

In any case, coming from television with its aura of easy glamour did me no good with hard bitten MPs who can only get a little glamour if they buy it from makeovers and public relations agencies. Most are suspicious of television, probably because they cannot get on it. Soon after I was elected I sat next to an old veteran in the bar. Staring at the wall he said to me 'That's a good programme you do about science.' I purred. He added 'You should stop doing it. You shouldn't do TV now you're an MP.' That reaction demonstrated the love hate relationship between politicians, who only love television when they are on, and television people. Politics and the media are, I was to find, as compatible as oil and water.

I had seen both as two approaches to the same job of popular education, reaching, informing and educating the people. This led me to the assumption that having mastered the theory I'd be able to do the practical with a certain amount of ease, and having learned how to present myself, eat bacon sandwiches and speak in public I would soon be on the plinth in Trafalgar Square. Neither was to be. The two professions have great similarities but they operate in very different fashion. The similarity is that they both depend on publicity, on reaching the people and producing a reaction in the audience. Neither television companies and programmes, nor Parliament and parties, can achieve anything if they do not reach the people. Parliament is not a government but a machine for drawing attention to problems, a platform for making a noise about them and a forum for publicity. Their grievances are raised and party cases put before the people in the hope that the exposure and the publicity will produce a public reaction which forces government to act.

Television is more successful at this job. It has the audience and that makes politics and parliament dependent on it. Unless MPs get the attention of the media they are impotent. Just 30 seconds on *Today*, a few minutes on *Calendar* or three weeks on *I'm a Celebrity Get Me Out of Here* are far better at reaching the people than an hour-long speech in Parliament or an adjournment debate in Westminster Hall to announce the end of the world. Indeed, the best way of keeping a secret is to announce it in the commons for if news were confined to *Hansard* it would never get out because Parliament speaks to (and mainly for) the small political class while television speaks to the world. So the politicians are dependent on the media and resent it. Which is why so many politicians turn to gimmicks to get on, a process I only discovered when I changed my name to Haddock to publicize National Fish Week. It brought endless TV appearances, usually eating fish and chips.

I was now in the game of drawing the attention of people like I had been to issues that I thought important in my new role. I was dependent, which brought home to me the fact that my former colleagues were not half as interested or concerned as I had been, and was. Damn them. This was why I introduced and carried the first bill for televising Parliament thinking that if Parliament had its own channel it could cut out the middleman of the media. We got our own channel but it did not get the audience because the nation still preferred the entertainment channels. Indeed its main effect was to persuade the main channels that they could do less politics.

The two groups, media folk and politicians, are similar in many ways: thick skinned, exhibitionist, ego maniacs are attracted to both occupations. Yet the medians are more liked and assumed to be safe and impartial while the politicians are under suspicion as selling something or trying to put one over on the public. Medians are there to talk with the public, politicians to be talked at by the public. That distinction was first brought home to me in the election campaign when after various attempts to get me down the fish dock to talk to the fish porters landing that day's catches – a process which revealed the Grimsby Labour party to be totally ignorant of the time the work was done since I was sent down at midnight to find no one there, then at 7.00am in the morning to find they had all gone home before we finally caught up at 2.30am.

With a television crew filming me I went round the hard-working lumpers (who were really too busy to be bothered) with a few cheery words but ran across one character who immediately started haranguing me loudly about Enoch Powell, the only man to run the country and the only one who understood its problems. I nodded and pursed my lips in my best *Man Alive* style to draw more from him until the director behind pushed me in the back and said 'Aren't you going to answer him?' I was not because I was doing my television job of getting him to talk. But that was no longer my function. I was there to reply, which I did half-heartedly: 'Oh I've met Enoch. He's a loner. Can't do anything on his own'; which produced another tirade about politicians being out of touch with people like him. I moved on.

That was an introduction to my new role as the punch bag of the British Constitution. Before, everyone had assumed that a television personality was their friend, someone who thought like them. Now an element of suspicion entered the relationship and reactions were cooler, even critical, because over half the population did not vote for you. So I had emerged from the TV closet and was committed to a cause rather than vacuous amiability. Just as people are suspicious of door-to-door salesmen and passing hucksters, so they are of politicians, and as a Labour man I began to realize that three out of every four people I met did not like my views and would not vote for me even if they might have liked me on telly. This created a distance which the 2008 expenses crisis later turned into a gaping gulf. Politicians need a thicker skin than television personalities but that row brought a massive surge of abuse greater than anything I could have produced on television, even if I had said that the entire Yorkshire cricket team should be shot.

There had always been a certain amount of abusive mail for MPs (television personalities got very little by comparison and much of that was admiring guff or requests for a lock of hair – from politicians they preferred the full scalp). Every town has a small quota of curmudgeons and lunatics but then e-mail and Twitter opened up a new world of opportunity for them to ventilate their mean misery on MPs by keeping up a steady stream of abuse and pouring out invitations to do anatomically impossible things. Indeed now we have closed the main lunatic asylums, Twitter may be the only form of therapy available and at least it keeps them off the streets. Yet the continuous drip, drip, drip of illiterate abuse can get depressing. The FBI used to send anonymous abusive letters to Martin Luther King to undermine him, and I sometimes wondered whether MI5 had used the same training manual.

I did not mind it all that much, though it provided a sad commentary on the effects of our education system on literacy levels. Yet early on I realized that many people had little idea what an MP was for. Television personalities are important just by being there. MPs have no visible clear role. People asked why I spent so much time in London, why I was not in Grimsby to deal with their drains. Others complained that I should not be travelling first-class, though Roy Hattersley, who was with me when one lad made that complaint, just told him to 'fuck off' which I would never have dared to do. However, it all made me realize why Tom Swain, MP for Derbyshire North East, and Dennis Skinner, MP for Bolsover, had competed to spend their time in their constituencies rather than in Westminster to the extent that Swain once tricked Skinner by getting the London train but then getting off at Newark and doubling back while Skinner travelled on.

It was not so much a question of changing glamour for graft, though MPs are the dogsbodies and sewer cleaners of the constitution unless they are privately wealthy like Michael Heseltine. The hours in Parliament are long and late, though in total probably no longer than the hours worked in television, but the difference is that television ('when I used to work for a living' was my standard joke) is mainly purposeful activity with an impact on screen but parliamentary activity is all too often hanging around in the tea rooms gossiping, grumbling, sleeping and waiting for something to happen as the brute votes are trundled out at 10.00 or 11.30pm, or even, in those days, the early hours of the morning. Nothing is more destructive to good looks and mental balance than all night sittings which on television only happen on election nights or long charity appeals. Television people are show ponies but MPs are like shire horses, there to pull things, not allowed out to speak. They must work hard for free, attending every party or constituency function, however useless or boring, on demand, whereas television personalities have to be invited and paid to grace functions with their presence and are infallibly well treated at them. They get deference. MPs do not. I well remember Bob Cryer's anger when I spoke to a branch of Keighley Conservative Association for the magnificent sum of £16. I do not think he ever forgave me. Media folk can make jokes and be as political as they want (my joke "As Tony Benn might say, 'thank you for your company'" always went down well at business dinners) but politicians must always be serious if they are not to be discounted and audiences have become more censorious.

The biggest difference between my old and my new job was personal. Politics is supposedly a team sport in our system of government by party, but parties are not teams, they are a collection of rivalries, antagonisms, ideological conflicts, jealousies, even hatreds, as indicated by the old joke about a new member announcing to a colleague that it was good to see the enemy. 'Those on the other side aren't your enemy,' the older member replied. 'They're your opponents. Your enemy is behind you and armed with knives.' Not quite that bad but politics is certainly the lonelier role. Television is a team operation and every member of the team relies on the rest. It is tightly structured: get a programme on the air at 6.00pm or fail. In politics an MP gets a little platform from which to speak, raise issues, put views and help constituents, but that is it – no deadlines, no guidance, little supervision, so that he stands or falls, succeeds or fails, on his own and does as much or as little as he wants to. On that platform the MP can achieve things but only by publicity. The audience will always assume he is doing nothing and that his aesthetic posing is just for show, which makes the MP a loner, balancing between constituency and parliament, local party and national, and all the while clamouring to catch the attention of the media he has to live by. MPs have no line manager except illiterate Whips, no HR Department, no adviser and if they seek help on speech making it is always 'Shut up', whereas the television personalities' few words will always be well received, however rubbishy.

In traditional terms, of course, the job of MP has, or should I say had up to the expenses scandal, the greater prestige, conferring as it does membership of the world's most exclusive club and a ticket to play the great game of power. Yet the club is pretty third rate and tatty like the railway tea rooms in *Brief Encounter*, the denizens

Best of Enemies: Tebbit and Mitchell on Target.

are smelly socks while television folk expect and get the best and the great game can be very petty and vicious. The pay is peanuts as appropriate to monkeys. When I was elected, MPs' pay was low at £6,000 while my television salary was double that and supplemented by all sorts of extras.

I found that the great debating forum had become a stage for a four-year election campaign. This turned MPs into the foot soldiers of the battle, kept in line by Whips and the lure of promotion. The parties do not want glamour-painted TV stars, and intellectuals are a nuisance. They need conformists able, like barristers, who can argue whatever brief the party is preaching at the time, not crusaders for causes who are a nuisance. Climbing the party ladder is more important than crusading for any cause.

All of which makes the MP's job less fun than the media man's. Duty is the important driver in politics. It has to be to put up with its disciplines. But the biggest driver for many is ambition, not to serve the party but to climb the slippery pole of power. Here I was at a disadvantage. I had been successful enough already, did not want the narrowing that ambition requires and was more of an observer than a climber, happy to be sitting in a ringside seat on the great struggle for power. I had always believed that the principle which had boosted me in academe, and in television, of ability attracting its own promotion would also operate in politics: Which goes to show how naïve I was in a world of pushiness, plotting, sycophancy and self-promotion.

Fortunately, I never really wanted to be a minister: a wish readily granted. The job is too tough, too hard work and too narrowing, when the MP's job done properly is tough enough already. There are many satisfactions for the backbencher. I have had a ringside seat on thirty years of power struggles and the pleasure of select committee work on the economy and on public spending which acts like a very selective adult education class. I have travelled the world to educate me to be the minister I never became. I have had the pleasure of doing several jobs at once because politics provided opportunities for doing media work as well. I made TV programmes for Yorkshire and for Sky. Norman Tebbit and I did an angry old men show called *Target* which was the best unwatched programme on telly for ten years. It produced one of my best jokes: 'What's the difference between *Target* and the Loch Ness monster? Some people claim to have seen the monster.' I also got to do radio programmes such as the regular election commentaries I did for BBC with Julian Critchley and Charles Kennedy (Critch, Mitch and Titch) and the phone-ins for LBC and talkSPORT which put me on air on the day of the mortar attack on the cabinet and on the week the twin towers were brought down. So I am not complaining, though it would have been nice to be asked and offered a job: even one as lowly as opposition spokesman on the 'Cones Hot-line'. In any sane party I would have been. But then I was Labour.

Promotion might have been nice – I shall never know because it did not happen – but I am happy as a backbencher. I joked 'I don't tell my mother I'm in politics. She thinks I'm in prison and she's happier that way,' but politics is a necessary and noble profession. It is not as glamorous or as powerful as television. It is more dutiful than delightful. It is harder work and less rewarding because the political

Age hasn't wearied us. Yet: The survivors in 1988.

task is Sisyphean and tough rather than sexy and for each yard you roll the stone upwards it rolls back a couple of feet, where television gives instant acclaim. But at the end of the day you can help people, you can serve your constituency, you can make minor changes to policy and you can plant seeds of thought which may grow. I am glad I jumped out of the studio and on to the Grimsby train. In any case there is not much alternative now except keeping pigeons.

No use grumbling and I am not going to. As a true 'Tyke' I had chosen my bed and I have been happy lying on it for nearly four decades (and do not go interpreting lying). Serving the best constituency in the country, one of the few real communities left, and pursuing my various causes has kept me both active and happy, even though too much of my career has been a long and failing rear-guard action to defend the welfare society and the kind of good industrial society Yorkshire had been against the free market 'Thatcherite' efforts to destroy it. It was the right battle to be fought. I have enjoyed fighting it. Still am. So say not the struggle naught availeth. Anyway it is not over yet. Cannot go back and no use regretting. But I did and do miss my Calendar days.

BYE BYE YTV

While I embarked on my fighting retreat, Yorkshire Television and *Calendar* were going from strength to strength doing a whole series of successful programmes I would have loved to be part of. Not *Countdown*, a programme for which Richard was perfect, but their national political programme, *First Tuesday. Calendar Sunday* continued and there was every opening a Yorkshireman could want with Duncan's science programmes and Barry Cockcroft's wonderful documentaries; none of them now for me. I could not have replaced Les Dawson or played Jack Frost in that wonderful series, but I watched Yorkshire's sustained success with a little envy. How could they do so well without me?

Yet while *Calendar* continued to dominate the ratings and Richard became Mr Yorkshire, the original team was beginning to fall apart. By the early 1990s, John Wilford and John Fairley had been pushed out after a failed bid for the Midlands contract, and though Fairley was brought back as director of programmes, Wilford went to work for Sky. Barry Cockcroft retired and Duncan Dallas left to set up his own company, XYTV. So the team, which had been such a pleasure to work with, broke up. Worse still that was followed in the 1990s by the first *felo de se* in television history. Yorkshire television killed itself.

Finance became tighter as the regional monopoly became worth less and more channels took slices of static advertising revenue. Indeed a latecomer, Google, was eventually scooping the pool, making more advertising revenue than ITV by 2010. Television was digitalized so that the regional monopolies were worth less when people could receive anything from anywhere. But even before that YTV damaged itself. In the 1992 round of licence renewals, which Mrs.

Thatcher stupidly turned into an auction, YTV's managing director, Clive Leach, former English cricketer and chief executive of Tyne Tees who had replaced Paul Fox on his retirement as chairman and chief executive and was paid a salary of over £400,000 a year, misguidedly put in a cripplingly-high bid. Fearing a big rival bid from Granada (which was bribing potential competitors not to compete, so that its own bid for the Northwest was remarkably low) Leach overbid for Yorkshire's. This subsequently forced huge economies which saw staff numbers drastically reduced, Duncan's science unit scrapped and *Calendar* made cheaper and meaner.

This disastrous overbid was the beginning of the end. Quality television is heavily dependent on money. From the start Yorkshire Television had benefitted from the strong cash flows coming from its regional monopoly of advertising. Now it had overspent on its future. Retrenchment, which always means reduction of both output and quality, began. Even worse, to conceal the disaster he had created Leach began to oversell advertising, selling £15,000,000 more than YTV could actually deliver. This forced the station into its first ever loss and the bubble burst. A meeting of hard faced non-executive directors, held significantly in the Athenaeum Club in London not in Leeds, decided that Leach had to go.

He went to be replaced by a resuscitated Ward Thomas (who had chaired the Athenaeum meeting) as chairman. He brought in Bruce Gyngell, the Australian who had rescued TV AM (at the price of permanently locking out the strikers, some of whom had been recruited from Yorkshire) as managing director. Showbiz was Bruce's remedy. He moved the company away from regional programming, current affairs and the science programmes which had long been its forte. He took Richard Whiteley off *Calendar* with the promise of a national chat show of the type Richard had always wanted. It never materialized so Richard was restricted to the hugely-successful *Countdown* which Yorkshire produced for Channel 4. For *Calendar* 'think pink', which in Manchester might have been interpreted differently, meant bringing in female presenters and fluffier items. *Calendar* became a news programme rather than the 'all Yorkshire life is here' magazine it had been.

Ratings began to slip. More importantly, so did the advertising revenue from the regional monopoly. More television channels were competing for advertising and Rupert Murdoch's Sky was winning bigger shares of the advertising pool. Ward Thomas, ever the imperialist who believed that bigger is better, sought a solution in merger with Granada, hoping to become the chairman of the united company. He did not and YTV was made a subordinate part of a Granada empire which once again covered the North as it had in 1968. Misguidedly Charles Allen, CEO of the 'new' Granada, combined with Michael Green, CEO of Carlton, to squander millions. Carlton had been created as Mrs. Thatcher's revenge on Thames for *Death on the Rock*. It turned out to be the worst of all the television companies, despite the emollient efforts of its young PRO, David Cameron, to present its dross as quality. Together Green and Allen decided to take on Murdoch by launching ITV Digital. This wasted over a billion pounds but flopped and crippled the network financially.

The result of this disaster and the shrinking revenues from the regional monopolies was that YTV-Granada was merged into the one national ITV. Its chief executive, Michael Grade, then began a game of bluff, pleading poverty as the justification for threatening to close regional programmes altogether. They did not pay. The bluff did not work because MPs rose to the defence of their regional programmes and government and its nervous new regulator, Ofcom, insisted on the maintenance of the regional commitments made in the contracts on which the original regional companies had got their region. So the new company economised. The staff on *Calendar* was slashed by 25 percent. The separate sections devoted to Lincolnshire, Hull and Sheffield were jettisoned to save money. Quality and ratings declined with it. The BBC lured away Christa Ackroyd, the best woman presenter in British TV, by offering more money, something they had never been able to do before. That gave *Look North* not only the more populist fun appeal which had always characterized *Calendar* but the opportunity to start a separate *Look North* from Hull. The combined BBC audience was soon winning a bigger share than *Calendar*.

Calendar survived but in a meaner, paler, less well-staffed form, doing less politics. When advertising revenues fell in the 2008 recession the whole of ITV was endangered, fearing a Murdoch takeover which fortunately never materialized. The new chairman of ITV, Archie Norman, who had built-up ASDA, took over and soon advertising began to grow again while quality productions, most in drama, began to reap their rewards in higher profits and serious overseas sales. *Downton Abbey* had replaced *Yorkhire Dales*. *Calendar* began again to produce two programmes for different parts of the region and in 2013 the recovery saved the magnificent Kirkstall Road studios. Built as the most modern in Europe they had become a 'white elephant' as drama production moved out of expensive, overstaffed studios to the great outdoors where God could provide the lighting less expensively than the ETU, and the scenery without NATKE. ITV had contemplated selling the studios as a warehouse, a drive-in brothel, or anything which would yield cash.

At the suggestion of Yorkshire MPs, Film Yorkshire looked at converting the studio to offices and production facilities for Yorkshire independent producers and visiting film companies but eventually they decided that this would be uneconomic: the machinery was outdated and dusty and, its director reported,(looking squarely at me) that they had found dirty magazines on the Telecine machines. So the studios sat there empty and unheated until Archie Norman decided to reinvigorate them. He moved *Calendar* back in from the bowling alley next door where it had been for ten years, brought *Emmerdale* back from its own studios on the other side of the Kirkstall Road viaduct, and opened a new glass-panelled studio in what had formerly been the bar.

There a revived *Calendar* lives on to fight another, more competitive, day but, like all today's regional magazines, it's a cut price magazine with fewer staff on lower pay. If those staff did need a drink afterwards they cannot even go to the Queen Victoria, as we did in the early days. It's closed. The streets its customers lived in have all been pulled down. YTV and its next door neighbour, Aire Radio, built in the 1970s, are left sitting on the waste-land site created by the clearance of the 'Alphabet' streets. There still is a TV Centre in Kirkstall Road but it is now a production facility for London, not an empire in itself, and it employs less than a third of the numbers there in 1969. A sad outcome, but still survival.

SO LONG, IT'S BEEN GOOD TO KNOW YOU

The team which started YTV has been more successful than the company itself, though sadly winnowed down by death. Two, possibly three, became millionaires. All did well for themselves, Richard Whiteley the most successful of all. He became Mr Yorkshire, a major figure in the county, a member of the county cricket club and a Deputy Lord Lieutenant with a page-boy uniform, a millionaire and munificient Mayor of Wetwang. Richard rose from Yorkshire figure to national treasure through *Countdown*. He was just right as its presenter: amiable, relaxed, with a liking for puns. He had been chosen for rather different reasons. The two producers who came back from Paris, having purchased the rights from the French investor, went with Graham Ironside to survey the *Calendar* staff in their search for a presenter. Ironside, ever contemptuous of 'luvies,' scanned the team, pointed to Richard and said 'Take him, he's fucking useless'. They did. Richard grew to the job and Ironside was furious when he found his 'luvy' was being paid £1,000 a day to present *Countdown*. Peanuts to what he was being paid on *Calendar*.

Countdown was the first programme to appear on Channel Four when it began transmission, and the only one which continues today. It brought Richard the national attention he had craved as one of what his friend, Gyles Brandreth called 'the middle England middle brow presenters of our time, living at what we called 'the shallow end of the pool'. He enjoyed splashing there. See his excellent (and modest) autobiography, *Him Off*. Richard was the most lovable of people, adored by *Countdown* enthusiasts who used the programme as an intellectual exercise to keep ageing brains alive. He was good at it and loved it. Brandreth observed in his malevolent way: 'Richard Whiteley loves the show so much he hopes it will last forever. It probably will. And if it does

Richard will have spent his own life on Earth simply sitting behind a desk growing fatter while repeating the words 'and the Countdown clock starts now.'

Countdown allowed Richard to achieve his ambitions, the most endearing of which was to be invited to David Frost's great annual party for anyone who is no one in British television. He also became a member of a London club and an active patron and governor of the old school he adored, Giggleswick, where he had been taught by Russell Harty. He became a father and, with his partner, Kathryn Apanowicz, who had started out on *Junior Showtime,* bought a large old house in his favourite corner of North Yorkshire to live like a new squire. On his visits to Grimsby he exhorted the town and the Labour Party to keep re-electing me. 'We don't want the bastard back on *Calendar.*' I think he was joking.

The drawback was that his exhausting role on *Countdown* took him off *Calendar.* He never realized his long-standing desire to revive *Down Your Way* with himself as Wilfred Pickles, (though Christa Ackroyd did not look like a new Violet Carson and Paul Fox would not have been happy as 'Give Him the Money Barney.') At the height of his powers and popularity, he died suddenly and mysteriously in 2004, victim of a strange infection acquired in Africa but badly treated in Leeds. His death was a tragedy and a real loss to TV and Yorkshire. The county commemorated it suitably, as Richard would have liked, with a memorial service in York Minster. The ferret which made him famous had died in obscurity some years before.

Others have also died. John Meade, Richard's producer on *Countdown,* died 'exiled' in Malta. John, an aggressive populist from Scarborough, had joined the *Calendar* team after the start and quickly showed himself an incomprehensible presenter but an energetic and original producer. He took over *Countdown* at its start but as an exuberant drinker, he became an alcoholic, a decline chronicled by Gyles Brandreth, then a regular YTV guest earning big fees on *Countdown.*

This did not stop him biting the hand that fed him so well. On 23 March 1983 he wrote in Leeds:

'It's pretty much a shambles here. The Producer (John Meade) is a nightmare - principally because he's a drunk and out of control (he also visits prostitutes. He is quite proud of this. In Leeds he says you're spoiled for choice. Quality totty)'.

On 26 November 1986, 'Long drive to London with the Producer, John Meade, who spent every minute of the journey telling me what a remarkable and undervalued talent he has.'

On 15 July 1987, 'Our Producer is a nightmare, a heavy drinker, a heavy smoker, and the other day he was subpoenaed as a witness in the trial of a notorious Leeds 'Madam.' As Derek (Nimmo) said: 'Countdown is such a cosy programme if only the viewers knew'. They did not but YTV did and John was pensioned off to die of his addiction in Malta.

Barry Cockcroft has also died. As a senior producer he devoted an increasing amount of his time to filming in the Dales, first for *Calendar,* eventually as producer of his own network programmes. Much of his work was done with YTV's discovery, Hannah Hauxwell, whose frugal life, alone on the small family farm in Baldersdale, was immortalized in Barry's great film, *Too Long a Winter.* This was followed by a whole series of films with Hannah, expounding her simple wisdom and good sense like a British Chauncey, as Barry took her to London, to Europe, to the US and to Asia. Had she not been old and frail she might have visited the moon and produced another film and a book for Barry. Hannah lives on and is now 87 years-old, looking 100. Barry moved on to more films in the Dales and one on Morecambe Bay for which he spectacularly sank a tractor (which was actually so old it had to be towed out on to the sands where it took three days to sink) providing an impressive end. After making over a hundred documentaries, Barry retired to everyone's great surprise to Cornwall not the Dales. There he died in 2001 of Motor Neurone Disease.

That was after his cameraman, the great Mostafa Hammuri, had fled the country to escape creditors. Mostafa was a sensitive and skilled cameraman but an extravagant spender and a slow worker. He gravitated from *Calendar* where very little artwork was possible in the rush of news gathering, into documentaries. Nothing but the best was good enough for Mostafa in films, objects, and possessions. If he had a watch it had to be a gold Rotary, a Hasselblad camera, and a Jaguar sports car, but all these possessions were above his pay grade and the extravagance eventually caught up with him. He fled back to Jordan, having wittered on when we filmed with him about how we should film in Arabia rather than Otley because grateful sheikhs would present us all with gold Rolex watches just for going. I hope he got one.

Alcohol is the curse of the television classes. Our presiding genius and creator, Donald Baverstock, succumbed in 1995, having been pushed out of YTV in 1974. Having failed to get the job of BBC controller Wales, which he craved, he wrote reports for BBC and Granada and retired. He died in a retreat in Keighley, his restless genius stilled at last but still in the adopted county for which he had done so much.

A more arresting spectacle (joke!), Alan Hardwick, reported Lincolnshire, hoped to present *Countdown*, then left to run a charity. In 2012, he was elected police commissioner for Lincolnshire and promptly suspended the chief constable for no very clear reason. This was condemned and reversed by a judge. Not a brilliant start to a new career in a curious and undefined job which he is still doing.

The newsroom staff went more gently unto that good night we call retirement. Graham Ironside, the dour, canny Scot who had kept the show on the road for so long, went to Sri Lanka to develop a new television station's news coverage. He came back, did various advisory jobs and still lives in Bramhope where he is writing the history of YTV.

John Wilford, head of news, editor and producer of a YTV documentary *Richard Whiteley, Television Man* in 2003, retired, and still lives, though not in good health, in Horsforth where he is writing books and plays.

Duncan Dallas, after directing the opening documentaries and an evocative film about his childhood holidays in Scarborough, *It Never Seemed to Rain*, produced items for *Calendar* and full-length documentaries for the network. The first was Whicker's *Journey to the South Pacific*. When Donald was told to fulfil YTV's commitment to science he made Duncan (the only one of us with a science degree – in chemistry) the head of it. Duncan recruited an interesting and lively team of young producers, most of them Oxbridge educated, which surprised me because though Duncan himself was a Balliol man I constantly annoyed him by repeating Lindsay's dictum that at the top of every tree there is a congested arboreal slum of Balliol men, and pointing out that, as a socialist, Duncan should have chopped down the tree. He produced very successful science programmes, such as *Don't Ask Me* and was tied to YTV with golden handcuffs, but once the contract was won the company could no longer afford him or his science department. Everything was cut to the bone and Duncan took redundancy, set up his own company called, appropriately, XYTV, producing programmes for Channel Four and began to develop and run science cafes all over the country and round the world. He promoted and financed both the Joe Kenyon Prize for social initiatives in Barnsley and the annual Baverstock Lecture at the Ilkley Literature Festival but died suddenly and tragically in April 2014.

Sid Waddell, Calendar's populist genius, enlivened the programme and invented a series of successful programmes culminating in *The Indoor League* in 1976. This went to six series but after a row about his expenses (he had sold his YTV car) he moved on to become the 'Voice of Darts' as darts commentator, first for the BBC then for Sky. He wrote several books, including a moving one about growing up in his pit village. He lived in Pudsey with his second partner, Irene Cockcroft, but died of bowel cancer in 2012.

Rod Lofthouse, an excellent sound recordist, went to New Zealand in the 1970s with Whicker, fell in love with that country, and with his new partner a YTV make-up artist, took redundancy, went back to New Zealand and used the money to buy a vineyard which now produces high-grade wines, including the wine for Princess Diana's wedding. Now he is a NZ-dollar millionaire living the Kiwi life of sailing, wine producing and staying happy.

Mike Wood came to *Calendar* late, left a year after me, and went on to fame and fortune as a brilliant TV historian. He has filmed in South America, India, Egypt and Britain to make wonderful and historic documentaries which combine high-speed hiking with expert commentary and lavishly illustrated books. A very serious lad and an Oxford history graduate with a rather posh accent, Mike was well suited to serious academic work, less well so to demotic *Calendar*, though he mucked in well, particularly when he was sent out to do silly items with me such as dressed in a toga chasing a girl in a bikini, for some reason I cannot now remember but was probably a classical allusion. That was about my level but well below his. When I reminisced to him about it much later I detected a slight shudder.

Peter Jones, our solid, ever reliable director, retired and died in 2008.

Eliza Seed, Calendar's efficient secretary and eventually John Fairley's secretary and gatekeeper in his absences, left in 1973 to do Voluntary Service Abroad (VSO) in Rhodesia. She came back in 1979 with Micky Chittenden, former district commissioner, as her partner. After organizing me in the Commons, she became a teacher while Micky became my assistant, bringing a wonderful upper-class tone to my office having been Churchill's constituency secretary in Epping.

John Willis, son of the more famous Ted, was recruited by Donald, a friend of his father, to cut his teeth on *Calendar*. He went on to produce major documentaries, such as the 1975 exposé of a paedophile operating at Kings Cross pretending to rescue young lost boys who had run away from home. His film *Johnny Go Home* won a BAFTA award. John did a moving documentary, *Shake hands with a Bum* about a Halifax boxer of promise who became a violent alcoholic, and became one of those television people who gravitated from production to management as someone obviously destined for higher things. John left to take senior administrative positions with the BBC, commissioning programmes rather than producing them and has now disappeared somewhere into the misty heights of TV administration and the chairmanship of BAFTA. He is now chief executive of Mentorn Media.

Michael Deakin, producer, ideas man and company spy, came with Tony Essex and began by making a series of serious documentaries for him, as well as *Tom Grattan's War*, a brilliant series of twenty-six episodes. More Cambridge than Leeds and never the most productive producer, he was too esoteric to stay in the North and did not. He helped form TV AM where he became director of programmes during that company's travails and brought back Jonathan Aitken to run it. Later he became a partner in Griffin Productions and now lives in France.

Tom Adam was the scion of a Scottish landowning family whose father managed to lose the family fortune and died owing £1,000,000 which Tom nobly struggled to pay back. Public school educated, instead of gravitating to the top like most of his class, Tom worked up from the bottom as floor manager for Yorkshire, with ambitions to be producer. As well as being the best of floor managers running the studio with efficiency and charm, he was one of a very rare species at YTV, a Liberal (another was Terry Ricketts, the sound recordist, and Les Dawson, but there may have been others who had the good sense to keep quiet about their abnormality). Married to an aristocratic Italian, Tom left to join TVAM at its start, working still as a floor manager. When Bruce Gyngell took over to break the union and force down wages, Tom (though neither a socialist nor a natural trade unionist) was one of the most loyal in the year-long strike. It cost him his job, his income and his prospects. He left to work in Italian television but later came back, fruitlessly seeking work in a television system grown meaner and nastier. He now lives in Rome.

Andrew Kerr's abilities were not stretched by his work on *Calendar*. His contract ran out at the end of May 1969 when he went back to London, bought a house and resumed working part-time on the 'Churchill' biography, as well as writing his own book. Both were the prelude to his greatest achievement – conceiving and creating the Glastonbury Festival, a tale fully told in his biography, *Intolerably Hip*. This was a far greater contribution to popular culture than anything he had achieved on *Calendar*.

Jonathan Aitken's brief interlude at YTV and in the politics of the late 1960s were a career dip for a young meteor. Jonathan was not a natural or effective TV performer and his political career got messy when he took the side of Biafra in the Nigerian civil war and copied (on YTV's premises) secret government documents on British supplies of arms to Nigeria to send to Sir Hugh Fraser, husband of Lady Antonia Fraser. As a result Jonathan was prosecuted for breaking the Official Secrets Act and, though acquitted, was dropped as candidate by the Thirsk and Malton Constituency Party.

He redeemed himself with the party, was elected as MP for Thanet in 1974 and briefly courted, then dropped, Mrs. Thatcher's daughter, Carol, which did not endear him to Mrs. T. Eventually he was made a minister, only to fall from grace, or Mrs. T, when he lied about dealings with Saudi Arabia over arms and a stay in Paris at the Ritz financed by them. Jonathan threatened to cut through the 'lies' with 'the simple sword of truth'. It buckled when *The Guardian* proved its case and his wife and daughter refused to support him. He was charged with perjury, sentenced to eighteen months, served seven and lost his office and seat. Since then he has written a book on his experiences and an excellent biography of Mrs. Thatcher. He lives a quiet, useful, religious life out of the headlines.

Peter Moth, a later recruit to *Calendar* as producer/reporter was a former congregational church minister and teacher at Garforth Comprehensive. A nice,

Old Codger toasts the last days of YTV.

clever man, Peter later moved as a producer to Tyne Tees where he rose to become programme controller, then created a scandal by announcing his gay marriage (highly publicized in Sunday scandal sheets) before gay marriages existed. He was beaten up by homophobic thugs and dumped on the moors in 2003. Since then he has disappeared from view.

Marylyn Webb joined the team in 1972, first as Lincoln reporter, then from 1975 effectively as a replacement of Liz Fox. A serious journalist, she presented more specialized items like *The Vet* and *The Gardener*, who she eventually married. Marylyn died in 2014.

Our brilliant cameramen alternated between *Calendar*/drama and documentaries: Frank Pocklington (who had started out at *Picture Post*), Peter Jackson (christened 'Crème de la Crème' by the secretaries), Brian Wilson and Charlie Flynn. All retired one-by-one in the 1980s and 1990s. Graham Barker, who trained up from assistant, was killed in the YTV helicopter which crashed while filming in Hull. Pocklington lives in France. Peter Jackson died in 2006.

John Fairley rose irresistibly, eventually becoming programme controller at Yorkshire, a position from which he resigned on a matter of principle but was later brought back by Paul Fox only to eventually resign again over Ward Thomas's plan to merge with Granada. He took over the horse-racing franchise for Channel Four and operated it successfully until 2013. He now lives at his stables near Malton.

John McFayden. After being fired from YTV, 'McFad the Bad' reappeared at the Hull office demanding £20 to join a Hull trawler heading for Iceland. He got it but has not been heard of since.

Two secretaries who tried to produce some order in my chaotic life at YTV, Chris Wilkinson and Dorothy Box, came down to London for brief periods to impose order on my life as an MP. I insisted that they went back, Chris to the warm certainties of YTV and Dorothy to Pennine Radio, where she had started work right at its beginning in 1975. Chris became a production assistant and has now retired. Dorothy became a mainstay of Pennine Radio and a regular broadcaster, almost the mother of the station. She too has retired. Chris and Dorothy were among the best of the bunch at *Calendar*. Both saved me from many a pitfall, Chris by keeping me organized, Dorothy by sheer common sense, as when I asked her to find out something about 'Crag Iron-jawed Alderman Blenkinsop of the Bradford Arts and Tramways Committee' as reported in *The Daily Telegraph's* Peter Simple. 'It's a joke' she explained. I had not realized.

Liz Fox, heaven's gift to YTV, provided fun for all for *Calendar's* first three years, leaving in 1970 to join ITN, a programme too serious for her talents. She then appeared regularly and beautifully on *Stars on Sunday*. She married a cameraman and went to work in TV in the West Country but has now disappeared from view: A great loss to the medium.

Paul Dunstan, was recruited from Central TV as journalist/presenter. Paul's all-purpose talent was soon being used on documentaries and science programmes, as well as on *Calendar*. He was the narrator on many of Barry Cockcroft's great documentaries and his mallifluous tones have narrated more documentaries than most people have had hot dinners. He has also produced several network programmes of his own, but is now retired.

Michael Partington was born and bred in Harrogate. He started out as a journalist on the local paper and the *Pudsey News*, going from there to the *News Chronicle* which died under him, then the *Daily Express*. He joined ITN and moved on to Anglia TV from where he came to Yorkshire as an experienced, safe and solid presenter. Michael had a sardonic wit which brightened our lives but was unhappy that he was not the lead presenter on *Calendar*. He left to join Tyne Tees as their senior presenter, political and industrial correspondent and producer until his retirement. He died in 2004 at the young age of 69 years.

Bob Warman, a Midlander, a smooth and effective anchorman and newscaster. His brother, Mike Warman, was news editor for Central (ATV), John Wilford's favourite recruiting ground. Bob eventually moved back there.

Gwyn Ward Thomas DFC, former RAF bomber pilot based at Immingham in the war started his television career as air-time salesman whence he moved to the new Grampian as sales director and then quickly chief executive where he was a scourge of the unions, threatening at one stage to close the station. He brought this reputation with him to Yorkshire where he became managing director, scheming remorselessly to merge the company with Tyne Tees and Anglia, the third prong of Trident. The IBA refused to allow it and after the 1982 contract bids forced Trident to sell off its two television stations. It purchased a number of casinos and betting shops, including the Playboy Casino in London and, amazing combination, Windsor Safari Park. Out of television, Ward Thomas became a gambling king, a role which hardly satisfied him. He retired in 1984 but then came back to the chairmanship of Yorkshire Television in 1993 and agreed to a bid of £771,000,000 from Granada where he hoped to become chairman of the joint companies. Instead, he was pushed into retirement at the ripe old age of 74 years. Still active, he lives in Weybridge.

Stuart Wilson, was the founder of the feast. He had won the contract and created YTV. After that life was something of an anti-climax as deputy managing director with heavy responsibilities, such as purchasing number plates like YTV1 and YTV2 (which Donald Baverstock refused to use and sold). Stuart became joint managing director but with the arrival of Paul Fox, who took over as managing director, Stuart was pushed out to run a sports shop in Leeds. In the 1982 bidding round, he attempted to repeat his success, becoming part of the consortium bidding for the Midland contract. They failed to get it. Now retired, Stuart lives near Harrogate.

Sir Geoffrey Cox, my saviour, was deputy chairman and responsible for setting up the news operation. In 1972, he became chairman of Tyne Tees, retiring from there in 1981. He died in 2008.

Kevin Sim. Yet another Oxford chap, Kevin joined us in 1972. Full of bright ideas at YTV and producer of *Through the Keyhole*, Kevin has since gone on to produce a whole series of major programmes and several editions of *Despatches* and won several BAFTA and Royal Television Society awards.

Simon Welfare. Married to the daughter of the Earl of Aberdeen, Simon moved straight from Oxford University into YTV as an active and inventive member of the Calendar team. He began to produce documentaries, invented *Don't Ask Me* and also invented a powerful series with Arthur C. Clarke, the science fiction writer living in Sri Lanka. This also produced a successful best-selling book in 1980. Simon then became an independent producer with his own company, Granite Productions, which produced blockbuster documentaries such as *Red Empire*, the history of the Soviet Union, and *China Rising* about the history of China, as well as further documentaries on Arthur C. Clarke, *The Lost Vikings* and *The Day the Earth Was Hit*. This mammoth output of monster programmes made Simon one of the most successful and serious independents until, just as the movies grew too small for Gloria Swanson, ITV became too small for Simon's blockbusters. He now writes and makes films from the ancestral home in Scotland. His legacy to Yorkshire could be health because he brought back from Clarke the idea of massive doses of Vitamin C for longevity. So far it has worked on me.

Anne Gibbons, the senior production assistant in my Calendar years. Anne later became a producer and produced *Emmerdale* and a series of other programmes for YTV.

Edwina Tarpley was our Lincolnshire reporter in the early 1970s but the only trace left today is memories of her lisp: 'Edwina Tarpley weporting from the Wiver Twent'.

Reverend Brandon Jackson, Vicar of Shipley (where he had been my milkman for a week's work experience) and religious adviser to YTV, took a brave stand behind our rival bid for the contract in 1982 and was fired in consequence. Mrs. Thatcher made him Dean of Lincoln to clean up the 'Trollopian' corruption in the cathedral. His opponents tried to discredit him in a sex trap which failed. Brandon officiated at Donald Baverstock's funeral.

Monseignor Michael Buckley, was the catholic religious adviser to YTV with a taste for ecumenism, peace in Ulster and alcohol. He later became 'Agony Aunt' for the *Catholic Herald*.

That is the lot, though I have missed a few latecomers. I could not have had a nicer set of colleagues. Team YTV 1968 to 1977. Bless 'em all.

NUNC DIMITTIS

My best friend, Duncan Dallas, reading the first draft of this walk down memory lane just before he died, suggested that it needed an intellectual thread. What were we trying to achieve? Did we succeed? I thought that this was to over-intellectualize a set of random recollections of happy days long gone. We were just enjoying ourselves, not working to a plan. Everyone involved in the formation of Yorkshire Television was trying to do something different. Yorkshire money wanted to make a bob or three and the money men did that, though not as much as Lord Thomson of 'Moneyprint' might have made them hope. Producers wanted to make programmes free of London bureaucracy in a company where they had the money to do what they wanted. Ward Thomas wanted to build a television empire over the east coast. Those of us lower down the hierarchy wanted to learn an exciting new job, make programmes and have fun. As for me, a television addict, I just wanted to be in, and on, television, the most exciting job in the world. I wanted to do things that interested me, have the fun, the ego massage and the excitement not available in academe and do all that at home in the North, the best part of benighted Britain.

Yorkshire was pretty new territory for television, just as New Zealand had been when we started it there, but prospects in Leeds were far better. At YTV we had more money, the great fertilizer of good television, an inspiring (and infuriating) guru in Donald Baverstock, the freedom to do anything we wanted. Yorkshire had more characters, stories and achievements so it could offer more than anywhere else. Here was all the excitement of a new team building a new station which could put the 'Broad Acres' on the nation's screens, and on its own. Nothing interests Yorkshire folk more than Yorkshire.

So what did we achieve? The Labour Party of the 1950s would have accused us of commercializing a county of community and solidarity. J. B. Priestley would have felt that we were intruding 'admass', the manipulation of the masses for profit and debasing his native county of blunt, honest, independent folk you could not push around. Culture vultures would (and did) accuse us of vulgarity and populism because we were not catering for the esoteric or the elite. All balls; we were stimulating and exciting our little corner of the world, talking to it in its own language and giving it a mirror to its great qualities as well as projecting them to a wider world. Yorkshire was much the better for *Calendar* and better still from having its own TV Centre and company as a focus and stimulus to create opportunities and careers for young people with ambitions to work in the media. YTV became a focus for local talent, writers, reporters, artists and even politicians, encouraging and stimulating them all to create a flourishing media life the area had never had before. We even brightened up Yorkshire politics, jolting them into lively debate and out of the dull and deep potations of two big taciturn blocks into a new lively individualism.

We achieved all that and *Calendar* gave the area a shared common experience, a Northerness and Yorkshireness they'd not had before. By winning a majority of the audience and giving it the populist television it wanted, we provided a unique civic space for news information and entertainment; in short a daily dose of Yorkshire. As for the Calendar team, of which I was a small part, we got the biggest and best privilege young people can have: that of creating something new and the leadership, the money and the opportunity to seize it. My Calendar years were more exciting and much more fun than anything I have done before or since. They live in my memory with a happy glow, which, I hope, suffuses this book.

What's left today? The programmes we made live on in scattered archives, mostly in a building on Kirkstall Road from where ITV is keen to dump them into some national archive. No one sees them. Calendar's successor programme goes out in attenuated form, its studios quieter, its crews cut, its manning levels down and its expenses tightly controlled. It is no longer in its old studio but in what used to be the bar of the 1968 Television Centre. The company itself, YTV (as Donald hated calling it) is dead and buried in Companies House. Much of its TV Centre is empty and unused. Some of the Calendar team are dead, as must be a sizeable proportion of the audience which watched it. The golden lads and girls who appeared on it, while not yet turned to dust, will be grey rather than golden.

In its two and a half channel system *Calendar* could reach audiences of up to 2,500,000 a night. Its successor struggles to reach 1,000,000 in a 200-channel system and ITV is now one company centralized on London, just like the BBC. Inevitably, Yorkshire features less on the nation's screens and its own. No one now has the power to clear the local schedules to put sudden Yorkshire news stories or programmes on. The Harold Wilson interview and the Clough/Revie debate were put on at a moment's notice. That could not happen now nor can a powerful local-programme director bargain with the network to get good Yorkshire programmes put on nationally, a sad outcome to the great hopes of 1968.

Being a politician I put much of the blame on the replacement of the social democratic consensus we shared in the 1960s by the free market imperatives and

'Thatcherite' economics of the 1980s and later decades. These damaged the North and its basic industries, all of which were run down too quickly and too massively in a process misnamed 'creative destruction' which was really just vandalism. This process of regeneration by ash production was greatest in the North, destroying much of its uniqueness. Cry the beloved county.

As well as undermining both regions and regionalism, free-market economics undermined good television. Auctioning the contracts drained money from production and while the free market can provide multiple cheap channels and a plethora of imports it cannot sustain expensive regional structures and quality local production. Good quality TV and regional service need regulation and a firm financial base. British television had both in the 1960s but both are weaker today. The new cheapjack local television stations all run on a shoestring for small local audiences and are no substitute for the great regional companies which survive only in Scotland in the shape of STV.

The creation of Yorkshire Television was a small step in the process of decentralization. Britain needs to scatter power, production, in our case TV production, and move things out of London. For three decades it succeeded. Then it succumbed to the new financial centralization begun by Margaret Thatcher. YTV's demise and its absorption into national ITV were a small part of this process of centralization through free market economics and deregulation which have characterized the last three decades. They leave regionalism, regional feeling, regional institutions, regional media and the North generally all weaker. Britain has been deprived of the healthy diversity of vigorous regionalism and lively media.

That damaging process has swept away too much of what we were trying to do. But I do not want to conclude my retrospective *Calendar* story with the geriatric maunderings of a left behind Leftie. Nor can I claim that the world was better when I was famous as the 'Clown Prince of Yorkshire'. I have just tried to show that what we were doing was good and right for Yorkshire, and that we had fun doing it. So *ave atque vale*, as they say in Harrogate. For Barnsley, Ah'll si thee.

INDEX

Figures in italics refer to captions. 'AM' indicates the author.